KV-638-322

Introduction to Computers

Introduction to COMPUTERS

KEITH LONDON

FABER AND FABER
London Boston

First published in 1968
by Faber and Faber Limited
3 Queen Square London WC1
Revised in 1970 and 1973
This new edition first published in 1979
Phototypeset in V.I.P. Times by
Western Printing Services Ltd, Bristol
Printed in Great Britain by
Whitstable Litho Ltd., Whitstable, Kent

British Library Cataloguing in Publication Data

London, Keith Robert
Introduction to computers. – 4th ed.
1. Electronic data processing
I. Title
001.6'4 QA76

ISBN 0-571-04995-8
ISBN 0-571-04975-3 Pbk

To Maureen, Paul and Graham

Acknowledgements

The assistance given by International Computers Limited in providing illustrations is gratefully acknowledged. Figures 44, 53, 55, 56, 58, 60, 63 and 74, and Plate 5a are based on computer devices in the ICL 1900 Series. Figures 43, 80 and 84, and Plates 1 and 4 are also reproduced by permission of ICL.

Plates 2 and 5b are reproduced by courtesy of IBM United Kingdom Limited.

Plate 3 is reproduced by courtesy of the Burroughs Machines Limited.

Plate 5c is reproduced by courtesy of UNIVAC, a division of the Sperry Rand Corporation.

Contents

Illustrations

PLATES

TEXT FIGURES

Preface to the First Edition

To the majority of people, computers are still a novelty surrounded by mystery. In industry and commerce computers are becoming accepted as valuable tools for everyday use but they still tend to be regarded as exotic luxuries. The average person is vaguely aware of their existence, but generally only as a result of science fiction stories and the news reports of the uses of 'electronic brains'. Greater publicity is given to electronic computers when they are misused. Incredible 'mistakes' purport to be the result of a computer's failing and ignorance: bills sent to customers for the sum of £99,999,999 instead of £17.00; bills submitted for £00.00 with final demands repeatedly being sent to the bewildered customer for payment until a cheque for £00.00 is despairingly sent and duly receipted! Such is the lot of most innovations; publicity is given primarily to the misuse of these new techniques. But what of the ordinary day to day usage of computers giving satisfactory service and reliable results? Most people have only a vague notion of what computers are and how they are used. This is surprising since most people are involved with a computer, or 'automatic data processing', in some way. Electricity or gas bills, for example, are probably produced by a computer, as are many of the invoices and statements from commercial companies. Equally probable is that a person employed by a large organization may be contributing to the work performed by a computer in that organization. To a large extent, however, 'the computer' still remains a machine of mystery.

The main aim of this book is to represent the basic facts about computers, and, by doing this, the myth of 'electronic brains' can be dispelled. The idea that the computer can make only mistakes can be set right, and the misconception that computers are highly specialized machines which are used by the privileged few can be corrected. Above all else it is hoped that this book will show, by explaining what computers can and cannot do, how and why they are becoming accepted tools in commerce, industry, government and research. It is often said that with the present growth in computer usage, the basic nature and organization of commerce and industry and even our way of life may slowly change.

There are two important points to be made both about the nature of the subject and the content of this book: firstly, a word of encouragement to the non-technical reader. There is a common misconception that to understand computers one must have a good knowledge of mathematics. In my opinion this is not so; a basic appreciation of arithmetic is usually more than adequate for an understanding of modern computers. The preoccupation with mathematics is due to the fact that early computers were developed and used almost exclusively by universities or research institutes. Secondly, there is a word of warning. This book is concerned neither with the engineering aspects of a computer nor the internal working of its electronic circuits. With any relatively new invention (computers have only come into prominence since the Second World War) there tends to be a preoccupation with 'how does it work?' rather than with 'what can it do and how can it be used?' The fact that we need not be concerned here with a *detailed* study of the internal workings of a computer can be made clear by a simple analogy. We understand how to drive a car by manipulation of the controls with only a meagre knowledge of the theory of the internal combustion engine and the gear system. When we use a car to get from point A to point B, we think more of 'road sense', route and petrol consumption. If we study a route, our primary concern is the economics and feasibility of using various roads. Thus, in our simple study of computers, we need only basic arithmetical calculations. There is no necessity to make a detailed study of the computer's logic.

The structure of this book is simple: Chapters 1, 2, and 3 explain what a computer is and how it works; Chapters 4 and 5 describe how a computer can be used to solve simple problems. Finally, Chapters 6 and 7 show how a computer is used in commerce, industry and scientific research.

I would like to acknowledge the assistance given by International Computers and Tabulators Limited who have supplied many illustrations, C. Hampson-Evans, whose encouragement was primarily responsible for me attempting this book, joined B. J. Knight in reading the whole book in typescript, thereby providing valuable criticism. Their ideas and the stimulus of much discussion with Miss M. Bevan, J. Graham and E. Housden are acknowledged with considerable appreciation of my debt to them. I am deeply grateful to Mrs. J. G. Boyce and Miss G. Hussey for the secretarial aid necessary in preparing the typescript. Finally, I am indebted to my wife for her moral support and forbearance while this book was being written and for her aid in reading the proofs.

Preface to the Fourth Edition

In the ten years since the first publication of this book there have been tremendous advances in computers. In the preparation of this new edition I have taken the opportunity to completely update the book to reflect these changes in technology. At the same time I have tried to make the book more relevant to the *user* of computers by including more on input techniques, the role of the systems analyst and the project work to develop and implement a computer-based system.

In making these revisions, however, I have tried not to change the basic approach or format of the book and thereby destroy its validity as a school text or a first guide for a businessman.

In the preparation of this new edition I am indebted to the assistance of Miss Jenni Carter for all secretarial services.

1. The Concept of Computers

In his book, *Handbook of Experimental Psychology*, S. S. Smith says 'When description gives way to measurement, discussion is replaced by calculation.' 'Calculation' means many things. It is, for example, the process of determining the amount of change to be received in a shop or the process of estimating the flight path of a space craft. These ideas of calculation are based on the *formal* approach of using the simple rules of arithmetic or the complexities of higher mathematics. The process of calculation may appear to have an informal aspect. A good card player can assess his chances of drawing a favourable card from a pack or his chances of winning a game. In the former instance, the player may have an exceptional memory, such that he can remember the cards drawn, or those he has seen, in a game of rummy. He may be a mathematician who can estimate the probability of the cards he requires being available in the pack and so on. Some part of a card player's assessment may therefore be calculation in the sense of the formal application of a mathematical procedure. Another part of his assessment is the general trend of a game, and his chances of winning may be based on 'instinct and experience'. He may calculate how his opponent is faring by experience and the formula:

'If Fred's jaw sags or his left nostril twitches after drawing a card, then he has drawn a "bad card" because he has just changed suits,' and so on.

As a further example of the meaning of calculation, we may read in a 'spy-thriller' that 'Agent 9X, with icy calm, quickly calculated whether he could wrest the ·45 from Brodvich's hand and pull beautiful blonde Serina free'. I doubt whether Agent 9X's calculation would have been a formal assessment of the situation based on an 'event-action' reaction time of Brodvich firing the gun, and his own ability to dive through ten feet of space within this time, therefore requiring a diving speed of '*x* inches per sec.' and so on. More likely,

his calculation would be pure guesswork which would be biased by such intangible factors as the value he places on his own life and the value he places on Serina's life. Reference to calculation in this book, means *formal* calculation; calculation that is not biased by irrational or emotional thought.

Calculation is a purely mechanical process. Consider a research scientist who is investigating certain physical phenomena. He observes the phenomena, makes notes and generally collects 'data'. He feels, although at this time he is not certain, that one phenomenon is related in some way or other to another phenomenon which he has also observed. Having collected sufficient data about the two phenomena, the scientist decides to 'calculate' the number of instances when they occur together. This decision having been made, the calculation is simply the comparison of dates and times and the listing of the number of instances when there is agreement. This process of calculation is purely a mechanical procedure of matching and counting. The scientist may be acclaimed, and perhaps rightly so, as a great thinker because he has established, with a reasonable degree of certainty, that the two phenomena are causally connected. The acclaim would be for the original observation and realization that there was a causal connection, and not for the process of calculation which could be performed by an intelligent seven-year-old. Alternatively, a scientist or mathematician may discover or formalize a new method of calculation, e.g. a procedure for solving a complex mathematical problem. Once the method or procedure has been established and accepted, it can be used as a mechanical process for calculation on the basis of: given factors x and y, and calculation procedure z, result a is correct.

Calculation, then, as used in this book, is not only a formal procedure but a mechanical procedure as well. The term mechanical procedure does not imply that it is a process performed by machine; it implies that the procedure can be performed in a 'machine-like' manner. Simple addition can be performed as a formal mechanical procedure. A young child, if given a table thus and taught how to use it, could perform simple addition without understanding the concept of number.

$$1 + 1 = 2$$
$$1 + 2 = 3$$
$$1 + 4 = 5$$
$$1 + 5 = 6$$
$$1 + 6 = 7$$

$$2 + 1 = 3$$
$$2 + 2 = 4$$
$$2 + 3 = 5 \text{ etc.}$$

Bearing in mind this description of calculation, let us consider some of man's simple 'aids-to-calculation'.

Perhaps the simplest aid-to-calculation is the hand. Books on country life sometimes include descriptions of the village idiot adding and subtracting by means of counting the fingers on his hands. To add two numbers, say 2 plus 4, first two fingers are raised and then another four; the total number of raised fingers is then counted thus giving the sum. When subtraction is performed, the reverse procedure is applied. Problems naturally arose when the sum of the numbers was greater than 10, and the result of the subtraction say 2 − 4 could be very perplexing.

A natural progression would be to identify numbers with a collection of external objects. Piles of stones could be employed. For example, the symbol 6 could mean

and the symbol 4

The symbol '+' means push the two piles of stones together and the resulting pile of stones could be identified by the symbol 10. For subtraction (say 6 minus 4) two piles of stones were made. From the pile 6 stones, another pile was created to match the 4 pile, the number of stones left in the original 6 pile representing the required answer. The identification of numbers with collections of physical objects presents serious problems. In fact, no 'number' could exist and take part in a calculation unless identified as a number of physical objects, thus, theoretically, limiting man's advancement.

The next aid-to-calculation to be considered is the abacus as shown in Figure 1. Again, numbers are represented by objects but this time in a manner which offers wider scope for number representation and calculation.

The aids so far described require the human calculator to perform operations which can be classified as follows:

(i) representing the number in a certain form (a grouping of fingers, stones or balls on wire etc.);

(ii) moving or rearranging the grouping in a prescribed manner.

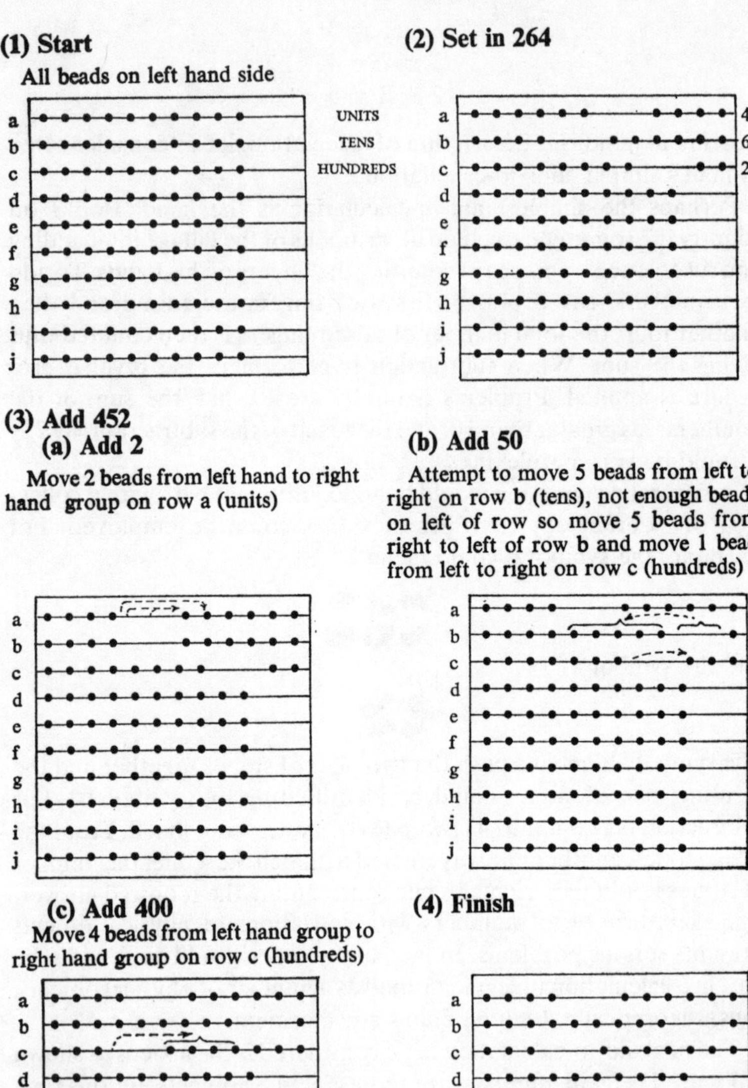
(1) Start
All beads on left hand side
a
b
c
d
e
f
g
h
i
j
UNITS
TENS
HUNDREDS
(2) Set in 264
4
6
2
(3) Add 452
(a) Add 2
Move 2 beads from left hand to right hand group on row a (units)
(b) Add 50
Attempt to move 5 beads from left to right on row b (tens), not enough beads on left of row so move 5 beads from right to left of row b and move 1 bead from left to right on row c (hundreds)
(c) Add 400
Move 4 beads from left hand group to right hand group on row c (hundreds)
(4) Finish
6
1
7

Fig. 1. The Principle of the Abacus. Addition of 452 to 264

The operation (ii) is based on the principle of 'merging' object groupings for addition or multiplication and 'dispersing' object groupings for subtraction or division.

There is a radical change in this principle when the slide rule is considered; see Figure 2. There is still the problem of number representation, but it is achieved in 'symbol-symbol' matching rather than 'symbol-object grouping' matching. To multiply two numbers, say 3 × 5, requires the selection of the symbols '3' and '5' on the scales; the product can be identified directly in like symbols, i.e. 15. The actual calculation is performed by moving the centre slide of the rule an appropriate distance, as for example in Figure 3. From the operator's point of view, there is no 'merging' or 'dispersal' procedure.

Finally, a big jump may be made to the desk calculating machine. A hypothetical machine is shown in Figure 4. Number representation is by a symbol-symbol matching procedure. For example, to add 241 to 3721 the operator presses keys, 2, 4, 1 and then the 'IN' key, followed by the keys 3, 7, 2, 1 and the 'IN' key. This causes the two numbers to be stored within the calculator by means of notched wheels with ten teeth as shown in Figure 5a. When the '+' key is pressed, the two numbers are added together. Addition can be achieved by a simple gear method whereby the wheels representing 241 are rotated back to the 'zero point' and the corresponding 3721 wheels are *advanced* the same distance (see Figure 5b). With further mechanical ingenuity the wheels may be connected in such a manner that subtraction and multiplication can be performed.

From the aspect of operating the device, there is a vast difference between the stone grouping and the desk calculator. In the latter instance, to multiply two numbers, the operator merely presses a series of keys to input the numbers and one key, '×', to perform the multiplication; the *procedure* for calculation is affected by gear wheels etc. inside the machine.

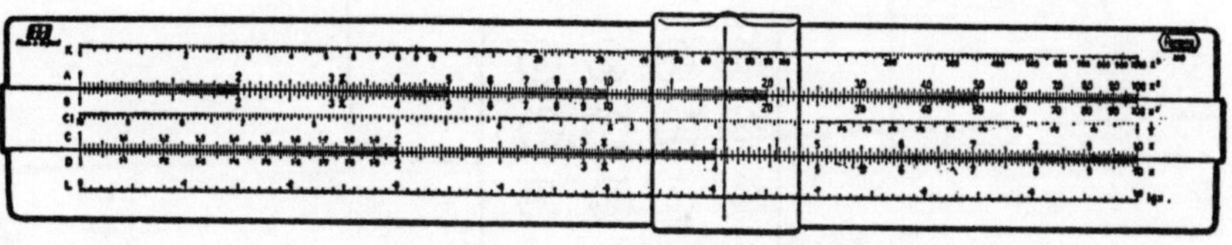

Fig. 2. A Slide Rule
(*By courtesy of Blundell Rules Limited*)

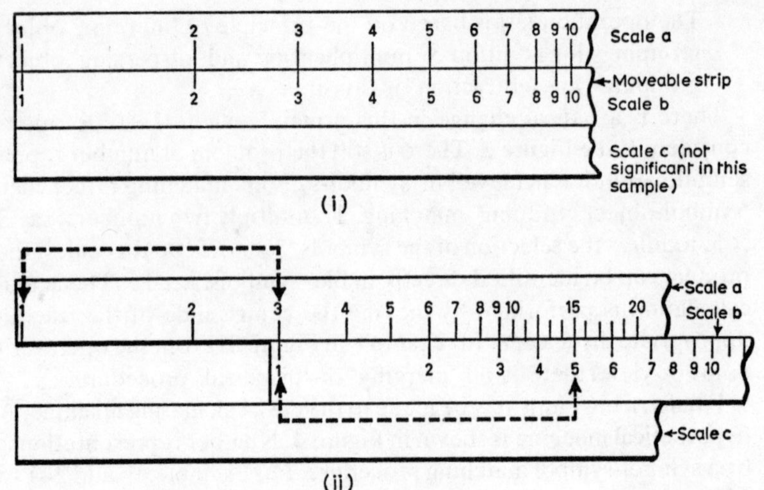

EXAMPLE:
The example (ii) shows the calculation 3×5. The moveable strip (scale b) is set so that '1' is beneath '3' (the multiplicand) on scale a.
The product (15) is read off scale a by the position of the multiplier, 5 on scale b.

Fig. 3. A Slide Rule Calculation

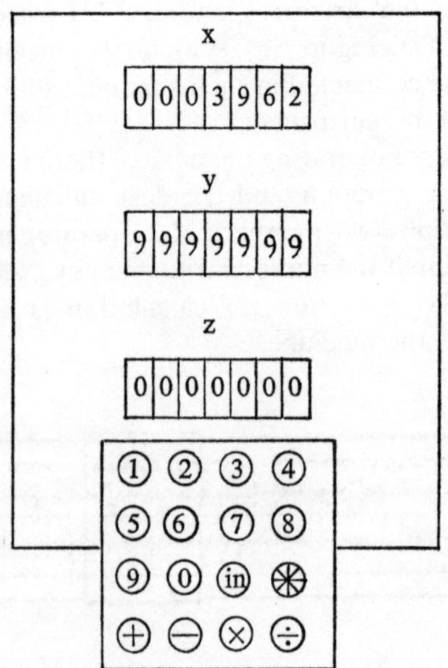

Fig. 4. Example Desk Calculator

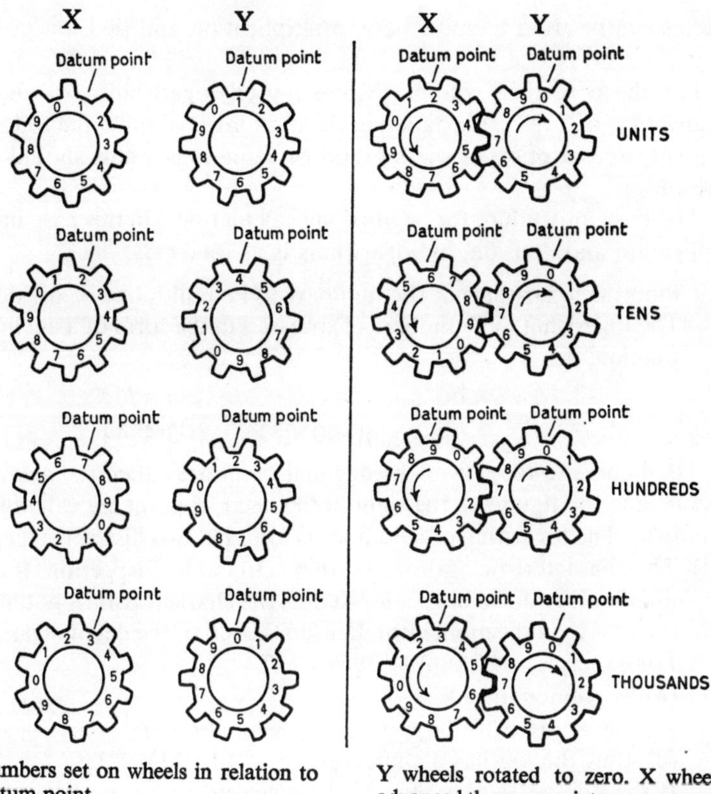

Numbers set on wheels in relation to Datum point.

(a)

Y wheels rotated to zero. X wheels advanced the appropriate amount and, in relation to the Datum point hold the sum.

(b)

***Note:* When point '1' is opposite the Datum point, it is displayed in a window.**

Fig. 5. Example Desk Calculator – Number Storage and Calculation

The jump from the simple desk calculator to the modern electronic computer is a large one and is comparable to jumping from balloon travel to flight by jet aircraft. To lessen the impact of this transition, a closer analysis of how a calculation is performed will be useful.

CALCULATION – MAN AND MACHINE

Let us consider one of the simplest and most widely used of all aids-to-calculation: logarithm tables. We are not concerned here with the theory of logarithms but rather with how pre-printed logarithm tables can be used to solve basic multiplication and division problems.

For those readers who have never used logarithms, or whose knowledge of 'logs' is shrouded in the dark mists of time, the following short description of the method of using logarithms should be useful.

The basic procedure for performing calculations, in this case multiplication and division, by logarithms is as follows:

1. Find the logarithms of the numbers to be multiplied or divided. The logarithm of a number is expressed in the form of a decimal fraction, e.g.

   the log of 251 is 2·3997
   the log of ·003051 is $\bar{3}$·4844

The figures to the left of the decimal point are called the *characteristic* and the figures to the right of the decimal point are called the *mantissa*. The logarithm of a number is found in two distinct stages:

(i) The characteristic of the logarithm is found by inspection. If the number is equal to or greater than 1, the characteristic is equal to one less than the number of digits to the left of the decimal point. For example, the number 3952·0127
 (a) is greater than 1,
 (b) has 4 digits to the left of the decimal point,
 (c) thus the log has a characteristic of (4 − 1) = 3.
 If the number is less than 1, the characteristic is equal to one more than the number of significant zeros which follow the decimal point. For example, the number 0·000127
 (a) is less than 1,
 (b) has 3 zeros to the right of the decimal point,
 (c) thus the log has a characteristic of (3 + 1) = 4.
 This characteristic is negative and is usually written as $\bar{4}$ and pronounced as *bar* four.

(ii) The mantissa is found by means of log tables, an example of which is shown in Figure 6. The mantissa is found thus:
 Log of 330·7

 Horizontal column where x = 33
 Vertical column under 'O' = ·5185
 Plus vertical column under 'ADD 7' = 9
 Mantissa = ·5194
 Characteristic 2
 Log = 2·5194

Logarithms of Numbers

	0	1	2	3	4	5	6	7	8	9	ADD 1	2	3	4	5	6	7	8	9
10	·0000	0043	0086	0128	0170	0212					4	8	13	17	21	25	29	34	38
						0212	0253	0294	0334	0374	4	8	12	16	20	24	28	32	36
11	·0414	0453	0492	0531	0569	0607					4	8	12	16	19	23	27	31	35
						0607	0645	0682	0719	0755	4	7	11	15	18	22	26	30	33
12	·0792	0828	0864	0899	0934	0969					4	7	11	14	18	21	25	28	32
						0969	1004	1038	1072	1106	3	7	10	14	17	20	24	27	31
13	·1139	1173	1206	1239	1271	1303					3	7	10	13	16	20	23	26	30
						1303	1335	1367	1399	1430	3	6	10	13	16	19	22	26	29
14	·1461	1492	1523	1553	1584	1614	1644	1673	1703	1732	3	6	9	12	15	18	21	24	27
15	·1761	1790	1818	1847	1875	1903	1931	1959	1987	2014	3	6	8	11	14	17	20	22	25
16	·2041	2068	2095	2122	2148	2175	2201	2227	2253	2279	3	5	8	10	13	16	18	21	23
17	·2304	2330	2355	2380	2405	2430	2455	2480	2504	2529	2	5	7	10	12	15	17	20	22
18	·2553	2577	2601	2625	2648	2672	2695	2718	2742	2765	2	5	7	9	12	14	16	19	21
19	·2788	2810	2833	2856	2878	2900	2923	2945	2967	2989	2	4	7	9	11	13	15	18	20
20	·3010	3032	3054	3075	3096	3118	3139	3160	3181	3201	2	4	6	8	11	13	15	17	19
21	·3222	3243	3263	3284	3304	3324	3345	3365	3385	3404	2	4	6	8	10	12	14	16	18
22	·3424	3444	3464	3483	3502	3522	3541	3560	3579	3598	2	4	6	8	10	11	13	15	17
23	·3617	3636	3655	3674	3692	3711	3729	3747	3766	3784	2	4	6	7	9	11	13	15	17
24	·3802	3820	3838	3856	3874	3892	3909	3927	3945	3962	2	4	5	7	9	11	13	14	16
25	·3979	3997	4014	4031	4048	4065	4082	4099	4116	4133	2	3	5	7	9	10	12	14	15
26	·4150	4166	4183	4200	4216	4232	4249	4265	4281	4298	2	3	5	6	8	10	11	13	14
27	·4314	4330	4346	4362	4378	4393	4409	4425	4440	4456	2	3	5	6	8	9	11	13	14
28	·4472	4487	4502	4518	4533	4548	4564	4579	4594	4609	2	3	5	6	8	9	11	12	14
29	·4624	4639	4654	4669	4683	4698	4713	4728	4742	4757	1	3	4	6	7	9	10	12	13
30	·4771	4786	4800	4814	4829	4843	4857	4871	4886	4900	1	3	4	6	7	8	10	11	13
31	·4914	4928	4942	4955	4969	4983	4997	5011	5024	5038	1	3	4	5	7	8	10	11	12
32	·5051	5065	5079	5092	5105	5119	5132	5145	5159	5172	1	3	4	5	7	8	9	11	12
33	·5185	5198	5211	5224	4237	5250	5263	5276	5289	5303	1	3	4	5	7	8	9	10	12
34	·5315	5328	5340	5353	5366	5378	5391	5403	5416	5428	1	3	4	5	6	8	9	10	11

Fig. 6. An Example 'Log' Table

Log of ·002171

Horizontal column where x = 21
Vertical column under '7' = ·3365
Plus vertical column under 'ADD 1' = 2
Mantissa = ·3367
Characteristic = $\bar{3}$
Log = $\bar{3}$·3367

Note that in the second example, the significant zeros are ignored when finding the mantissa. This and the characteristic are written together as shown above, thus giving the 'log' of the number.

2. Multiplication and division are performed according to the two simple rules:

   To multiply, the logarithms of the quantities to be multiplied are added together.

   To divide, the logarithm of the divisor is subtracted from the logarithm of the dividend.

   (Note: in the example 3 divided by 4, 4 is the *divisor* and 3 the *dividend* and the result is the *quotient*.)

   Let us look at two simple examples.

(a) 2516 × 37,010 log 2516 = 3·4007
log 37,010 = + 4·5683
7·9690

(b) 37·12 ÷ 1·917 log 37·12 = 1·5696
log 1·917 = − 0·2825
1·2871

3. The result of the addition or subtraction gives the logarithm of the result. We must now reverse the procedure described in 1. to convert the logarithm of the result to a 'conventional' number. Usually, antilogarithm tables are provided, 'antilog' tables for short, an example of which is shown in Figure 7. Since an antilog table is a mere restatement of a log table in reverse format, the original log table can be used to find a conventional number. However, for simplicity and convenience, the use of an antilog table can be assumed.

   As in 1. above, we find the value of the result in distinct stages.

   (i) The mantissa is inspected and the equivalent value in conventional form is found on the antilog table. For example:

Find antilog of ·1923

Horizontal column where x = ·19
Vertical column under '2' = 1556
Plus vertical column under 'ADD 3' = 1 = 1557

(ii) The characteristic is then inspected to determine the position of the decimal point. The two simple rules described in 1. still apply. Thus, for example:

antilog of 2·2567 = 180·6
antilog of 1·2567 = 18·06
antilog of $\bar{1}$·2567 = ·1806
antilog of $\bar{3}$·2567 = ·001806

and so on.

Some time has been spent describing this method of calculation because it shows how a relatively simple procedure can be described, with only a few embellishments, as a purely mechanical one. The procedure is a process of simple inspection, consultation of tables and addition and/or subtraction; it is a process of simple calculation which is, in fact, a means of performing more complex calculations. For the moment, the fact that it is a process of calculation to perform calculation, can be ignored. The mechanical process of calculation by logarithm tables is a valuable guide to the basic characteristics of a computer.

Consider the following application of logarithms to calculating results, based on figures derived from an experiment. There is a team of four people (Figure 8) performing an experiment and preparing the results. A and B are actually performing the experiment. The experiment involves two factors, factor a and factor b. Essentially, A sets factor a on a dial and B reads off the corresponding factor b on another dial. Certain calculations must then be performed on factors a and b. It is the task of C to perform these calculations (producing result c) by means of logarithm tables. Result c is entered on a work sheet and passed to D who is preparing a graph and interpreting the results. We now come to a very important assumption, namely that C is a very junior clerk, somewhat of an automaton, who does only what he is told. C is provided with:

(i) a set of comprehensive and explicit instructions
(ii) a set of log/antilog tables
(iii) a pencil and jotting pad
(iv) a ruled work sheet
(v) a sheet of paper with two constants written on it.

His basic task is to:

x	0	1	2	3	4	5	6	7	8	9	ADD 1	2	3	4	5	6	7	8	9
·00	1000	1002	1005	1007	1009	1012	1014	1016	1019	1021	0	0	1	1	1	1	1	2	2
·01	1023	1026	1028	1030	1033	1035	1038	1040	1042	1045	0	0	1	1	1	1	2	2	2
·02	1047	1050	1052	1054	1057	1059	1062	1064	1067	1069	0	0	1	1	1	1	2	2	2
·03	1072	1074	1076	1079	1081	1084	1086	1089	1091	1094	0	0	1	1	1	1	2	2	2
·04	1096	1099	1102	1104	1107	1109	1112	1114	1117	1119	0	1	1	1	1	2	2	2	2
·05	1122	1125	1127	1130	1132	1135	1138	1140	1143	1146	0	1	1	1	1	2	2	2	2
·06	1148	1151	1153	1156	1159	1161	1164	1167	1169	1172	0	1	1	1	1	2	2	2	2
·07	1175	1178	1180	1183	1186	1189	1191	1194	1197	1199	0	1	1	1	1	2	2	2	2
·08	1202	1205	1208	1211	1213	1216	1219	1222	1225	1227	0	1	1	1	1	2	2	2	3
·09	1230	1233	1236	1239	1242	1245	1247	1250	1253	1256	0	1	1	1	1	2	2	2	3
·10	1259	1262	1265	1268	1271	1274	1276	1279	1282	1285	0	1	1	1	1	2	2	2	3
·11	1288	1291	1294	1297	1300	1303	1306	1309	1312	1315	0	1	1	1	2	2	2	2	3
·12	1318	1321	1324	1327	1330	1334	1337	1340	1343	1346	0	1	1	1	2	2	2	2	3
·13	1349	1352	1355	1358	1361	1365	1368	1371	1374	1377	0	1	1	1	2	2	2	3	3
·14	1380	1384	1387	1390	1393	1396	1400	1403	1406	1409	0	1	1	1	2	2	2	3	3
·15	1413	1416	1419	1422	1426	1429	1432	1435	1439	1442	0	1	1	1	2	2	2	3	3
·16	1445	1449	1452	1455	1459	1462	1466	1469	1472	1476	0	1	1	1	2	2	2	3	3
·17	1479	1483	1486	1489	1493	1496	1500	1503	1507	1510	0	1	1	1	2	2	2	3	3
·18	1514	1517	1521	1524	1528	1531	1535	1538	1542	1545	0	1	1	1	2	2	2	3	3
·19	1549	1552	1556	1560	1563	1567	1570	1574	1578	1581	0	1	1	1	2	2	3	3	3
·20	1585	1589	1592	1596	1600	1603	1607	1611	1614	1618	0	1	1	1	2	2	3	3	3
·21	1622	1626	1629	1633	1637	1641	1644	1648	1652	1656	0	1	1	2	2	2	3	3	3
·22	1660	1663	1667	1671	1675	1679	1683	1687	1690	1694	0	1	1	2	2	2	3	3	3
·23	1698	1702	1706	1710	1714	1718	1722	1726	1730	1734	0	1	1	2	2	2	3	3	4
·24	1738	1742	1746	1750	1754	1758	1762	1766	1770	1774	0	1	1	2	2	2	3	3	4
·25	1778	1782	1786	1791	1795	1799	1803	1807	1811	1816	0	1	1	2	2	2	3	3	4
·26	1820	1824	1828	1832	1837	1841	1845	1849	1854	1858	0	1	1	2	2	3	3	3	4
·27	1862	1866	1871	1875	1879	1884	1888	1892	1897	1901	0	1	1	2	2	3	3	3	4
·28	1905	1910	1914	1919	1923	1928	1932	1936	1941	1945	0	1	1	2	2	3	3	4	4
·29	1950	1954	1959	1963	1968	1972	1977	1982	1986	1991	0	1	1	2	2	3	3	4	4

Fig. 7. An Example 'Antilog' Table

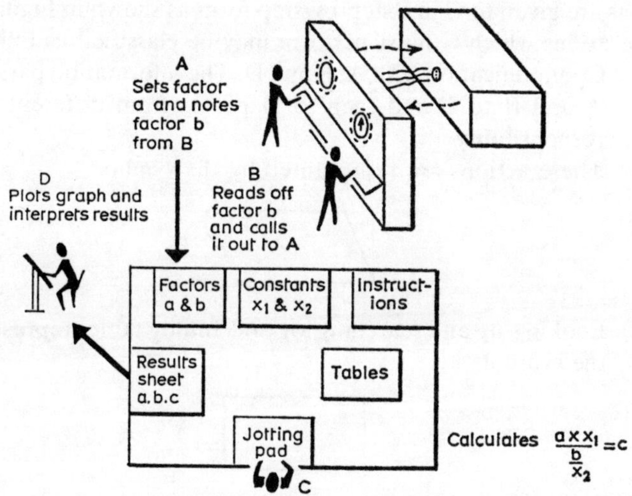

Fig. 8. The Experiment

(vi) Receive a sheet of paper from A and B which states factors a and b.

(vii) Perform the calculation

$$\frac{\dfrac{a \times x_1}{b}}{x_2} = c$$

where x_1 and x_2 are the two constants mentioned in (v). During this calculation, C looks up the logarithms of a and b (we may assume that x_1 and x_2 have been provided as logarithms), writes down the intermediate calculations on the jotting pad, looks up the antilogarithm of the result to give c and, lastly, enters factors a and b and c on the final work sheet.*

Now, since C has the mentality of an automaton, he must be provided with detailed instructions but in a simple explicit form. The instruc-

* This could be written as

$$\frac{a \times x_1 \times x_2}{b} = C$$

and could be calculated by giving C log $(x_1 \times x_2)$ thus leaving him to perform (log a + log $(x_1 \times x_2)$) − log b. For explanatory purposes however, the above method of calculation will be used here.

tions are given to C in a step-by-step form as shown in Figure 9. The operations which C must perform may be classified as follows:

(i) Communication with A, B and D. The information passing from A and B to C and then to D passes from different areas of responsibility.
These actions are represented by the symbol:

(ii) Looking-up and searching log and antilog tables represented by the symbol:

(iii) Performing simple mental calculations, e.g. determining the characteristic, performing the addition and subtraction of logs, placing the decimal point in the result etc. are also represented by the symbol:

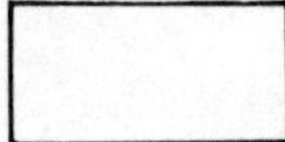

(iv) making simple decisions is represented by the symbol:

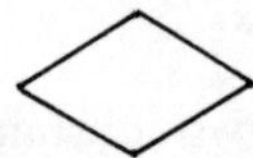

C has a 'repertoire' of basic capabilities, such as reading, adding, subtracting and writing etc. Thus, for C to perform his task, his inherent capabilities are utilized and 'channelled' by means of the instruction list. A closer examination of the list shown above will reveal that certain fine distinctions may be made. The memory of C may be such that the jotting pad is necessary; C may, however, be endowed with an excellent memory so that the intermediate calculations are performed completely in his mind. The jotting pad therefore acts as an 'extension' to C's memory. The same may be said of the written instructions and log/antilog tables. If C had a photographic memory, then after initially reading through the instructions and tables, he would have them stored in his memory and no further reference need be made to the sheets of paper. A situation can thus

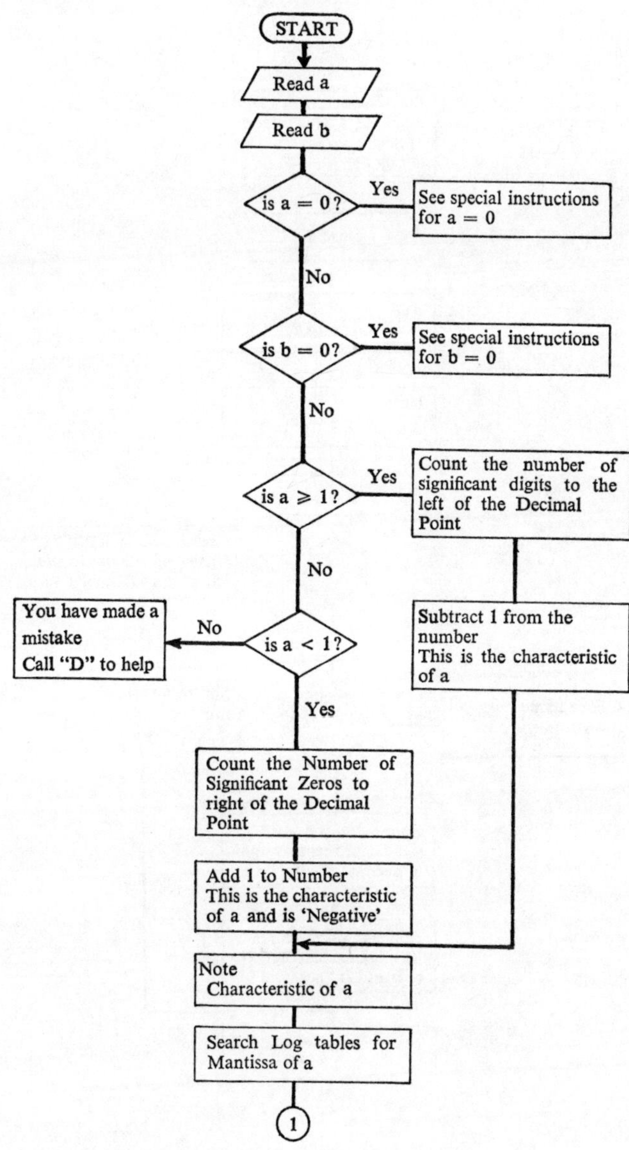

Fig. 9. C's Calculation Procedure

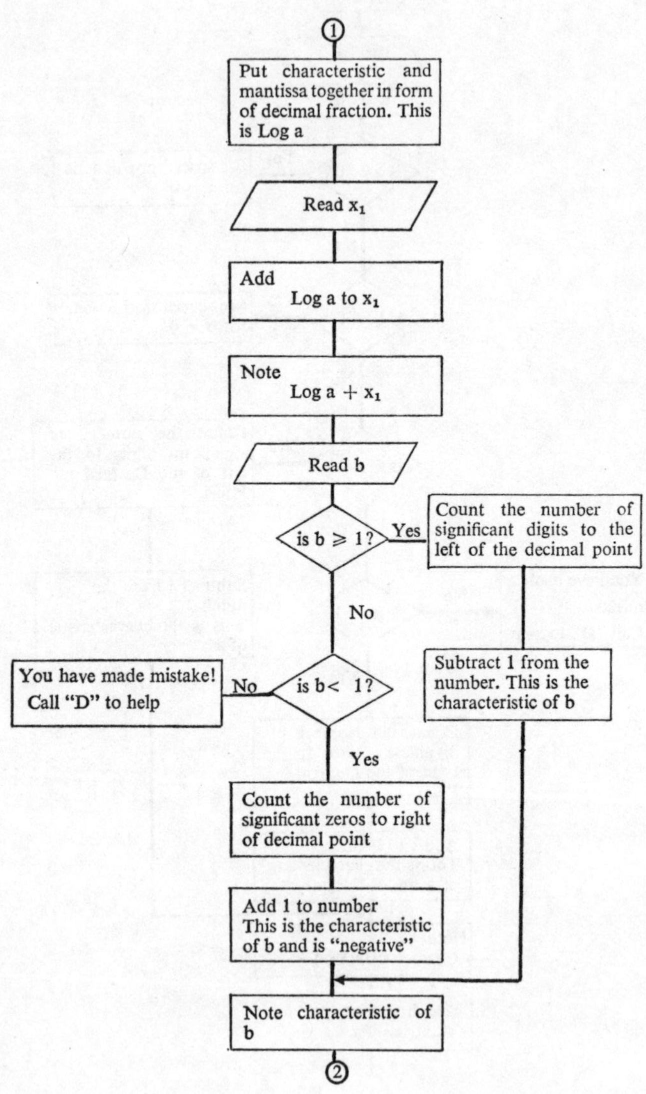

Fig. 9. – *continued*

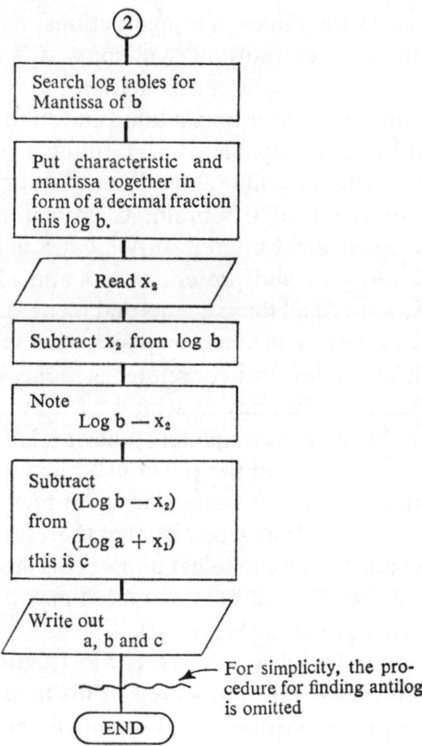

Fig. 9. – *continued*

be imagined in which C performed functions (ii), (iii) and (iv) in his own mind with no continual reference to outside sources such as tables etc. Point (i) in the list is however a separate case; or so it may first appear to be. C may perform the task of calculation after all the results from the experiment are available, i.e. after A and B have completed their part in the experiment and all the values a and b are complete. C could then read the list of the experiment results, the a's and b's, and memorize them. The only external contact that C would have to make during the calculation phase would thus be the writing out of the factors a and b and the results c.

For the moment however, C's memory will not be taxed too hard and it can therefore be assumed that the factors a and b are read before each result is calculated. The characteristics which have been attributed to C and the peculiar method in which he approaches his work may now be summarized. Firstly, C reads all the required data, i.e. x_1 x_2 and the tables, and instructions; data and instructions are then held in C's extraordinary memory. C's memory also holds the results of the intermediate calculations. C is capable of performing simple arithmetic: counting, adding and subtracting; C therefore has a part of his mind capable of performing arithmetic and this can be called the 'arithmetic unit'. Finally, one last observation may be made on the operation of C's brain; C's 'awareness' of what is in his memory must be considered. Inside your memory, for example, are memories of past and present events and ideas. You are not consciously aware of all these events and ideas at one and the same time. There is a selection mechanism which places the required memory of an event into a level of conscious awareness. If you were asked to remember your first day at school, you would (before reading this sentence) have been completely 'unaware' of the memory of such an event. If you had read the previous sentence assiduously, a vivid or vague memory of that particular event may have flashed into your 'conscious' mind. It may be assumed therefore that C has in his brain a control unit which can select items in his memory and that C will be 'aware' of the selected item. C's mind may be represented diagrammatically as shown in Figure 10.

C performs his job as follows. The instructions which specify how C is to perform his task are stored in his memory in the sequence in which they are to be obeyed. The control unit selects the first instruc-

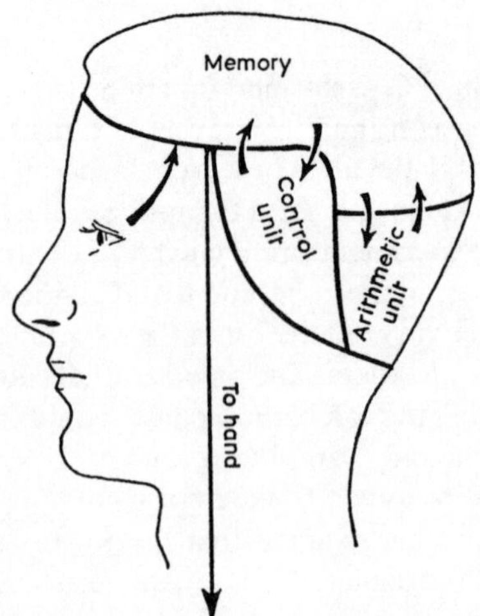

Fig. 10. Diagrammatic Representation of C's Mind

tion and brings it to a 'level of awareness'. It is inspected and is obeyed, i.e. the eyes focus on the sheet of paper and factors a and b are read. C obeys all the instructions in sequence until the last instruction is reached and C's hand is activated to write out the final results. The complete cycle is then repeated and the next values of a and b are read and result c is calculated.

So far in this example, a procedure for performing a calculation has been defined and the process of calculation has been related to a particular circumstance. In the experiment described above, there were three distinct stages, namely:

(i) the origination of data, which is the function of A and B,
(ii) the calculation of certain results from the data, which is the function of C,
(iii) the interpretation of the results, which is the function of experimenter D.

The function of calculation, performed by the automaton C, can now be summarized as follows.

C had a number of inbuilt abilities which included:

the ability to read and write,
the ability to add and subtract,
the ability to 'understand and obey' a limited number of processes, such as 'select next instruction in sequence', 'inspect instruction' 'obey instruction',
the ability to remember instructions and data.

However, C *did not have the ability to reason.*

Since, by the end of the above example, C had been relegated to mere automaton status, he may now be made redundant, and can be replaced by a machine closely resembling the broad outline picture of C as presented earlier. The machine is a collection of electronic circuits which may be considered as comprising six parts, namely:

(i) a memory,
(ii) an arithmetic unit,
(iii) an input unit,
(iv) an output unit,
(v) a control unit,
(vi) a switch panel unit.

The machine is shown diagrammatically in Figure 11.

The physical construction of each of the component parts need not be considered at this particular moment; an initial analysis must first be made of the *functions* of the component parts.

The machine is an inanimate object, a collection of electro-

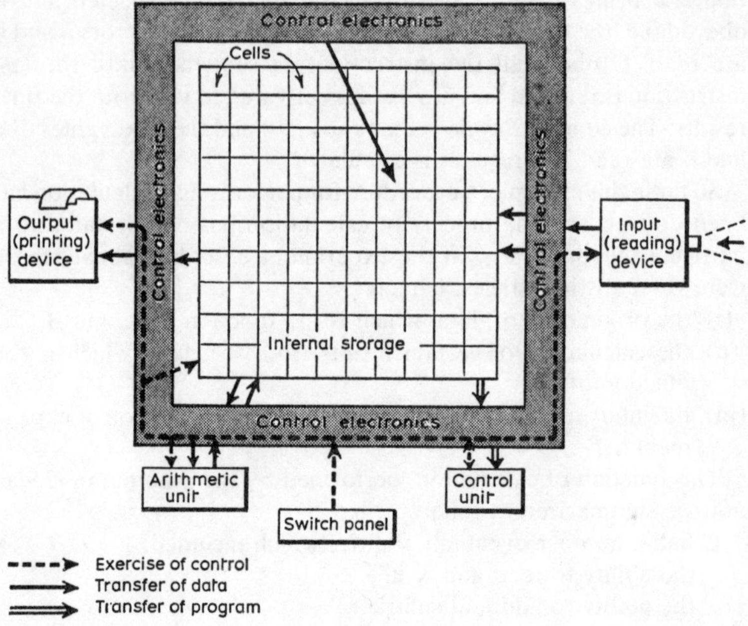

Fig. 11. Machine X

mechanical devices. To perform any operation, the machine must be provided with precise instructions, similar to those given to the human calculator C. These instructions are fed to the machine via the input unit and are held in the memory or *store* as it will now be called. These instructions are called a *program*. An instruction is in this case a statement which is inspected by the control unit so that the appropriate circuitry of the machine is activated. In this example machine, the basic repertoire of instructions that can be obeyed is:

(i) add, subtract, multiply and divide two quantities,
(ii) transfer one unit of information within the store to another position within the store,
(iii) read one unit of information on the input device,
(iv) output, in this case 'print', one unit of information on the output device.

In addition to these basic capabilities, the machine can:

(i) select any instruction within the store,
(ii) transfer it to the control unit,
(iii) inspect the instruction in the control unit and obey it.

The entire storage of the machine is divided into 'cells' and each cell is said to hold one unit of information. The 'information' may either be data to be processed or instructions to process the data. Let us first consider the latter instance, namely the storage of instructions.

The experiment described above is to be performed using our 'machine X' to execute the calculation phase. Some modifications must be made to the basic procedure of the experiment. Before the experiment is performed, a program (the 'list' of instructions) is prepared to perform the calculation on the machine. The calculation is

$$\frac{a \times x_1}{\frac{b}{x_2}}$$

where a and b are derived by experiment and x_1 and x_2 are two constants. Result c is to be calculated for all values of a and b. The instructions are prepared in a special form which can be read by the input device and the complete program is read into storage so that each instruction occupies one cell of storage. The program, in this particular instance, comprises ten instructions as follows:

Instruction No.	
1	read value x_1
2	read value x_2
3	rcad valuc a
4	read value b
5	multiply a by x_1
6	divide b by x_2
7	divide $a \times x_1$ by $\frac{b}{x_2}$ (= c)
8	print a
9	print b
10	print c

For simplicity, this program may be represented in a stylized form as shown in Figure 12.

When the program is read into the store, one program instruction per cell, there is the problem of: 'into which cells are the program instructions to be placed?' For explanatory purposes, it is assumed here that a program may be loaded by means of a series of switches on the switch panel unit; see Figure 13. The principle of reading a program into the store is now as follows.

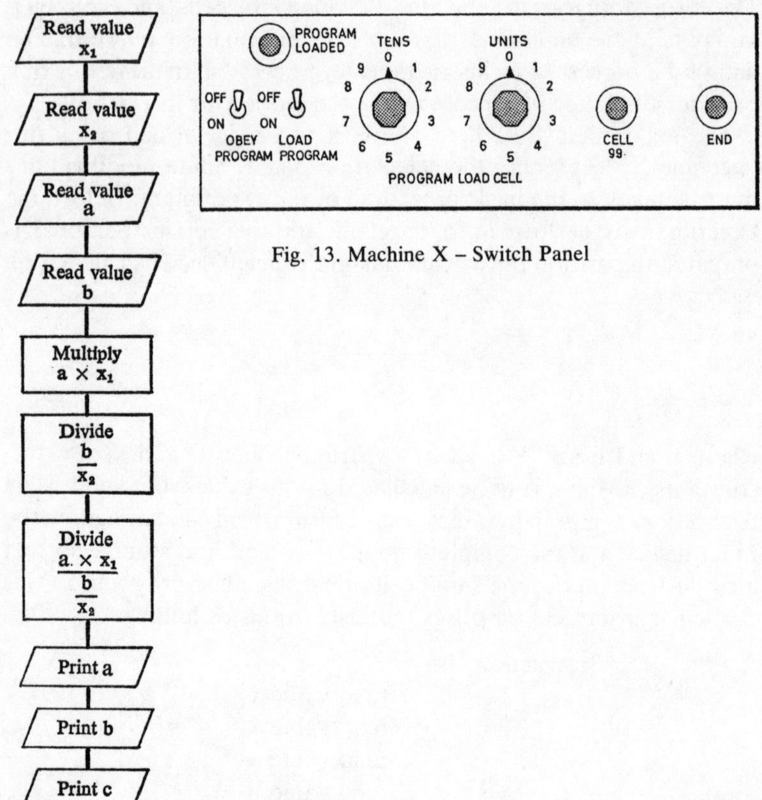

Fig. 13. Machine X – Switch Panel

Fig. 12. Example Program in Flowchart Form

The program is prepared in a form that can be read by the input device. The machine is made in a state of readiness, i.e. power supplies are switched on, and the program is presented to the input device to be read. The store of this particular machine consists of 100 cells; each cell is uniquely identified by means of a two digit number. The cells are numbered in the range 00 to 99 and each number which identifies a cell is called an *address*. When the program is ready to be read, the PROGRAM LOADED CELL dials are set to the number of the cell into which the *first* program instruction is to be read. When the LOAD PROGRAM switch is placed *on*, the input device is activated and the first program instruction is read into the specified cell. The second and subsequent instructions are read into the adjacent cells. An example program input procedure is shown in Figure 14. The program having

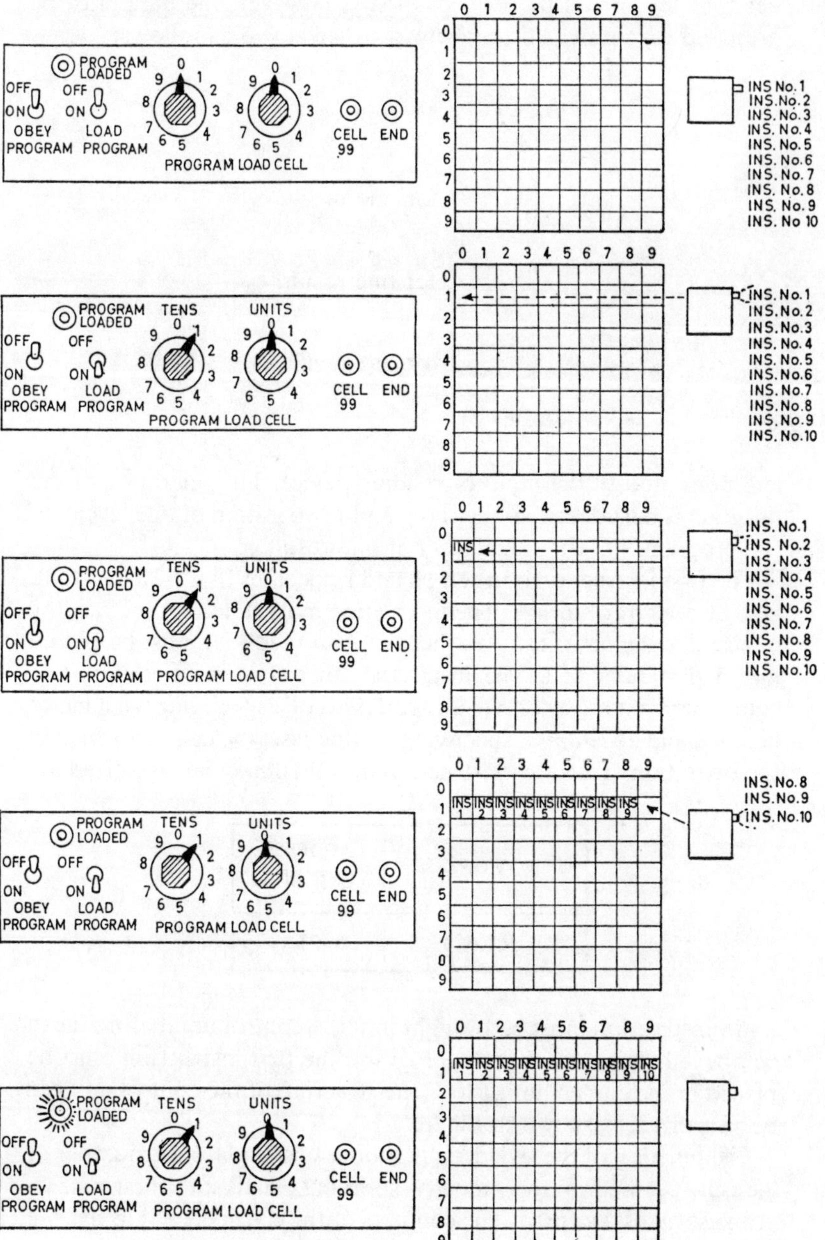

Fig. 14. Machine X – Program Input Procedure

been loaded, it can be obeyed. Firstly, however, the data must be prepared for input. All the factors are arranged as follows:

$$\left.\begin{matrix} x_1 \\ x_2 \end{matrix}\right\} \quad \text{constants}$$

$$\left.\begin{matrix} a_1 \\ b_1 \end{matrix}\right\} \quad \text{for one result, } c_1$$

$$\left.\begin{matrix} a_2 \\ b_2 \end{matrix}\right\} \quad \text{for one result, } c_2$$

$$\left.\begin{matrix} a_3 \\ b_3 \end{matrix}\right\} \quad \text{for one result, } c_3$$

etc.

and presented to the input or reading device. The operation of the program is best described by showing the operation of one 'cycle' of the program, i.e. the calculation of one result c.

The first instruction is in cell 10 and it specifies that x_1, a constant, is to be read into storage. The instruction must state that the reading device is to be activated and that the data read (x_1) must be placed into a particular cell. The instruction therefore must contain two components; it must contain an *operation code* specifying what has to be done and an *address*, specifying, in this case, the cell concerned in the operation. Thus, the instruction in cell 10 may be visualized as:

OPERATION CODE	ADDRESS (Cell No.)
READ	01

An instruction must be brought into the control unit before it can be obeyed. Thus, to start the program, the first instruction must be placed in the control unit. Now, the structure of the control unit can be visualized as shown in Figure 15.

The function of the switch OBEY PROGRAM is to place the number of the cell specified on the PROGRAM LOAD CELL dials into the PROGRAM ADDRESS REGISTER (PAR). The contents of the cell specified in the PAR are placed in the PROGRAM REGISTER. The contents of the PROGRAM REGISTER are inspected and analysed; the operation code and address cause the appropriate circuitry to be activated and the required action is taken. In the case of the first instruction the control unit functions as shown in Figure 16. Once the instruction has been obeyed, one is added to the contents of the PAR and the whole process is repeated. The contents of the PAR are now 11, and the contents of cell 11 are transferred to the PROGRAM REGISTER and the instruction ('READ 02') is obeyed; one is added to the contents of the PAR and the process is repeated. Note that:

(i) the contents of a cell are not altered after a transfer to the PROGRAM REGISTER, i.e. an instruction is still in the cell after a transfer;

(ii) the previous contents of the PROGRAM REGISTER are overwritten by each new instruction transferred from the store.

The state of the store after instructions 1 to 4 (in cells 10 to 13) have been obeyed is as follows:

0	1 x_1	2 x;	3 a	4 b	5	6	7	8	9
10 read x_1	11 read x_2	12 read a	13 read b	14 multiply a by x_1	15 divide b by x_2	16 divide $\frac{a \times x_1}{\frac{b}{x_2}}$	17 print a	18 print b	19 print c
20	21	22	23	24	25	26	27	28	29
30	31	32	33	34	35	36	37	38	39
40	41	42	43	44	45	46	47	48	49
50	51	52	53	54	55	56	57	58	59
60	61	62	63	64	65	66	67	68	69
70	71	72	73	74	75	76	77	78	79
80	81	82	83	84	85	86	87	88	89
90	91	92	93	94	95	96	97	98	99

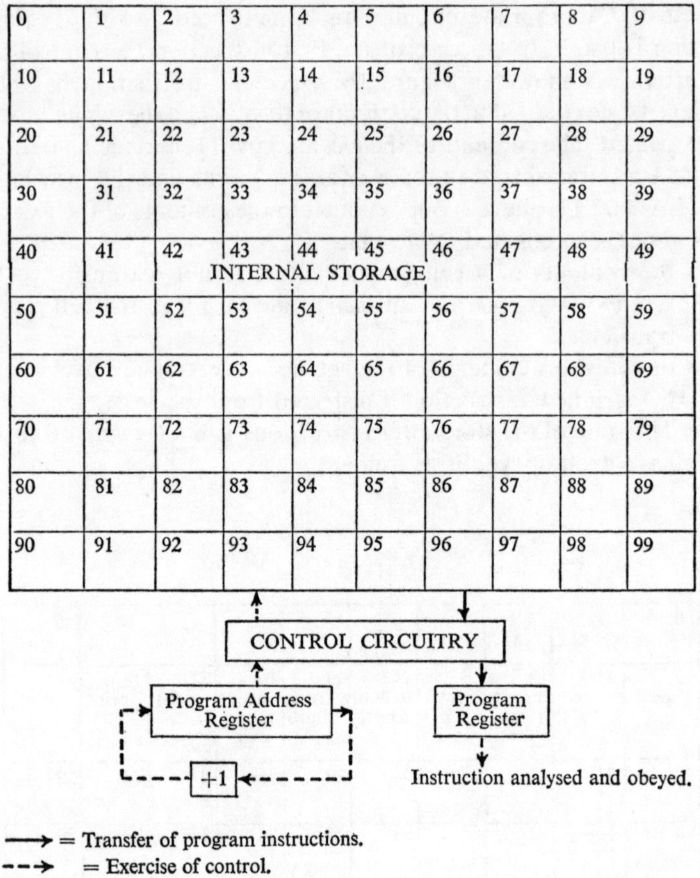
0 1 2 3 4 5 6 7 8 9
10 11 12 13 14 15 16 17 18 19
20 21 22 23 24 25 26 27 28 29
30 31 32 33 34 35 36 37 38 39
40 41 42 43 44 45 46 47 48 49
INTERNAL STORAGE
50 51 52 53 54 55 56 57 58 59
60 61 62 63 64 65 66 67 68 69
70 71 72 73 74 75 76 77 78 79
80 81 82 83 84 85 86 87 88 89
90 91 92 93 94 95 96 97 98 99
CONTROL CIRCUITRY
Program Address Register
Program Register
+1
Instruction analysed and obeyed.
= Transfer of program instructions.
= Exercise of control.

Fig. 15. Machine X – Control Unit

assuming that the program states:

OPERATION CODE	ADDRESS	
Read	01	x_1
Read	02	x_2
Read	03	a_1
Read	04	b_1

and that each READ instruction causes the one factor to be read into storage. The operation of the reading device may be visualized as

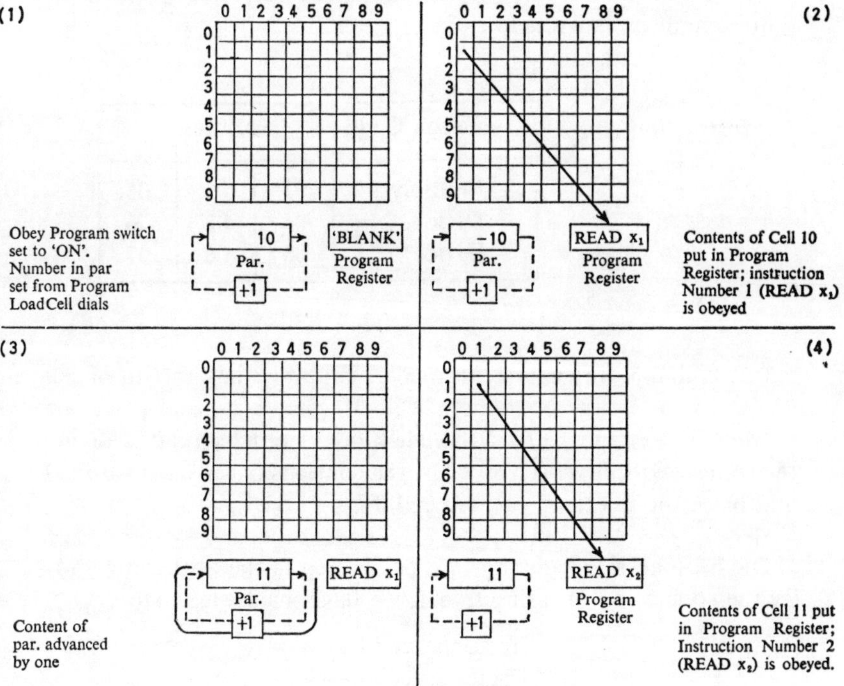

Fig. 16. Machine X – Operation of the Control Unit

follows. Each item of data, in this case a 'factor', is written on a separate line of a sheet of paper. A read instruction causes the first line to be scanned and the data to be read into storage. A subsequent read instruction causes the paper to move forward one line; the contents of that line are scanned, placed into storage and so on.

The next three instructions are arithmetic and present new problems. Instruction number 5 stored in cell 14 must state that factor a, in cell 03, is to be multiplied by factor x_1 which is in cell 01. To perform this operation it is necessary that

(i) the operation code must specify 'multiply';

(ii) When the instruction is held within the PROGRAM REGISTER to be obeyed, the cell numbers or addresses, holding factor a and factor x_1, must be apparent;

(iii) when the instruction is held within the PROGRAM REGISTER to be obeyed, the number of the cell (address) which is to hold the result of the multiplication must be apparent.

The instruction format which illustrates the 'three addresses' requirement is shown below.

Instruction No.	Operation Code	Address		
5	Multiply	03	01	05
6	Divide	04	02	06
7	Divide	05	06	07

Instruction 5, for example, is read as 'multiply the contents of cell 03 (factor a) by the contents of cell 01 (factor x_1) and place the product ($a \times x_1$) into cell 05'. Similarly, instruction 6 is read as 'divide the contents of cell 04 (factor b) by the contents of cell 02 (factor x_2) and place the quotient $\left(\frac{b}{x_2}\right)$ in cell 06.'

The arithmetic calculations are performed in the arithmetic unit. By the conclusion of instruction 7, we have available in store:

factor a (cell 03)
factor b (cell 04)
factor c (cell 07)

Instructions numbered 8 to 10 held in cells 17 to 19 specify that the contents of cells 03, 04 and 07 are to be printed. One 'cycle' of operations has thus been performed and one result has been calculated.

To produce further results, the sequence described above must be repeated for each calculation of result c. However, certain modifications must be made to the basic cycle. At the conclusion of the first 'cycle' there are two possibilities. Firstly, further instructions may be placed in storage in the cells 20, 21, 22 onwards. At the end of the first cycle, only two new factors a and b need to be read in; the constant x_1, and x_2 are still held in storage and thus need not be read a second time. In fact, unless the constants x_1 and x_2 are repeated before each factor set of a and b, x_1 and x_2 could not be read again. Further, the format x_1, x_2, a_1, b_1, x_1, x_2, a_2, b_2 etc. would not conform to the specification laid down on page 39.

If the sequence of *instructions* is:

Instruction No.	in Cell No.	Description of Instruction
1	10	READ x_1 into Cell 01
2	11	READ x_2 into Cell 02
3	12	READ a_1 into Cell 03
4	13	READ b_1 into Cell 04
8	17	PRINT a_1 from Cell 03
9	18	PRINT b_1 from Cell 04
10	19	PRINT c_1 from Cell 07
11	20	READ a_2 into Cell 03
12	21	READ b_2 into Cell 04
16	25	PRINT a_2 from Cell 03
17	26	PRINT b_2 from Cell 04
18	27	PRINT c_2 from Cell 07

the sequence of operations is:

First Cycle
- READ x_1 and x_2
- READ a_1 and b_1
- CALCULATE c_1
- PRINT a_1, b_1 and c_1

Second Cycle
- READ a_2 and b_2
- CALCULATE c_2
- PRINT a_2, b_2 and c_2

The instructions comprising the second cycle can be identical to those of the first cycle with the exclusion of the first two read instructions. The factors a_2 and b_2 read on the second cycle can be input to cells 03 and 04 respectively. This will 'overwrite' or replace the existing factors a_1 and b_1. This method will require eight cells to store the eight instructions for each cycle. There are ninety cells available for the program and therefore instructions for eleven cycles can be stored and only eleven calculations of c can be performed.

Instructions for Cycle No.	Store in Cell Nos.
1	10 to 19
2	20 to 27
3	28 to 35
4	36 to 43
5	44 to 51
6	52 to 59
7	60 to 67

8	68 to 75
9	76 to 83
10	84 to 91
11	92 to 99

Suppose however that there are twenty-two calculations of c to be performed. In this instance, arrangements will have to be made to repeat the series of ninety instructions. The repetition of the instructions could, for example, be initiated as follows. It will be remembered that the PAR (Program Address Register) is an integral part of the control unit. A lamp, 'CELL 99', is included in the switch panel unit and this lamp will glow when the contents of the PAR are 99, one is added and the contents becomes 100, too large for the PAR to hold. In this particular instance, the lamp will glow when the eleventh cycle is completed. To repeat the eleven cycles, the OBEY PROGRAM switch is placed *off*, the PROGRAM LOAD CELL dials are set to cell '12' and the OBEY PROGRAM switch is placed *on*. As described on page 42, this will cause '12' to be placed in the PAR and the series of instructions stored in cell 12 to cell 99 will be repeated.

This method has obvious disadvantages. If any 'program repeats' are required, the last instruction must be placed in cell 99 such that the 'CELL 99' lamp is activated. Further, consider the position when the last instruction to be obeyed in the complete series is not in cell 99. For example, suppose twenty-four calculations of c are required; how can the program be terminated at the end of the twenty-fourth cycle? If the twenty-fourth cycle is performed, or there is an attempt to perform it, a read instruction will be given to reading unit but there will be no data available to be read. If there are sixteen cycles (sixteen calculations of c), there are eight redundant cycles to be performed or rather to be attempted.

There are thus two major problems in the manually controlled repetition of program cycles as described above. A machine working on this 'push button' repeat system would be ludicrously inefficient. Besides the two obvious disadvantages described above, the operator (presumably a demoted human calculator C!) must be constantly at hand. The solution to all these problems is to devise a means whereby the program initiates a repeat of a program cycle itself. This will require certain basic modifications to be made to the program as previously described; it will also necessitate the inclusion of a new type of program instruction.

Assume that the program instructions are arrayed in store as described on page 43. In cell 20 however, there is an instruction of the form:

Instruction No.	Operation Code	Address
11	Jump	12

This instruction has the same effect as setting 12 on the PROGRAM LOAD CELL dials and placing the OBEY PROGRAM switch on. When the contents of the PAR are 20, the 'JUMP 12' instruction is placed in the PROGRAM REGISTER and obeyed. The instruction is obeyed as follows:

(i) The existing figure in the PAR is overwritten by the address 12.
(ii) The 'add one' function is inhibited.
(iii) The contents of the PAR are inspected and the relevant instruction is entered from store into the PROGRAM REGISTER, in this case the contents of cell 12 – 'READ 03'.
(iv) The instruction in the PROGRAM REGISTER is obeyed.
(v) One is added to the contents of the PAR and the next instruction placed in the PROGRAM REGISTER is obeyed and so on.

Thus the 'JUMP' instruction causes an interruption to the sequence in which the program instruction is obeyed. The jump is *unconditional*, i.e. it will occur every time instruction number 11 in cell 20 is obeyed. Our program may now be shown as in Figure 17. When the program is initiated, the entire series of instructions is obeyed; when the first 'cycle' is completed, a jump is made and the complete series of instructions is repeated, with the *exception* of those two instructions which cause factors x_1 and x_2 to be read into storage. Once the program has been initiated, the basic cycle 'READ 03' to 'JUMP 12' will be repeated indefinitely. There is still the problem therefore of relating the number of times the basic 'cycle' is performed to the number of calculations of result c required. This can be achieved, with further modifications to the basic program as shown, by means of counting and the use of a *conditional jump* instruction. This method requires that the exact number of calculations of c to be performed is known and constant. Suppose 150 calculations of c are to be performed, then –

(i) Instruction No. 1 and No. 2 ('READ x_1' and 'READ x_2') are to be obeyed once.
(ii) Instructions No. 3 to No. 10 ('READ a' to 'JUMP') are to be obeyed 150 times.

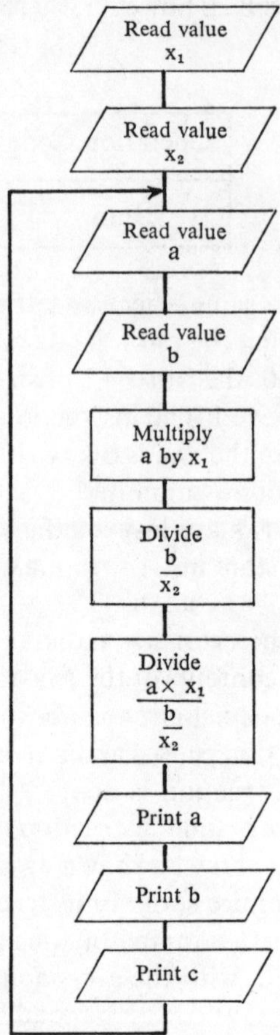

Fig. 17. Revised Program with an Unconditional Jump

By the inclusion of a simple procedure it is possible to count, by program, the number of times the 'READ a' to 'JUMP' cycle is performed. This process of counting can be achieved as follows:

(i) The list of input data is modified so that x_1 is preceded by two constants of 1 and 150.

1
150
x_1
x_2
a_1

b_1
a_2
b_2
a_3
b_3
etc.

(ii) The first four instructions in the program become

Cell No.	Operation Code	Address
08	Read	90
09	Read	91
10	Read	01
11	Read	02

This places the constant 1 into cell 90 and the constant 150 into cell 91; constants x_1 and x_2 are placed into cells 01 and 02 as before.

(iii) The program instructions in cells 12 to 19 can remain unaltered Three new instructions are placed in cells 20, 21, and 23, namely:

Cell No.	Operation Code	Address		
19	Print	07		
20	Subtract	90	91	91
21	Jump = 0	91	23	12
23	End			

The three new instructions perform the following functions: SUBTRACT 90 91 91 operates in a manner similar to the MULTIPLY and DIVIDE instructions previously described, i.e. the contents of cell 90 are subtracted from the contents of cell 91 and the result is placed in cell 91. Thus, if the contents of cell 90 are 1 and contents of cell 91 are 150, after the instruction in cell 20 is performed, the contents of cell 91 are 149.

JUMP = 0 91 23 12 is a 'conditional jump' instruction and can be read as follows.

'If the contents of cell 91 *are* zero, jump to and obey the instruction in cell 23. If the contents of cell 91 *are not* zero, jump to and obey the instruction in cell 12.'

The jump is obeyed in a similar manner to the 'unconditional' jump instruction, i.e. the contents of the PAR are replaced bya new address. The address placed in the PAR is, in a conditional jump instruction, dependent on certain conditions. If the contents of cell 91 are zero, then a jump will be made to cell 23 which contains an 'END' instruction. Alternatively, if the contents of cell 91 are not zero, then the jump will be made to cell 12 holding the 'READ 03' instruction.

END is an instruction which stops the program; when it appears in the PROGRAM REGISTER, the operation of the PAR is suspended and the END lamp on the switch panel glows.

The operation of the program using these new instructions will now be a conditional 'loop'. The basic structure of the program is:

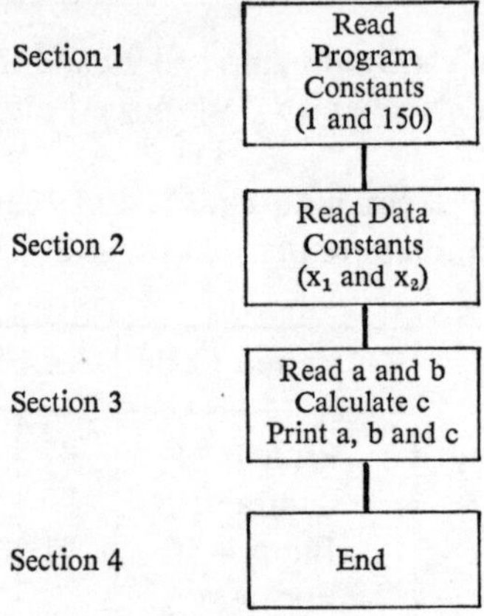

The revised program is shown in 'flowchart' form in Figure 18.

Sections 1 and 2 are to be performed once at the beginning of the program. Section 3 is to be performed one hundred and fifty times and Section 4 is to be performed once at the end of the program. At the start of Section 3, the contents of cell 91 are 150; at the conclusion of Section 3, one is subtracted from the contents of cell 91 and the contents of the cell are now 149. The jump instruction at the conclusion of Section 3 causes the instruction in cell 12 to be obeyed since the contents of cell 91 are not equal to zero. This process is repeated and when Section 3 has been repeated one hundred and fifty times, one has been subtracted from the contents of cell 91 one hundred and fifty times thereby reducing the contents to zero. The jump instruction at the conclusion of the one hundred and fiftieth passage through

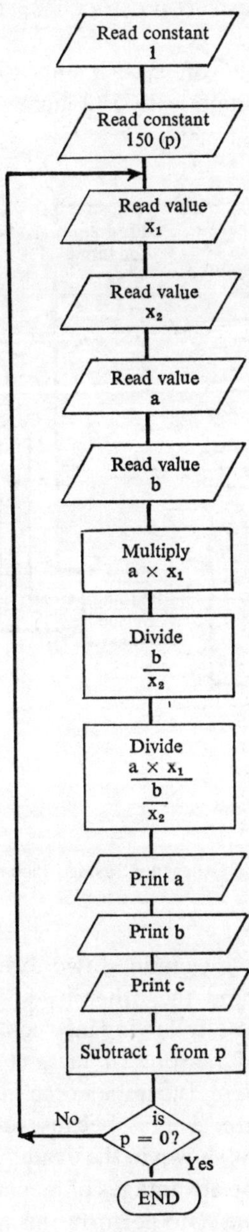

Fig. 18. Revised Program with a Conditional Jump

Section 3 causes the instruction in cell 23 to be obeyed and the program completed.

The complete process of experiment, calculate and interpret results is shown diagrammatically in Figure 19.

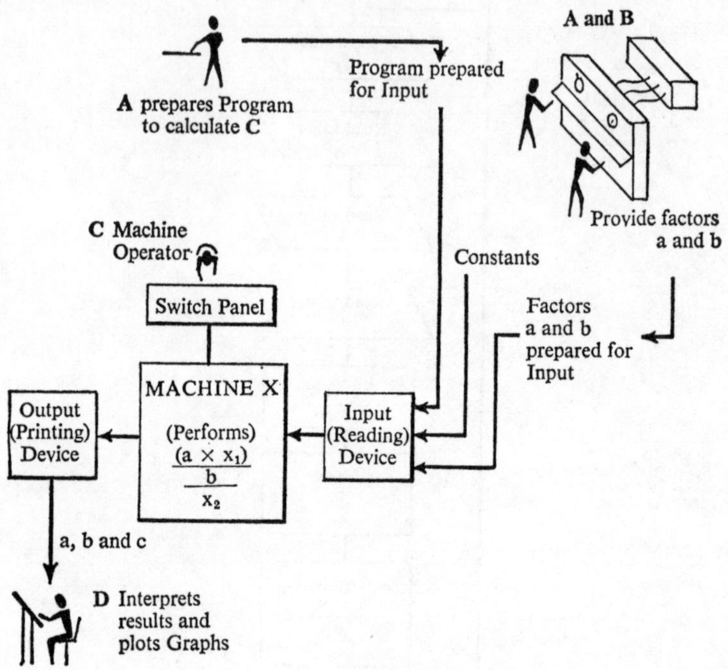

Fig. 19. The Experiment using Machine X

In this chapter we have examined two examples of calculation – one by an automaton and the other by a simple machine. Both involved a basic process of 'following instructions'. No one can claim that 'machine X' could reason. In fact, it may appear that the machine, as described here, is cumbersome in operation and unusually complex in structure. This is because of the volume and the nature of the calculations shown in the examples. If there are 10,000 calculations of c, then the advantages of machine X become clear. A realistic time for machine X to perform this number of calculations and print the results would be 10 to 15 minutes.

THE STORED PROGRAM CONCEPT

Machine X employed a *stored program*. Although the instructions have been shown here as 'READ 01' for example, an instruction when held within the store of the machine would be entirely numeric. A simple numeric operation code system can be employed thus:

00 — Unconditional Jump
01 — Read
02 — Print
03 — Multiply
04 — Divide
05 — Subtract
06 — Add
10 — Jump on 'x' equal to zero

and so on. A cell on machine X is capable of holding eight digits. A 'single address' instruction has the format:

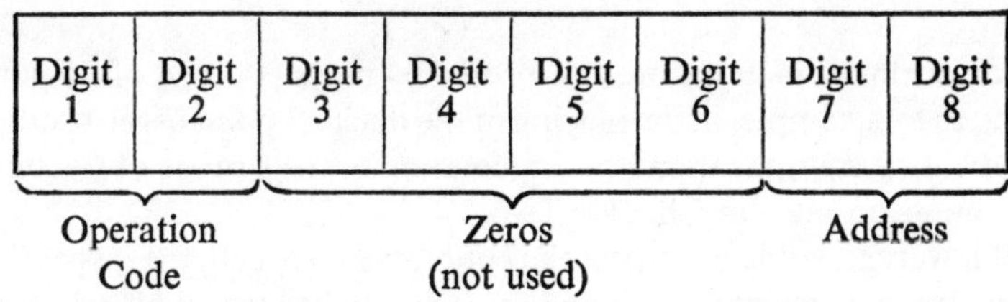

as for example in 'READ 03':

0	1	0	0	0	0	0	3

A 'three address' instruction has the format:

Digit 1	Digit 2	Digit 3	Digit 4	Digit 5	Digit 6	Digit 7	Digit 8
Operation Code		Address (1)		Address (2)		Address (3)	

as, for example, in MULTIPLY 03 15 87, multiply the contents of cell 03 by the contents of cell 15 and place the product in cell 87:

0	3	0	3	1	5	8	7

Numeric data is held in a cell in an eight digit form, right justified. For example, the figure 8,342 would be held in a cell as:

0	0	0	0	8	3	4	2

and 18,300,421 would be held as:

1	8	3	0	0	4	2	1

Since decimal fractions present problems in the storage of numeric data, as for example, in the placing of the decimal point in the product following a multiplication, the explanation of the storage of fractions will be given later in Chapter Two.

If it were possible to inspect the contents of one cell, the inspection would reveal an eight digit number. It would be impossible to determine if the eight digit number were an instruction or data. Machine X performed arithmetic on data cells and, since there is no distinction between data and instructions, arithmetic can be performed on instructions. The effect of this is that an instruction can be *modified*. Instruction modification is a characteristic of a machine operating with a stored program. It is often claimed that a machine operating with a stored program and capable of performing instruction modification can be classed as a 'computer'. Any machine *not* capable of performing instruction modification, so it is claimed, cannot be classed as a computer. This is a debatable point but, since the capability of instruction modification is ranked so high in the definition of a computer, an examination of what it is and how it is used is necessary. The reader can then assess the importance of instruction modification.

Returning to machine X, consider the following example. One

quarter of the total storage is occupied by program; the remainder is available to hold data. As the result of calculation, ten factors are produced and stored in cells 50 to 59. It is required to find the sum of the quantities in cells 50 to 59, store the sum in cell 60, and then print the sum. This could be achieved by ten instructions as follows:

Cell No.	Instructions: Operation Code	Address		
90	06	50	51	60
91	06	52	60	60
92	06	53	60	60
93	06	54	60	60
94	06	55	60	60
95	06	56	60	60
96	06	57	60	60
97	06	58	60	60
98	06	59	60	60
99	02	00	00	60

However, the following program, comprising only six instructions, performs the same task:

Cell No.	Instructions: Operation Code	Address		
90	06	50	51	60
91	06	52	60	60
92	06	97	91	91
93	05	99	98	98
94	10	98	91	95
95	02	00	00	60

The instruction in cell 90 adds two of the required quantities and places the sum into cell 60. The next instruction adds yet another quantity to the previous sum and the new sum is placed in cell 60. The action of the next instruction is to add one to the 'address (1)' part of the instruction. The contents of cell 91 are now 06 53 60 60. The instructions in cells 93 and 94 form a 'counter' which will cause the

Cell No.	Contents							
97	0	0	0	1	0	0	0	0
98	0	0	0	0	0	0	0	8
99	0	0	0	0	0	0	0	1

instruction in cell 91 to be performed eight times. Thus, at the conclusion of the eighth cycle, the instruction in cell 91 will be 06 59 60 60. Each time the instruction in cell 91 is obeyed, it relates to a different item of data and thus the contents of cells 53, 54 and so on to cell 59 are added to cell 60. This method requires nine cells; six for instructions and three for the program constants. If the contents of cell 60 were zero at the start of the first cycle, then only five instructions would be required.

Instructions

Cell No.	Operation Code	Address		
90	06	50	60	60
91	06	97	90	90
92	05	99	98	98
93	10	98	91	94
94	02	00	00	60

The contents of cell 98 will be, initially, 00000010. In terms of storage, the number of cells required to perform this operation has been effectively reduced by two. If there were twenty figures to be added together, the same number of program/constant cells could be used, only the contents of cell 98 being altered to give the required count of twenty.

From this example, it can be seen that instruction modification enables one set of instructions to perform several operations on different data. The complete address part of an instruction may be changed by adding a complex constant rather than just adding one. Although it is not true that the entire form of a program is usually altered by instruction modification, the basic structure of addressing can be altered as a program is obeyed.

The calculation processes shown in this chapter have been simple arithmetical procedures. However, calculation need not be related only to basic procedures of arithmetic. Let us consider another aspect of calculation – the role of 'decision'. In the initial discussion on calculation, it was shown that 'decision is an integral facet of calculation. Agent 9X's calculation was in fact a 'decision'; if we assume that agent 9X is a mathematically minded spy, the result of his calculations was a decision, 'leap' or 'no leap.' The decisions which are of interest here are those based on formal calculations. Consider the decision made in a supermarket by a housewife; she must decide between the purchase of two brands. The decision to be made is: 'Shall I buy brand x or brand y?' and it is based on data such as, 'I think brand x tastes better, but my husband likes brand y'; the decision may be biased by influential advertising. A calculating housewife on the other hand may be able to formalize her decision procedure. For example, the calculation could be: compare price – compare quantity – compare vitamin content – and so on. A computer can make such decisions provided that:

(i) the decision procedure is specified, that is, a comprehensive program is provided;
(ii) all the required data is provided.

A 'decision' procedure was shown in Figure 18. The decision in this program was basically – 'Has the calculation section of the program been obeyed one hundred and fifty times?' A 'yes' resulted in the 'end' section being entered and a 'no' resulted in the calculation section being re-entered. The decision was, of course, based on the 'inspection' of the contents of a specified cell. If a decision is represented by the symbol

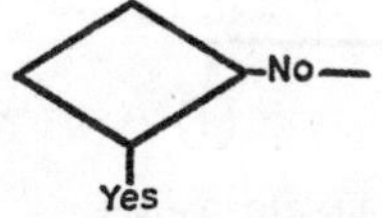

a simple set of related decisions may be shown as in Figure 20. The major decision is as follows: 'Should a tip be left after a snack and if so how much?' This major decision is based on a network of minor decisions. This rather exotic application has been shown to make a very important point. The computer can only perform this operation because the decision making procedure has been formalized. Note

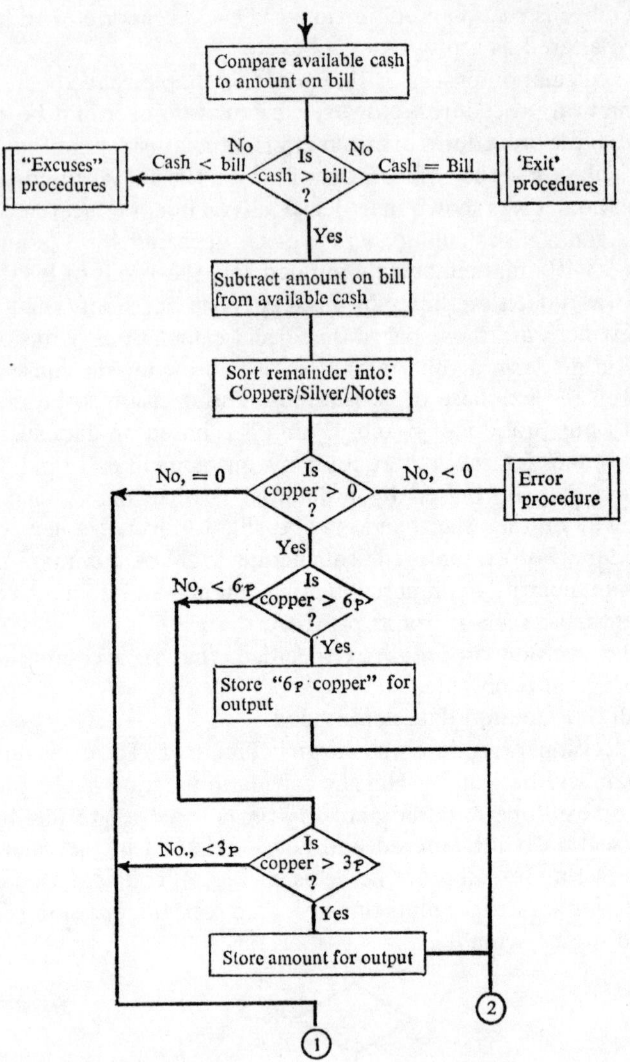

Fig. 20. Tipping

that this procedure can only be performed because the computer's users have to provide all the relevant data such as the amount of cash available, the analysis of the cash, time in/time out of restaurant, evaluation of waitress' legs and so on. Decisions, as can be seen, are 'made' by a simple process of comparison and 'yes' and 'no' branches of a program. A *complex* system of decision networks is possible only

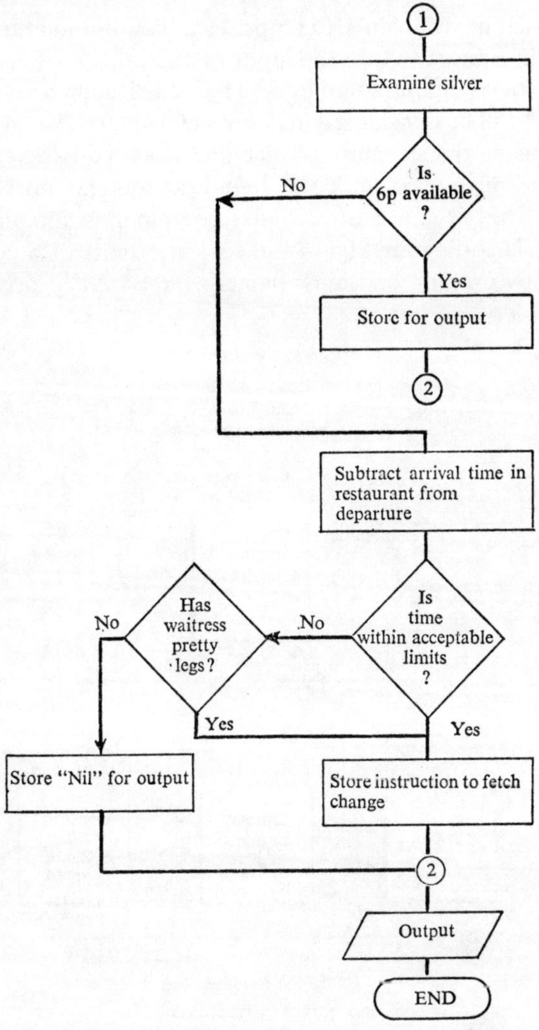

Fig. 20. – *continued*

because of the large internal storage of a computer and the versatility of a stored program.

THE MODERN DIGITAL COMPUTER

The example machine X represents an idea rather than an actual physical machine. Machine X comprises a 'micro-miniature' digital computer. Its basic structure and mode of operation is representative of most modern digital computers. The actual units are as yet ill-defined and will be considered in detail in Chapters Two and Three. However, using the structure of machine X as the basic guide, the capabilities and uses of modern digital computers can be briefly described. The structure of a digital computer is summarized in Figure 21. This diagram shows the six basic units of a computer. There are two major divisions, namely the *central processor* and *peripheral units*.

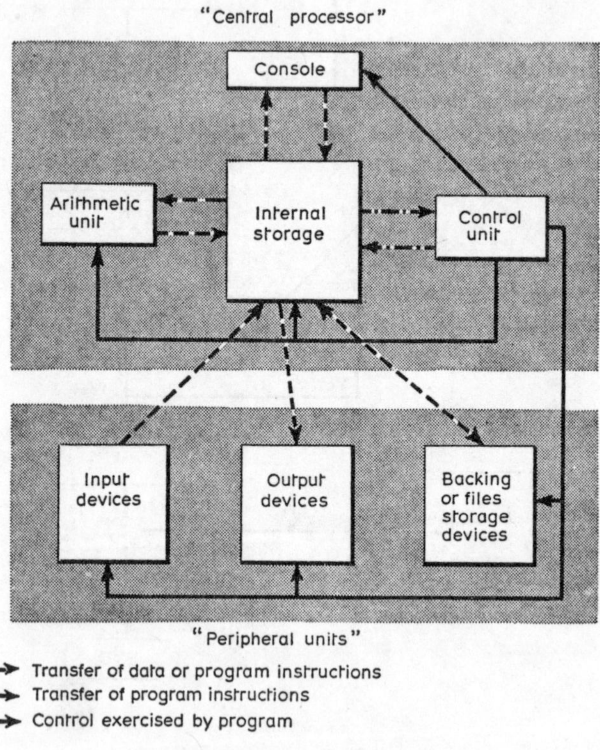

Fig. 21. Structure of a Modern Digital Computer

The central processor includes:

(i) internal storage
(ii) arithmetic unit
(iii) program controller or control unit
(iv) console or switch panel unit

and the peripheral units include:

(i) input devices

(ii) output devices

(iii) backing (file) store devices.

The previous discussion of machine X showed how the central processor could be used for calculation; the input and output devices were introduced merely as a means for reading in data and program and printing out results. The example experiment described on page 54, was primarily concerned with calculation; input and output were 'incidental' to the calculation of results.

In the terms of this book, a basic distinction may be made between 'scientific and mathematical' applications and 'commercial' applications of a computer. It may be assumed that the term 'scientific application' is synonymous with 'an application which is mostly concerned with calculation'. In a computer which is to be used for scientific work, the central processor will be of greater 'importance' than the peripheral (input/output) units. The central processor will probably have the characteristics of: large internal storage, fast speed of arithmetic calculations, the ability to perform arithmetic on large numbers and so on. Thus, the characteristic of scientific and mathematical work is the predominance of calculation.

The classification of 'commercial' is distinguished from the classification of 'scientific and mathematical' by the fact that calculation is less. It is difficult to give a precise definition of the term 'commercial' and in this book, 'commercial application' is defined only in terms of the characteristics of the type of work performed on the computer.

Widespread use of computers in commerce will be found in the preparation of company payrolls, the production of invoices and bills, the regulation of stock, the preparation of production/consumption statistics and so on. These applications usually involve calculation at a very elementary level such as 'hours × rate', 'quantity × price', 'net discount', 'sales figures of brand x in area y by adding sales of salesman a, salesman b, salesman c', etc. Since, as the previous part of this chapter implies, computers are capable of performing complex calculations in a very short period of time, what is the relevance of computers in commercial applications? The emphasis of the calculation aspect is reduced and the predominance of the capabilities of the central processor is replaced by the peripheral units and the function of input/output. In commercial applications the storage and access of data becomes the key factor. Consider the following simplified example of a commercial procedure.

A company (which we will call 'Beautiface') manufacturing and distributing cosmetics, supplies 5,000 retailers throughout the United Kingdom. The retailers are serviced by 500 Beautiface salesmen who call once a week. An average of 10,000 items of Beautiface products are ordered per week. Thus, assuming an average distribution of orders over the retailers, there are two items ordered per retailer per week. Naturally, some retailers will place no orders and some will place ten orders. The Beautiface company have conditioned their customers (the retailers) to plan ahead and to order at least a week in advance of the time when they will require the ordered items. The procedure for processing the orders is as follows.

(i) Monday to Wednesday – salesmen collect orders;
(ii) Thursday – orders are sent to head office. (Beautiface works on the 'centralization' of sales principle);
(iii) Thursday/Friday/Monday – orders processed at head office – stock despatch notices sent to stock department – invoices produced and sent to retailers.

Ignoring the production of stock notices and the receipt of payments etc., the production of the invoices requires the following documentation.

Salesmen complete orders in the field which contain

(i) a customer number (in the range of 1 to 5,000);
(ii) a salesman number;
(iii) a description of the items ordered (basically an 'item number');
(iv) the quantity of items ordered.

At head office there are a number of 'invoice clerks'. Each clerk has a ledger and each ledger sheet is identified by a customer number. The ledger sheet states:

(i) customer number;
(ii) name and address of customer;
(iii) terms of trade.

For each group of ordered items the clerk enters:

(i) date of order and order number;
(ii) invoice number;

(iii) date invoice despatched;
(iv) total value of invoice;
(v) amount paid.

There is also a 'stock item book', each item sheet being identified by an item number. The item sheet states:

(i) item number;
(ii) description;
(iii) price;
(iv) quantity discount.

The invoice sent to a customer states:

(i) number, name and address of customer;
(ii) invoice number;
(iii) order number;
(iv) date of order and invoice;
(v) the goods ordered, quantity, description, unit price, discount and price for items ordered, i.e. quantity × unit price – discount;
(vi) the total price.

The basic procedure to produce the invoices is:

(i) Clerk A consults Customer Ledger and writes out, on a separate sheet of paper, the invoice data (i) to (iv). Clerk A passes order and sheet of paper to Clerk B.
(ii) Clerk B consults Stock File, calculates and enters invoice data (v) to (vi) on the separate sheet of paper. Passes completed sheet of paper back to Clerk A.
(iii) Clerk A enters total price in Customer Ledger. Passes sheet of paper to invoice typing department.
(iv) Invoice typing department types invoice. Passes completed typed invoice to invoice despatch department.
(v) Invoice despatch department folds and posts completed typed invoice.

The above procedure is cumbersome, but it illustrates two important points. Firstly, the calculation of prices is a relatively simple procedure forming but a small part of the total procedure. Secondly, by far the greatest amount of work in the procedure is the effort expended in looking up records in the ledgers and files, amending or updating the records and preparing and typing the final document – the invoice.

Computers today can have vast storage facilities. These storage facilities are usually peripheral units which act as an extension to the internal storage of the central processor. In terms of the example given above, the computer must be capable of storing the details of every customer and the specification of every stock item. Usually, the internal storage of the computer is limited in size by high costs and certain technical problems in manufacture. The internal storage of the computer is therefore seldom, if ever, used for the mass storage of data. Mass storage devices used as backing or file storage are linked to the computer's central processor, and an interchange of data can take place between internal storage and external peripheral storage.

The invoicing procedure described could be transferred to a computer. A reading device can be used to input the orders, mass storage devices can hold the large customer and stock files, and a fast printer can produce the required invoices; see Figure 22. The program to perform the invoicing procedure will locate and access the required records from the mass storage device, make the appropriate calculation and return the updated records to the mass storage device.

The distinction made between 'calculation oriented jobs' and 'storage oriented jobs' was for explanatory purposes. It is possible to imagine a job which involves both long complex calculations and mass storage and access of data. For example, 40,000 records of events (say weather reports) can be stored and complex calculations can be performed to show the inter-relationship and similarities between these events. The amount of calculation and the amount of data storage/access will depend on the characteristics of the work to be performed by the computer.

The gap between the simple desk calculator and computer can now be seen to be very wide indeed. Only a brief summary of the capabilities of a computer has been given in this chapter. Despite the relative complexity of a computer when compared with the desk calculator, there still remain the three problems of: the method of character representation within the central processor, the method of calculation and methods of inputting and outputting data. These three problems are the subject of the next two chapters. It may be observed here, however, that the physical construction of a modern computer is radically different from any other calculating machine. Both data and program (in numerical form) are stored by means of

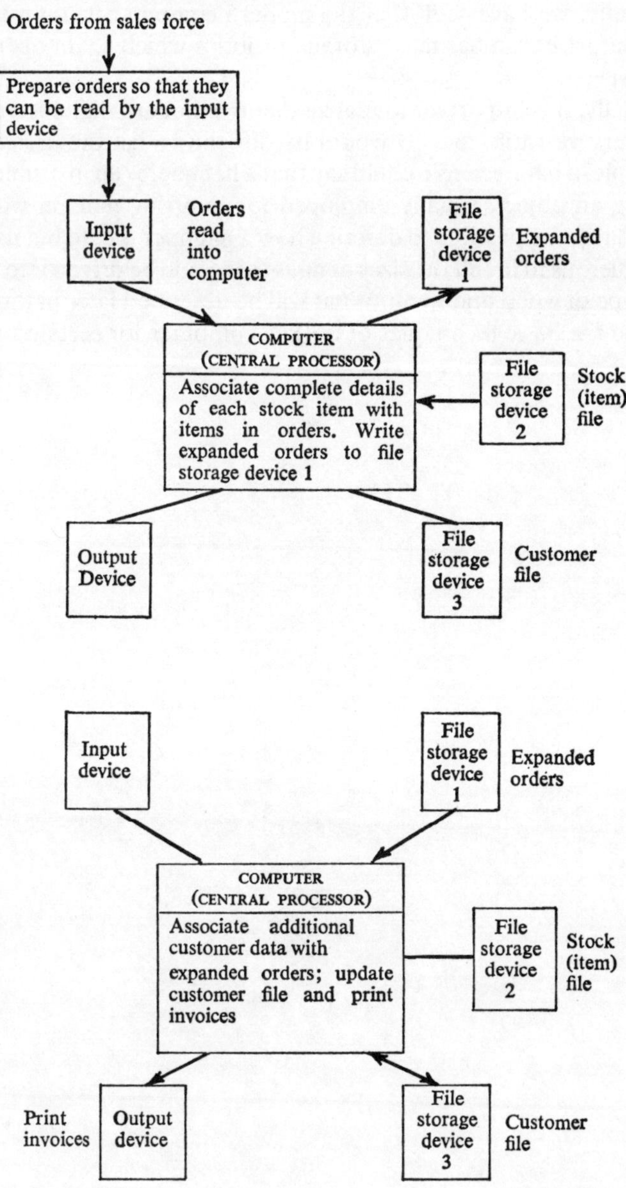

Fig. 22. An Example 'Commercial' Application

electronic units or circuits which operate at extremely high speed. Secondly, we have seen that the modern computer is not merely a calculator; it also has mass storage facilities which again operate at high speed.

Finally, it is important to realize that the modern digital computer is a very versatile tool. It would be difficult to list the uses of, for example, a hammer. We could say that a hammer is an instrument for hitting an object, usually employed for inserting nails in wood. It would then be possible to describe how a hammer is held but it would be ludicrous to list all the sizes of nails that could be driven into wood, the type of wood and so on. What will be described later in this book will be the basic techniques of using a computer for certain types of work.

2. The Central Processor

The central processor as defined on page 62, is that part of a computer which comprises: 'internal storage, arithmetic unit, control unit or program controller and console'. By far the most important aspect of the central processor to be considered is that of the representation of data inside the machine.

REPRESENTATION OF DATA IN THE COMPUTER

Analysis of the aids to calculation discussed at the beginning of Chapter One shows that there are two basic ways of representing or 'storing' numbers. There is the method of *direct* number representation and calculation by means of discrete 'object groupings' as for example a number of raised figures, a group of stones or a grouping of beads.

The methods of calculation which employ this direct system of *number* representation can be said to handle numbers in 'digital' form.

An alternative method of calculation is the method illustrated by the slide rule. This instrument does not handle numbers in digital form; calculation is done by combining quantities. Numbers are represented by *lengths* indicated by graduations along the scales. In fact, the number-length representation is by indicating lengths proportional to the logarithm of a number. Since multiplication can be performed by the addition of logarithms, the slide rule combines two scales for multiplication, the resultant length being proportional to the logarithm of the product. This is shown diagrammatically in Figure 23. In terms of electronic computer techniques, numbers can be represented by electrical quantities such as voltages. The term used for the 'quantity' representation and calculation of numbers is *analogue computing*, and we thus talk of 'electrical quantities as

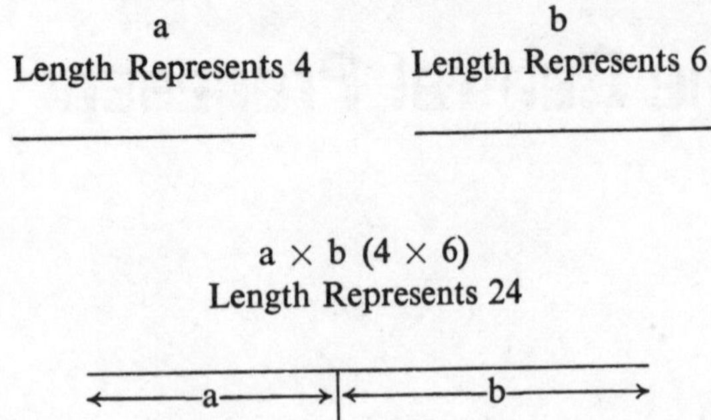

Fig. 23. Calculation by Lengths

analogues for numbers'. Simply then, an analogue is the representation of a numeric quantity by means of a physical variable such as length, rotation, voltage or resistance, etc.

What is the value of using an analogue computer? Consider again the experiment described on page 29. Suppose that the machine operated by experimenters A and B handled 'electrical quantities'. The electrical quantity registered on dial b was represented as a number in digital form. Calculator C, later replaced by machine X, performed calculations with digits. The result of the calculation, c_1 was in digital form and this number may have represented an electrical quantity. The machine operated by A and B could be attached to an analogue computer so that arithmetic could be performed directly on the electrical quantities. A problem can arise if there is a time function involved as for example when a calculation may have to be related to a 'time base'. Since the required calculation can be performed by analogue circuits, the resultant 'quantity' can be considered in terms of the time function.

Analogue computers are usually designed for use in specialized fields such as hydrodynamics, aerodynamics and industrial control. Analogue computers tend to be 'purpose-built' and since their construction and operation are usually extremely complex, they are not considered in this book.

The basic problem in digital computers is how to represent a *digit* by using modern electronic circuits. In early calculating machines, gear wheels with ten teeth were used to represent the digits 0 to 9, the value of a digit being denoted by the position of the wheel at any one time. If we consider an 'electronic circuit' replacing a gear wheel, the circuit can be visualized as a series of nine switches. Each switch is given one value and a closed switch represents the actual value in a digit position as shown in Figure 24.

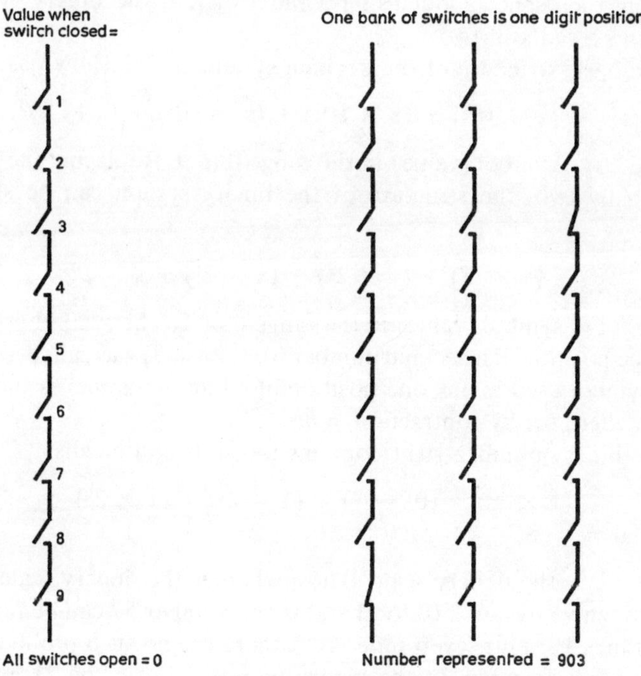

Fig. 24. Digit/Switch Representation

This method of digital representation is cumbersome and impractical. The method of number representation which is universally used in digital computers is based on the *binary* system.

The *decimal* system is generally used with complete acceptance but what in fact is the basis of this number system? Quite simply, the decimal system is based on a symbol combination such that the value of a number is represented by the type of symbol and the position of one symbol relative to another. For example, the number one hundred and fifty nine comprises three symbols 1, 5 and 9 written in the form 159 which signifies

9 units
5 tens
1 hundred

or $(9 \times 1) + (5 \times 10) + (1 \times 100)$ which may be written using indices as $(9 \times 10^0) + (5 \times 10^1) + (1 \times 10^2)$. The decimal system uses radix 10, where each digit position represents a function of ten. There is nothing sacrosanct about using a radix of ten; the binary system employs a radix of two.

The basic structure of the decimal system can be shown as:

$$\ldots + (x \times 10^3) + (x \times 10^2) + (x \times 10^1) + (x \times 10^0)$$

where x is a symbol (value) in the range 0 to 9. Replacing the radix of ten by two, the structure of the binary system can be shown as:

$$\ldots (x \times 2^3) + (x \times 2^2) + (x \times 2^1) + x \times 2^0)$$

where x is a symbol (value) in the range 0 or 1. The symbol used in any one position of a decimal number (0, 1, 2 . . . 9) was called a digit. The symbol used in any one position of a binary number is called a *binary digit*, or, by contraction, a *bit*.

The binary number 1011 contains four bits and means

$$(1 \times 2^3) + (0 \times 2^2) + (1 \times 2^1) + (1 \times 2^0)$$

$$\text{decimal} = \quad 8 \quad + \quad 0 \quad + \quad 2 \quad + \quad 1$$

and is 11 in the denary scale. Thus, whereas the denary scale employed ten values for x (0 to 9) and in the number 57 can be read as 'five times 10^1 plus seven times 10^0', there are no such problems in binary. For example, in the binary number above, the 1s meant, include 2^3, 2^1 and 2^0 and 0 meant, do not include 2^2. Further examples of decimal numbers represented as binary numbers of four bits are shown in Figure 25.

As the number of bits increases, so the maximum value which can be represented increases. For example, using six bits the maximum will be 111111, i.e.

2^5 2^4 2^3 2^2 2^1 2^0
1 1 1 1 1
(32)+(16)+(8)+(4)+(2)+(1) = denary 63

Using eight bits the maximum will be 11111111, i.e.

2^7 2^6 2^5 2^4 2^3 2^2 2^1 2^0
1 1 1 1 1 1 1 1
(128)+(64)+(32)+(16)+(8)+(4)+(2)+(1) = denary 255

There is a pattern in the relationship between the number of bits and the denary value that can be represented. For example:

DECIMAL	BINARY value of bit			
	2^3	2^2	2^1	2^0
0	0	0	0	0
1	0	0	0	1
2	0	0	1	0
3	0	0	1	1
4	0	1	0	0
5	0	1	0	1
6	0	1	1	0
7	0	1	1	1
8	1	0	0	0
9	1	0	0	1
10	1	0	1	0
11	1	0	1	1
12	1	1	0	0
13	1	1	0	1
14	1	1	1	0
15	1	1	1	1

Fig. 25. Four Bit Numbers

Maximum value represented (decimal)	Number of bits	Value of one additional bit
15	4	$2^4 = 16$
63	6	$2^6 = 64$
255	8	$2^8 = 256$

If the total number of bits is equal to n the maximum decimal number is equal to $2^n - 1$.

The basic concept of binary as described above relates only to whole numbers; fractional numbers can also be represented in binary. For simplicity, however, the representation of numbers in the computer's internal store is now explained only in terms of whole numbers.

There are various ways in which data can be held in the internal storage of the computer. Present day techniques employ the binary method of representation. The various methods differ only in the ways that the binary system is used and in the nature of the stores' 'cell'. The three most common methods that can be considered are:

(i) The pure binary – fixed word system,
(ii) The binary coded decimal (B.C.D.) system,
(iii) The seven bit character system,
(iv) The byte system.

Pure Binary System

The pure binary system is based on a cell structure such that each cell comprises a fixed number of bits. Each cell is called a *word* and we speak of 'fixed word lengths' meaning that each word comprises the same number of bits. Examples are the ICL 1900 Series with a word length of 24 bits and the UNIVAC 1100 Series with a word length of 36 bits. In the following discussion, a convenient word length of 24 bits will be used for explanatory purposes.

Consider a computer whose word length is 24 bits. The internal storage of the computer may be visualized as an array of many cells or words, each word comprising 24 bits. For reasons which will become apparent later only 23 bits are used to represent numbers; these 23 bits are commonly called *data bits*. By using the simple formula given previously, the maximum decimal value that can be represented by 23 bits is $2^{23} - 1 = 8{,}388{,}607$. Some example numbers represented in a 23-bit form are shown in Figure 26.

Number	Word Representing Number
1	0 00000000000000000000001
13	0 00000000000000000001101
512	0 00000000000001000000000
32,768	0 00000001000000000000000
32,772	0 00000001000000000000100
2,883,585	0 01011000000000000000001

↑ ↑ ↑
B0 B1 – – – – – – – – B23

Fig. 26. Twenty-four Bit Positive Numbers

The bit positions are identified by the symbols B_0, B_1, B_2 and so on to B_{23}. Note that in Figure 26, 24 bits are shown but B_0 is always zero.

The significance of the twenty-fourth bit (B_0) can now be explained. The numbers shown in Figure 26 are positive; the sign '+' is by convention omitted. There must be a method, however, of representing negative numbers. At its simplest, negative numbers can be represented by making B_0 equal to 1 and representing the number as shown in Figure 26. Thus +261 will be represented as:

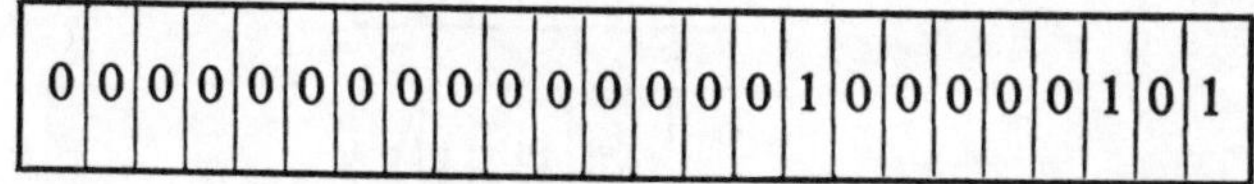

and −261 will be represented as:

1	0	0	0	0	0	0	0	0	0	0	0	0	0	0	1	0	0	0	0	0	1	0	1

The twenty-fourth bit, B_0, is called the *sign bit*.

The representation of negative numbers is usually more complex than this. Negative numbers are usually stored in *complementary* form. The basic technique of holding numbers in complementary form may be first explained by using the more familiar decimal system. The usual means of performing subtraction is by 'taking one number from another'. The fundamental form of a subtraction is 'x−y' which is equivalent to (+x) − (+y) or as an alternative form of representation (+x) + (−y). Consider the simple subtraction sum of 18−11. Computers, as will be seen later *cannot* perform subtraction in the sense of taking two numbers and forming the difference by inspection but they can perform addition. How then can −11 be represented in the process of (+18) + (−11)? One method is to write the complement of 11 which is formed by subtracting 11 from 100 and adding this figure to 18, i.e.

form complement of 11 = 100 − 11 = 89
add complement to 18 = 18 + 89 = 107

If we ignore the '1' in the hundreds position, we find the correct answer of 7. To subtract 110 from 180 the complement of 110 is formed and added to 180. The complement is formed by subtracting 100 from 1,000 and the complete calculation is performed as follows:

form complement of 110 = 1000 − 110 = 890
add complement to 180 = 180 + 890 = 1070

Again if the '1' in the thousands position is ignored, we find the correct answer of 70. The first example (18 − 11) may be shown in binary using a word length of seven bits thus:

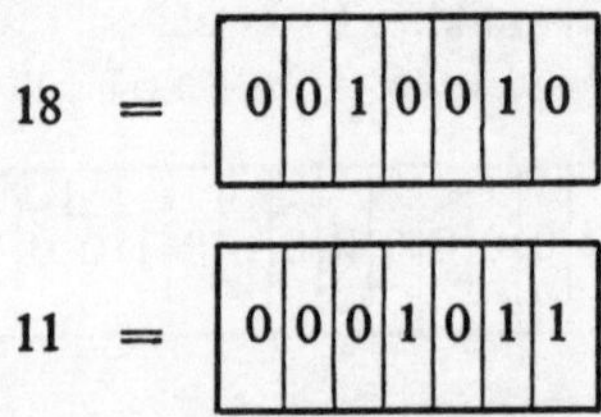

Now, the principle of forming the complement of a decimal number is to subtract the number from x^n where x equals the radix 10 and n equals the number of digits in the number. For example in 18 – 11, x = 10 and n = 2 giving 100. In dealing with binary notation, there is a different radix; it is now 2. In this case there are seven bit positions and thus 11 (binary 0001011) must be subtracted from 2^7 = binary 10000000 = decimal 128. The complement of denary 11 is denary 89. The complement of 11 in binary is formed thus:

```
 1 0 0 0 0 0 0 0
   0 0 0 1 0 1 1
 _______________
   1 1 1 0 1 0 1   =   128 - 11 = 117
 (64 + 32 + 16 + 0 + 4 + 0 + 1)
```

We have now reached the stage of:

18 =	0 0 1 0 0 1 0	—(i)
11 =	0 0 0 1 0 1 1	—(ii)
—11 =	1 1 1 0 1 0 1	—(iii)

The next stage is to add (i) and (iii). The addition is performed thus:

```
   0 0 1 0 0 1 0
   1 1 1 0 1 0 1
   _____________
(1)0 0 0 0 1 1 1 = 7
```

Again, it must be remembered that the radix is two. Taking any two bits there are six combinations:

0	1	1	0	1	1
1	0	1	1_1 carry	0_1 carry	$1_1 \leftarrow$carry
—	—	—	—	—	—
1	1	$1 \leftarrow 0$ carry	$1 \leftarrow 0$ carry	$1 \leftarrow 0$ carry	$1 \leftarrow 1$ carry

For example,

decimal 11 = binary 0 1 0 1 1
decimal 7 = binary 0 0 1 1 1

11	0 1 0 1 1
+ 7	$+0_1 0_1 1_1 1_1 1$
—	————
18	1 0 0 1 0

Before relating the principles shown above to the pure binary word of 24 bits, one important feature of the binary system can be explained. The process of complementing a number has been shown as a process of subtraction but as previously stated most computers cannot perform subtraction in the sense of 'taking x from y'. The computer can complement a number by 'inverting' certain bit values in a word. One method by which subtraction can be performed by a computer is as follows. Let us again consider the example of 18 − 11. The computer takes the number 11:

0 0 0 1 0 1 1

and inverts all the bit values thus

1 1 1 0 1 0 0

This is then added to 18:

   1 1 1 0 1 0 0
   0 0 1 0 0 1 0
   —————————
$1 \leftarrow$0 0 0 0 1 1 0

and the one carry is added back into the least significant bit

0 0 0 0 1 1 1

thus giving the required answer.

How is this inversion performed? Quite simply, the 0 and 1 notation of the binary system is ideal for use with electronic circuits where there are two states in a circuit – 'no pulse' or 'pulse', 'no magnetism' or 'magnetism' and so on. Inversion of bit values is therefore no more than changing a 'magnetized' area into a 'no magnetized' area. More will be said on this when storage devices are considered.

The simple principles of addition and subtraction by the addition of a complement may now be related to the example 24 bit word. Firstly, it is necessary to emphasize that of the 24 bits, 23 are data bits and one is a sign bit. If the number in the 23 data bits is positive the sign bit is '0'; if the number in the 23 bits is negative the sign bit is '1'. For general reference, the decimal value of each of the bits is shown in Figure 27. Some negative numbers are shown in Figure 28.

Bit Number	n	2^n	2^{-n}
B23	0	1	1·0
B22	1	2	0·5
B21	2	4	0·25
B20	3	8	0·125
B19	4	16	0·062 5
B18	5	32	0·031 25
B17	6	64	0·015 625
B16	7	128	0·007 812 5
B15	8	256	0·003 906 25
B14	9	512	0·001 953 125
B13	10	1 024	0·000 976 562 5
B12	11	2 048	0·000 488 281 25
B11	12	4 096	0·000 244 140 625
B10	13	8 192	0·000 122 070 312 5
B9	14	16 384	0·000 061 035 156 25
B8	15	32 768	0·000 030 517 578 125
B7	16	65 536	0·000 015 258 789 062 5
B6	17	131 072	0·000 007 629 394 531 25
B5	18	262 144	0·000 003 814 697 265 625
B4	19	524 288	0·000 001 907 348 632 812 5
B3	20	1 048 576	0·000 000 953 674 316 406 25
B2	21	2 097 152	0·000 000 476 837 158 203 125
B1	22	4 194 304	0·000 000 238 418 579 101 562 5
B0	23	8 388 608	0·000 000 119 209 289 550 781 25

Fig. 27. Decimal Values of Bits in a Twenty-four Bit Word

Number	Word Representing Number
—13	1 11111111111111111110011
—128	1 11111111111111110000000
—130	1 11111111111111101111110
−32,768	1 11111111000000000000000
−32,772	1 11111110111111111111100
−2,883,591	1 10100111111111111111001

↑ ↑ ↑
B0 B1 - - - - - - - - - B23

Fig. 28. Twenty-four Bit Negative Numbers

All the numbers considered so far have been whole numbers. The representation of fractional numbers must now be considered. In the denary system, decimal fractions such as ·256 are again based on the radix of 10 thus: $(2 \times 10^{-1}) + (5 \times 10^{-2}) + (6 \times 10^{-3})$. In terms of the binary system using radix 2, fractions are shown as

$$(2^{-1}) + (2^{-2}) + (2^{-3}) \text{ and so on.}$$
$$\tfrac{1}{2} \quad + \quad \tfrac{1}{4} \quad + \quad \tfrac{1}{8}$$

Thus ·5 is ·1 in binary, ·25 is ·01 in binary, ·75 is ·11 in binary, ·125 is ·001, ·875 is ·111 and so on. Mixed fractional numbers such as 105·125 can be represented by two bit patterns

105 = binary 1 1 0 1 0 0 1
·125 = binary · 0 0 1
105·125 = binary 1 1 0 1 0 0 1 · 0 0 1

It is not usually possible to store mixed fractions in the form shown above in a fixed length pure binary word. The position of the binary point would fall somewhere within the word e.g.

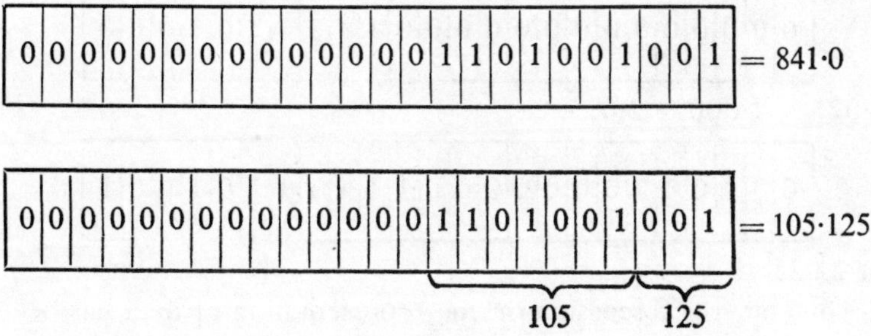

Circuits which enable multiplication to be affected would be extremely complex since:

(i) the point does not actually appear in a word;

(ii) the position of the point could alter in the product.

With modern pure binary computers, fractional numbers can be represented in two ways. One method is that of multiple length working; the integer and fraction are stored in two separate but adjacent cells. Thus, the number 105·125 will be stored as:

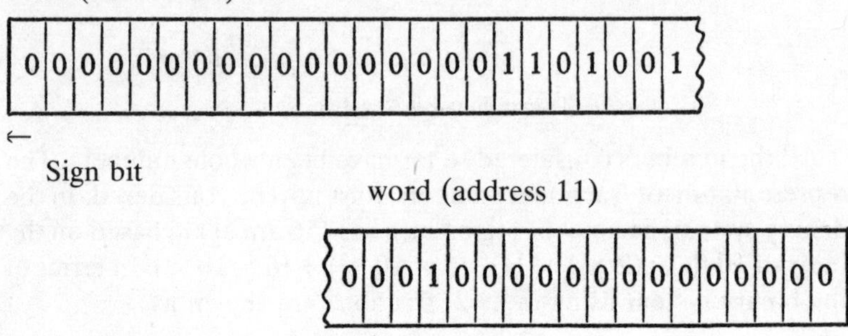

The binary point is understood to be between B_0 and B_1 in word 11; the sign bit B_0 is not significant in the value of the number represented. The other method is to ignore the binary point completely and store the number as an integer. For an example 1·025 can be stored as 1,025 thus

If this number is, say, to be added to 1, then the 1 must be stored as 1,000:

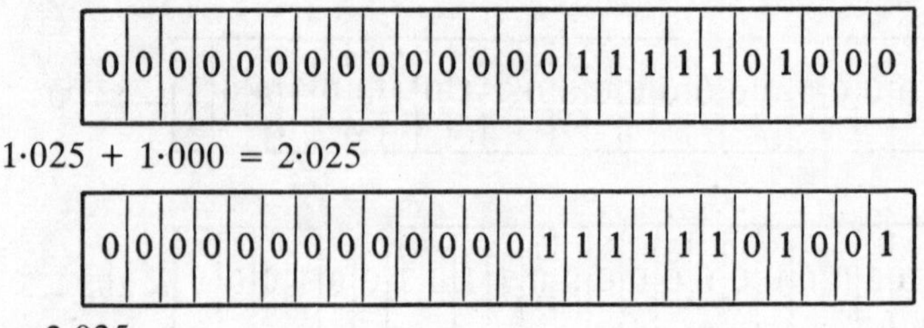

or 2,025

Thus far, the discussion on the representation of data has been restricted to data in numeric form. There must be provision to store alphabetic symbols (A to Z) and some special symbols (e.g. '+', '−', '·', '£'). In a pure binary computer, a special numeric coding system is employed to represent alphabetic symbols and special symbols. To illustrate the principle of storing non-numeric data, a simple coding system can be explained for the 24 bit word length shown previously. Let us consider the case when all data entering the computer's internal storage is in 'character' form. In other words, each symbol, numeric (0 to 9), alphabetic (A to Z) or special symbol (×, − etc.), is represented by a unique numeric code. This code comprises six bits; thus, four 'characters' of six bits each can be stored in one 24 bit word:

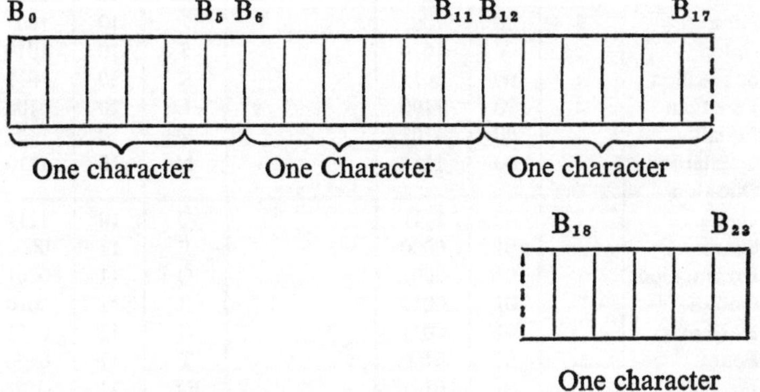

The six bits representing each character may be considered in two groups, one group of two bits and one group of four bits. For explanatory purposes, the six bits representing one character may be given the values:

2^1	2^0	2^3	2^2	2^1	2^0

The number (0 to 3) represented in the left-hand two bits is called the *zone* and the number (0 to 15) represented in the right-hand four bits is called the *numeric*. The zone and numeric digits are used to form a two digit code; for example:

Zone	*Numeric*	*Character*
0	0	0
0	1	1
0	2	2
0	3	3

A complete six bit character code is shown in Figure 29.

Character Description	Printed Symbol	Machine Code Zone	Machine Code Numeric	Character Description	Printed Symbol	Machine Code Zone	Machine Code Numeric
Zero	0	00	0000	At	@	10	0000
One	1	00	0001		A	10	0001
Two	2	00	0010		B	10	0010
Three	3	00	0011		C	10	0011
Four	4	00	0100		D	10	0100
Five	5	00	0101		E	10	0101
Six	6	00	0110		F	10	0110
Seven	7	00	0111		G	10	0111
Eight	8	00	1000		H	10	1000
Nine	9	00	1001		I	10	1001
Colon	:	00	1010		J	10	1010
Semi-colon	;	00	1011		K	10	1011
Less than	<	00	1100		L	10	1100
Equals	=	00	1101		M	10	1101
Greater than	>	00	1110		N	10	1110
Question mark	?	00	1111		O	10	1111
Space		01	0000		P	11	0000
Exclamation	!	01	0001		Q	11	0001
Quotes	"	01	0010		R	11	0010
Hash mark	#	01	0011		S	11	0011
Pound	£	01	0100		T	11	0100
Percentage	%	01	0101		U	11	0101
Ampersand	&	01	0110		V	11	0110
Apostrophe	'	01	0111		W	11	0111
Left Parenthesis	(	01	1000		X	11	1000
Right Parenthesis	)	01	1001		Y	11	1001
Asterisk	*	01	1010		Z	11	1010
Plus	+	01	1011	L.H. Bracket	[	11	1011
Comma	,	01	1100	Dollar	$	11	1100
Hyphen/ Minus	–	01	1101	R.H. Bracket	]	11	1101
Stop	.	01	1110		↑	11	1110
Solidus	/	01	1111		↓	11	1111

Fig. 29. Six Bit Character Code for use in a Twenty-four Bit Word Machine

Characters may thus be stored in a word system in the following examples.

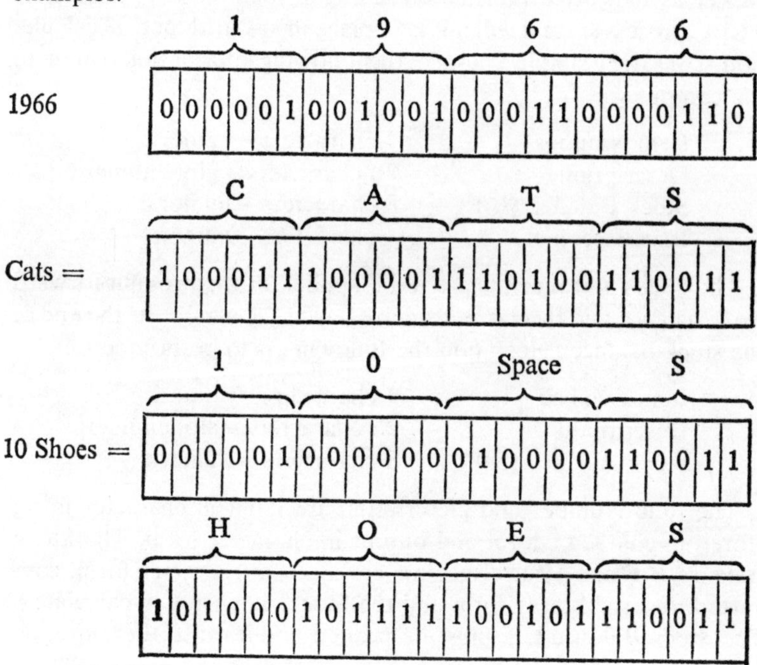

There is one problem; the word

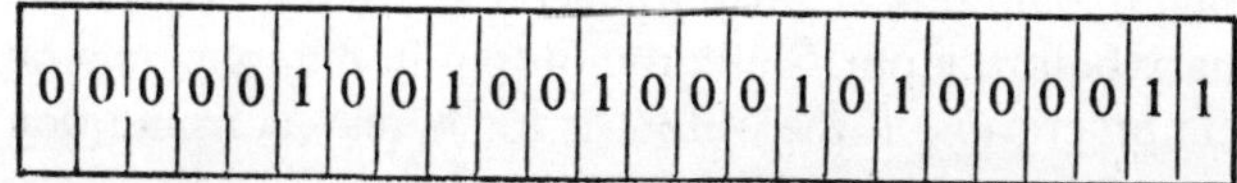

contains the number 1953 in character form. However, the number represented in the word in pure or serial binary form is 299,331. Obviously, if the number 1953 is to take place in an arithmetical calculation, it must be transformed into the pure (serial) binary form of:

0	0	0	0	0	0	0	0	0	0	0	0	0	1	1	1	1	0	1	0	0	0	0	1

In fact this may be achieved by a simple process of multiplication and addition as shown in Figure 30. This process can be called 'Character to Binary Conversion' (CBC) and must be applied to all numbers in character form which are to take place in an arithmetic operation. Some information passing into the computer may be classed as 'indicative information'. This information never undergoes a CBC process since it will not take place in any arithmetical calculation. Consider a simple example; the following information is input to the computer:

Item Number	–	4 characters – numeric
Description	–	28 characters – alphanumeric
Stock Balance (B/F)	–	8 characters – numeric
Issue/Receipts	–	4 characters – numeric

The issues and receipts are to be applied to the brought forward stock balance and the current stock balance calculated. At the end of the stock balance calculation the following is to be printed out:

Item number	–	4 characters – numeric
Description	–	28 characters – alphanumeric
Stock Balance (B/F)	–	8 characters – numeric

The Item Number and Description are input in character form, stored in character form and output in character form. The Stock Balance B/F and Issues/Receipts are input in character form, converted to serial binary form and the Stock Balance C/F calculated. The Stock Balance C/F must be printed and it must, therefore, be converted to character form.

As will be seen in Chapter Three, computers would be useless if their human 'data feeders' had to encode the contents of each word into binary before input. Similarly, output in binary would be completely impracticable if the output is for human consumption; thus there is usually an intermediate coding stage:

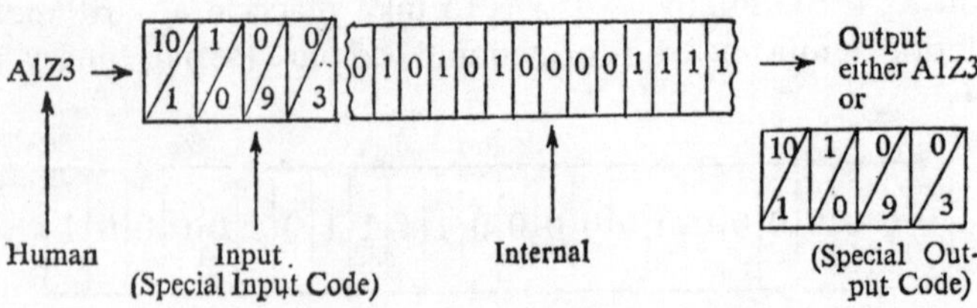

Convert 1,024 in character form to pure (serial) binary form, i.e.

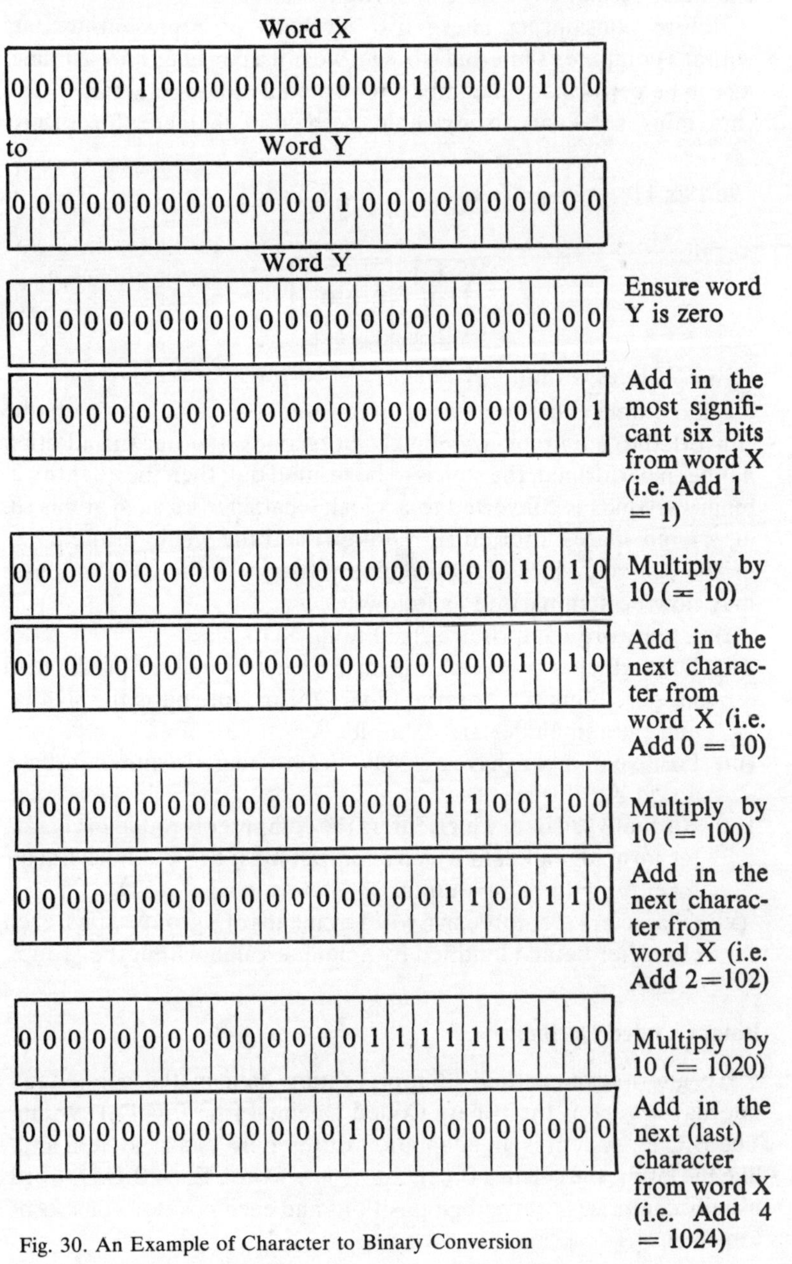

Fig. 30. An Example of Character to Binary Conversion

It is in the intermediate (input/output) coding stages that the character format in store is important.

Before considering alternative methods of representing data within a computer's internal storage, we must consider how arithmetic can be performed on numbers with mixed radices, e.g. time. Time (hrs, mins, secs) can, for example, be held in character form thus:

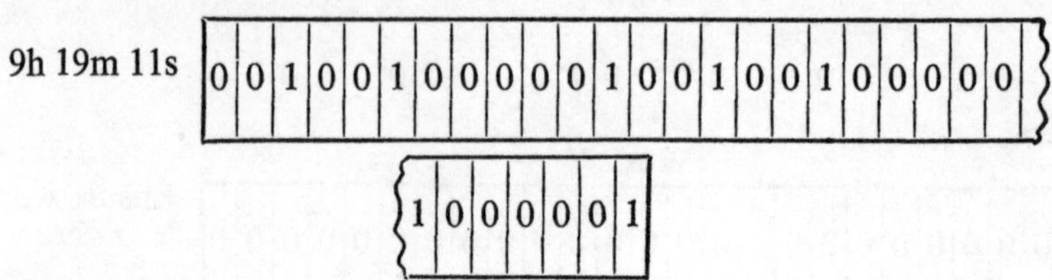

(symbols h, m, s omitted)
To add a time value to another time value, the values must first be converted to a pure binary number of seconds. If, after the addition has been performed, the sum is to be printed out, then the quantity in binary seconds is converted to a 'clock' character form, symbols (h, m, s,) and spaces inserted (if required) and the whole printed.

The characteristics of a pure binary fixed word length computer may now be summarized as follows.

(i) Each word comprises a fixed number of bits.
(ii) Data which is to take part in an arithmetic process must be held in 'pure numeric' or serial binary forms: one bit is the sign bit and the remainder are data bits.
(iii) Positive numbers have a sign bit of zero; negative numbers have a sign bit of one.
(iv) Normally, all data which enters the computer is coded in character form and all data which is output must be held in character form prior to being output.
(v) Characters are stored in a word by means of a group of bits, each character being identified by a unique value within the group.

Binary Coded Decimal

An alternative method of representing data in the computer's internal storage is the Binary Coded Decimal (the B.C.D.) system. The B.C.D. system is an adaptation of the pure binary system and, like the latter, the cell in a B.C.D. store is a 'word'. Each B.C.D. word usually comprises twelve digit positions and each position consists of four bits:

Bit Value 1→												
Bit Value 2→												
Bit Value 4→												
Bit Value 8→												
	1	2	3	4	5	6	7	8	9	10	11	12

Digit Positions

Numbers are stored in words as shown in the following examples:

	0	0	0	0	0	0	0	0	0	0	0	1
9	0	0	0	0	0	0	0	0	0	0	0	0
	0	0	0	0	0	0	0	0	0	0	0	0
	0	0	0	0	0	0	0	0	0	0	0	1
												9

	0	0	0	0	0	0	0	0	0	1	1	1
4,517	0	0	0	0	0	0	0	0	0	0	0	1
	0	0	0	0	0	0	0	0	1	1	0	1
	0	0	0	0	0	0	0	0	0	0	0	0
									4	5	1	7

	0	0	0	0	1	1	1	0	0	1	1	0
51,924,316	0	0	0	0	0	0	0	1	0	1	0	1
	0	0	0	0	1	0	0	0	1	0	0	1
	0	0	0	0	0	0	1	0	0	0	0	0
					5	1	9	2	4	3	1	6

Fractional numbers are stored without a decimal point actually appearing within the word; its position is 'implied' by an instruction which addresses that word. Thus 375, 37·5, 3·75, ·375 are all stored as:

0	0	0	0	0	0	0	0	0	1	1	1
0	0	0	0	0	0	0	0	0	1	1	0
0	0	0	0	0	0	0	0	0	0	1	1
0	0	0	0	0	0	0	0	0	0	0	0
									3	7	5

For the storage of characters, two digits must be used and a two digit code (with zone and numeric components) as shown in the example in Figure 31(a) is employed. The purpose and use of a character code is the same for a B.C.D. computer as for a pure binary machine.

Again, arithmetic must be performed on numbers in true numeric form rather than character form. If it is assumed that the zone and numeric components are positioned in a word as shown in Figure 31(b), the conversion process is simple.

Numeric Component	Zone Component 1	Zone Component 2	Zone Component 3	Zone Component 4	Zone Component 5
0	0	11	10	0	£
1	1	A	J	&	$
2	2	B	K	S	%
3	3	C	L	T	¼
4	4	D	M	U	–
5	5	E	N	V	/
6	6	F	O	W	½
7	7	G	P	X	.
8	8	H	Q	Y	@
9	9	I	R	Z	¾

Space = Zone 0 Numeric 0

Fig. 31. (a) B.C.D. Character Code for use in a Twelve Digit Word

Example method of Storing Characters in a Word:

Zone of Character 1	Zone of Character 2	Zone of Character 3	Zone of Character 4	Zone of Character 5	Zone of Character 6	Numeric of Character 1	Numeric of Character 2	Numeric of Character 3	Numeric of Character 4	Numeric of Character 5	Numeric of Character 6
1	2	3	4	5	6	7	8	9	10	11	12

Digit Positions

For example: 3 CATS stored in one word thus

1	1	0	0	0	0	0	1	0	1	1	1	0
2	0	0	1	1	0	0	1	0	1	0	1	1
4	0	0	0	0	1	1	0	0	0	0	0	0
8	0	0	0	0	0	0	0	0	0	0	0	0
	1	2	3	4	5	6	7	8	9	10	11	12

Digit Positions

Fig. 31. (b) B.C.D. Character Code for use in a Twelve Digit Word

The most significant six digit positions (1 to 6) contain ones (i.e. zone 1) and these ones are replaced by zeros, usually by a simple 'cyclic shift' inserting zeros. For example the number 356,987 is stored as

1	1	1	1	1	1	3	5	6	9	8	7

or in binary

	1	2	3	4	5	6	7	8	9	10	11	12
1	1	1	1	1	1	1	1	1	0	1	0	1
2	0	0	0	0	0	0	1	0	1	0	0	1
4	0	0	0	0	0	0	0	1	1	0	0	1
8	0	0	0	0	0	0	0	0	0	1	1	0

and is converted by:

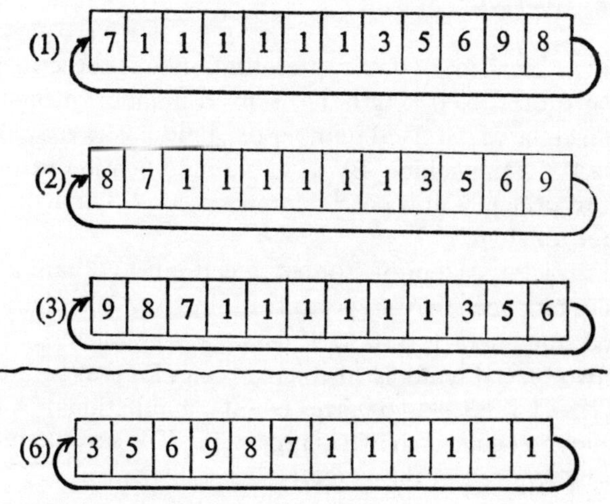

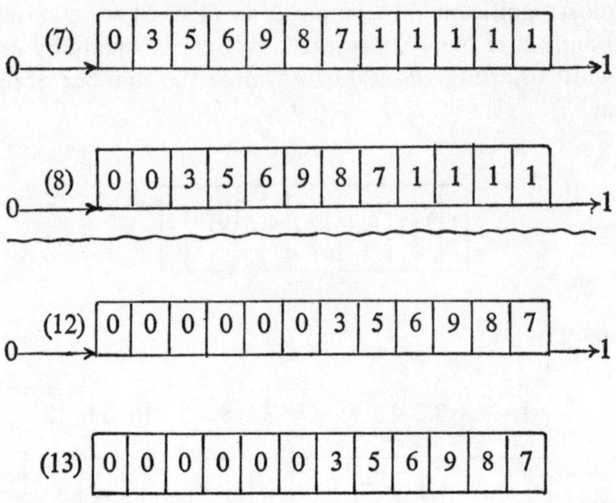

The B.C.D. word system for information storage was widely used in 'first generation computers', i.e., those computers which used valve storage built in the middle 1950's. Today, the B.C.D. word system is rarely used for the storage of information inside a computer. It has been mainly superseded by the serial binary word and the byte technique.

Seven Bit Character System

In the two methods of data representation so far described, the cell was a word of a fixed length, i.e. a fixed number of bits in a pure binary machine and a fixed number of 'digit' positions, each of four bits, in a B.C.D. machine. By a simple modification of the B.C.D. fixed word principle, it is possible to make a cell synonymous with a 'character' or 'byte'.

In a character system of storage, a cell must contain a sufficient number of bits, such that a repertoire of say sixty-four characters may be stored; ten characters, 0 to 9; twenty-six characters, A to Z and twenty-two special symbols. Six bits can cater for the required character set ($2^6 - 1 = 63$; 0 to 63 gives 64 bit combinations). An example six bit character code is shown in Figure 32. (The seventh bit, labelled 'P', can be ignored at this stage.)

Character Description	Printed Symbol	Machine Code							Character Description	Printed Symbol	Machine Code						
		P 2^6	Zone 2^5	2^4	Numeric 2^3	2^2	2^1	2^0			P 2^6	Zone 2^5	2^4	Numeric 2^3	2^2	2^1	2^0
Zero	0	1	0	0	0	0	0	0	Colon	;	1	0	1	1	1	0	1
One	1	0	0	0	0	0	0	1	Apostrophe	'	1	0	1	1	1	1	0
Two	2	0	0	0	0	0	1	0	Plus zero	+0	0	0	1	1	1	1	1
Three	3	1	0	0	0	0	1	1	Minus	—	0	1	0	0	0	0	0
Four	4	0	0	0	0	1	0	0	J	J	1	1	0	0	0	0	1
Five	5	1	0	0	0	1	0	1	K	K	1	1	0	0	0	1	0
Six	6	1	0	0	0	1	1	0	L	L	0	1	0	0	0	1	1
Seven	7	0	0	0	0	1	1	1	M	M	1	1	0	0	1	0	0
Eight	8	0	0	0	1	0	0	0	N	N	0	1	0	0	1	0	1
Nine	9	1	0	0	1	0	0	1	O	O	0	1	0	0	1	1	0
Space		1	0	0	1	0	1	0	P	P	1	1	0	0	1	1	1
Quarter	¼	0	0	0	1	0	1	1	Q	Q	1	1	0	1	0	0	0
At the rate of	@	1	0	0	1	1	0	0	R	R	0	1	0	1	0	0	1
Open Parenthesis	(	0	0	0	1	1	0	1	Pound	£	1	1	0	1	0	1	1
Close Parenthesis	)	0	0	0	1	1	1	0	Asterisk	*	0	1	0	1	1	0	0
Hash Mark	#	1	0	0	1	1	1	1	Dollar	$	0	1	0	1	1	1	1
Ampersand	&	0	0	1	0	0	0	0	Half	½	1	1	1	0	0	0	0
A	A	1	0	1	0	0	0	1	Oblique	/	0	1	1	0	0	0	1
B	B	1	0	1	0	0	1	0	S	S	0	1	1	0	0	1	0
C	C	0	0	1	0	0	1	1	T	T	1	1	1	0	0	1	1
D	D	1	0	1	0	1	0	0	U	U	0	1	1	0	1	0	0
E	E	0	0	1	0	1	0	1	V	V	1	1	1	0	1	0	1
F	F	0	0	1	0	1	1	0	W	W	1	1	1	0	1	1	0
G	G	1	0	1	0	1	1	1	X	X	0	1	1	0	1	1	1
H	H	1	0	1	1	0	0	0	Y	Y	0	1	1	1	0	0	0
I	I	0	0	1	1	0	0	1	Z	Z	1	1	1	1	0	0	1
Plus	+	0	0	1	1	0	1	0	Comma	,	0	1	1	1	0	1	1
Period	.	1	0	1	1	0	1	1	Per cent	%	1	1	1	1	1	0	0
Semicolon	:	0	0	1	1	1	0	0	Equals	=	0	1	1	1	1	1	0

Fig. 32. Six (Seven) Bit Character Code

Two numbers could be added together in a word machine merely by specifying the addresses of the appropriate two words holding the numbers. Since, in a character machine, the basic unit of addressing is a character, the addition of two numbers of say eight digits in length will require the addressing of sixteen character positions in the add instructions. Consider the example shown below; it is required to add the quantity held in cells or character locations 1,000 to 1,007, to the quantity held in cells 2,000 to 2,007.

BEFORE ADDITION

Locations

1000	1001	1002	1003	1004	1005	1006	1007	1008	1009	1010
1	3	7	5	7	4	9	6	A	2	X

Locations

2000	2001	2002	2003	2004	2005	2006	2007	2008	2009	2010
2	8	7	4	3	2	1	3	0	0	0

AFTER ADDITION

Locations

2000	2001	2002	2003	2004	2005	2006	2007	2008	2009	2010
4	2	5	0	0	7	0	9	0	0	0

Locations 1000 to 1010 – unchanged

Note: Number 13,757,496 (locations 1000 to 1007) and Number 28,743,213 (locations 2000 to 2007) are to be added together; locations 1007 and 2007 contain the least significant digits of the two numbers.

To illustrate the principle of addressing cells in a character machine, consider an instruction format of twelve characters:

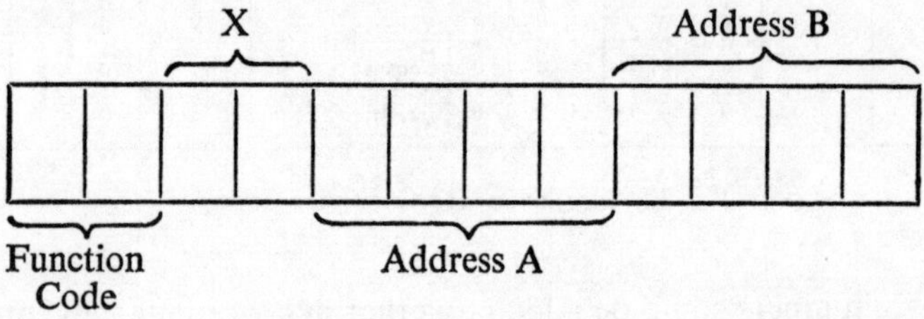

The function code for 'add' is, we shall say, 20 and the address of the two least significant digits of the two numbers to be added is specified in the A and B addresses. The effect of function code 20 is to add the two digits specified in the A and B addresses and place the result in the location specified in the B address part of the instruction. Thus, if the instruction was:

2	0	X	X	1	0	0	7	2	0	0	7

(ignoring the 'x' part) 6 would be added to 3 and the sum, 9, placed in location 2007. However, the problem is to add two quantities which are eight digits in length. The 'x' part of the instruction is set to eight and the instruction:

2	0	0	8	1	0	0	7	2	0	0	7

can be read as 'add the two quantities in cells 1000 to 1007 inclusive and cells 2000 to 2007 inclusive'; respectively – that is, eight characters as denoted by x. The 'x' part of the instruction is used to indicate the size of the quantities and the A and B addresses act as basic reference points in the instruction. A modification of this system is to build-in to the central processor a 'stop on specified character' facility. The operation specified by the operand commences at the locations specified in the A and B addresses. Depending on the type of operation, successive characters to the right or left of the specified addresses are processed. When a predetermined character is sensed in core storage, the operation is automatically terminated. Thus, the user must insert marker characters to delineate strings of data characters in store.

The character code shown in Figure 32 is a *seven* bit code; six bits are data bits and the seventh is a check or *parity* bit.

As will be seen later, parity bits are widely used in computers. A parity checking system may be on 'odd' or 'even' parity.

In checking *odd* parity, the number of bits comprising one character should always be odd. Thus, if the character represented in the six data bits has an even number of '1' bits, for example the character 3: 00011, then the parity bit is set to '1' (1000011). The parity bit is set when a character is first input to thc store. If any character is subsequently detected in store with an even number of bits, the character has 'dropped a bit'. The principle is the same for an even parity checking system except than an odd number of bits indicates an error character. Obviously, only single or treble bit dropouts can be detected. The single parity bit system is the simplest of the 'cell' parity checking systems. Most computers with word storage and addressing systems also have one or more parity check bits in addition to the data bits.

We may now consider completely variable length working. The character system of storage described previously had fixed length instructions. Data was handled in variable length units by means of a 'character length count' or 'stop on specified character'. An alternative system is the use of a system of 'markers' set in core storage by the user to define the length of the data. A 'word mark' defines the boundary of a field when it is used in a transfer, comparison or arithmetic operation. Thus, an ADD instruction in a two-address instruction machine with word marks placed in the most significant digit position could be stated as:

'Add the two digits whose addresses are specified, *and the subse-*

quent digits to the left, up to and including the digits with word marks.'

Additional marker characters may be included to delineate areas used in input/output transfers and so on. A machine working on this principle will require facilities such as 'set word mark' and 'clear word mark' instructions.

Not only can data be held and processed in completely variable length form within internal storage; a 'word mark' system may also be used to define the length of instructions. The system would require that the first (operand) character of the instruction contains a word mark. The transfer of an instruction to the control unit could thus be terminated by the detection of a word mark.

Depending on the character system of storage employed, a word mark could be a combination of bits set in character position. In all arithmetic operations, etc., the word mark bits would be set to terminate the operation but would have no effect in the actual result produced.

The Byte System

Byte storage has become one of the most popular methods of storage. It combines the advantages of both the fixed length word and the character method of storage. The major user of the method is International Business Machines (IBM) as in the System/360 and 370 computers. The basic unit of storage is a byte; that is, a group of eight data bits (with, often, a ninth parity bit). The eight data bits give great flexibility; a byte can be used to hold three different types of value:

(i) *an alphanumeric character*. This can be done by using six data bits as in the character method of representation as described on page 90. Note that in this case two bits in the byte are not used and a character set of 64 characters (2^6) is available. Alternatively, an extended coding system may be used which utilises all eight bits. This gives 2^8 code combinations or 256 characters. The extended character set can include not only upper case (capital) letters but also lower case letters, more special symbols and a range of control codes.

(ii) *two numeric characters without zone bits*. A numeric value needs four bits, i.e. 0 (decimal) = 0000 to 9 (decimal) = 1001. The eight bits in a byte can thus be used to hold two, four bit numeric values. For example, a byte can be used to hold the number 29 thus:

$$\left.\begin{matrix}0\\0\\1\\0\end{matrix}\right\}2 \qquad \left.\begin{matrix}1\\0\\0\\1\end{matrix}\right\}9$$

(iii) *any binary value*. In other words, the eight bits can be used to hold a pure binary number. Because there are eight bits, the maximum number which can be held in this manner is 255.

Method (ii) is known as *packed decimal*. In effect it doubles the capacity of the available storage when decimal digits are stored. A maximum binary value of 255 in method (iii) is of little practical use. In some computers the method is extended to enable four bytes to be used together as a 'word'. This means that the byte storage can be used, if required, as a fixed word length store with a word length of 32 bits.

The basic numeric coding employed by a computer and the nature of a 'cell' in the internal storage having been seen, the storage units may now be described.

THE CONSTRUCTION OF INTERNAL STORAGE

Most early commercial computers used a *magnetic drum* for internal storage. The drum (an example of which is shown in Plate 1), usually about six inches in diameter, revolves at high speed, say 3,000 to 6,000 revolutions per minute. The outer surface of the drum is covered by a coating which can be magnetized. A number of recording/reading heads are positioned over its surface. The drum consists of *channels*, each channel corresponding to that area of the drum positioned beneath one set of recording/reading heads.

To illustrate the mode of operation, let us assume that the drum is used to store data held in B.C.D. form with a fixed word length of twelve digits; each channel may therefore be considered as comprising four *tracks*, each track representing a bit position as shown in the diagram on page 96.

Note that there is no physical marking on the drum's surface; a

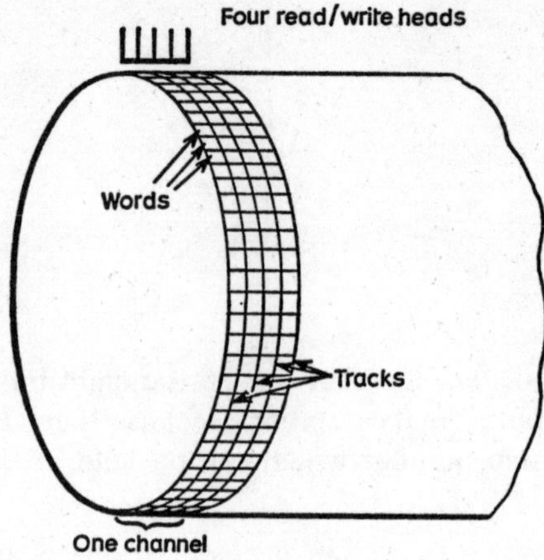

channel is defined by the position of four heads and a track by the position of one head. The position of a word on a channel and the digit position within a word is defined by a 'clocking' system. The operation of the drum can be described simply as follows. Consider a machine with a drum capacity of say 12,000 words.* There are sixty channels with 200 words per channel. In addition to the basic drum storage, there are three registers in the central processor: Registers X, Y and Z. Each register is capable of storing one word. If two numbers are to be added, the numbers are transferred from the drum and placed in two registers, say X and Y, and the addition causes the sum to be placed in the third register, Z.

Let us see how an addition can be performed with the above components. There are four basic instructions:

(i) transfer a specified location (word) on the drum to Register X – function code 01;

(ii) transfer a specified location on the drum to Register Y – function code 02;

(iii) transfer the contents of Register Z to a specified location on the drum – function code 03;

(iv) add the contents of Register X and Register Y and place the sum in Register Z – function code 04.

The instruction format is

* When referring to storage capacity the symbol K is used to denote thousands. The drum storage capacity in the example can be said to be 12K words.

1. Inside the CPU of a modern computer (ICL 2950)

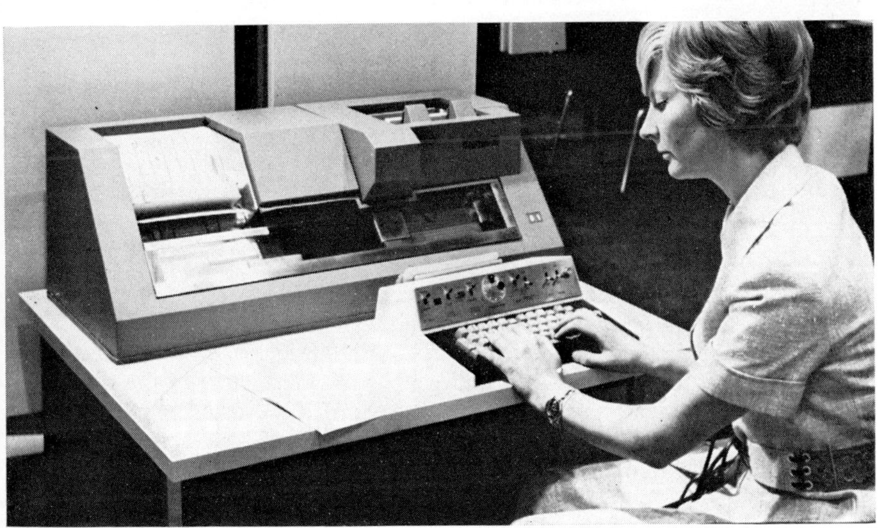

2. A Card Punch/Key Punch (IBM 129 Card Data Recorder)

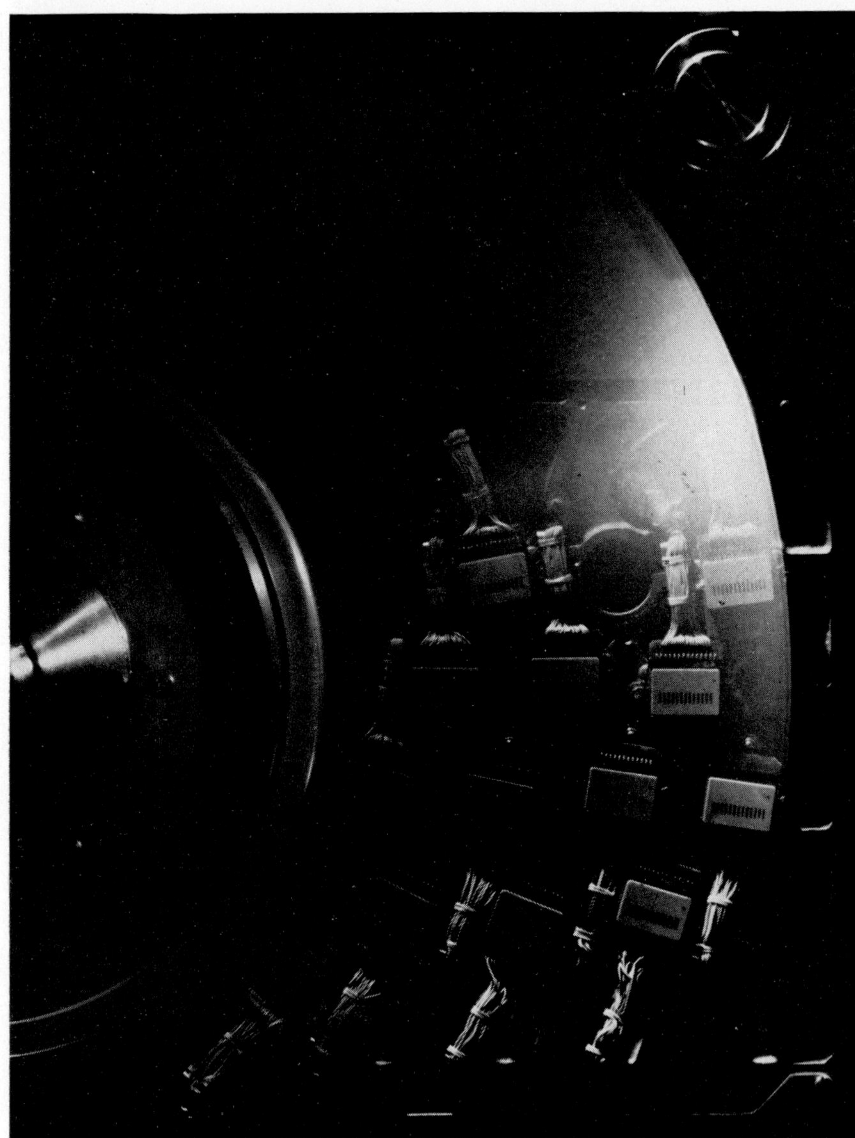

3. A Magnetic Disc Storage Device (Burroughs fixed head-per-track disc store). The photograph, taken by double exposure, shows the relationship between the recording surface and read/write heads. The disc (26·5 in. in diameter) rotates at 1,500 revolutions per minute. Opposite the disc are 156 read/write heads arranged in 12 groups of 13 heads each, which thus provide for recording data on 156 tracks. (Note the 6-head group—second in from right, middle row—is reserved for timing/checking purposes.)

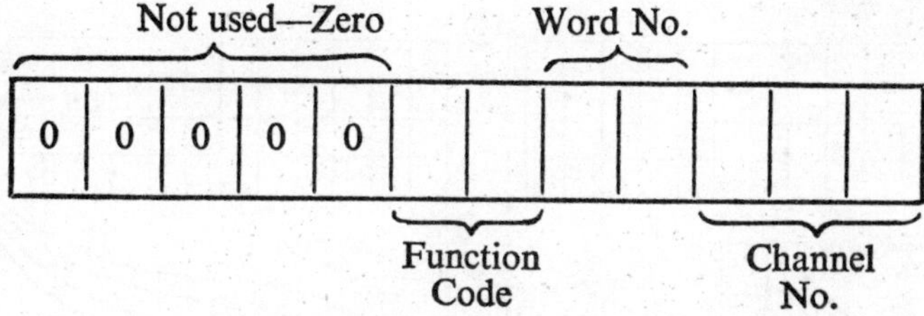

The problem is to add two numbers stored in locations 10 050 (i.e. word 10 on channel 50) and 15 050 and store the sum in location 30 050. The process may be performed by the four instructions

01 10 050
02 15 050
04 00 000
03 30 050

The first instruction is obeyed as follows.

The recording/reading heads on the appropriate channel (50) are selected and a 'highway' from the heads to Register X is opened; this is achieved by a simple switching of circuits. At the appropriate 'word time', the heads are activated and the word, 10, is read into the register (see Figure 33). The second instruction is obeyed in the same manner as the first, a highway being opened from the heads to Register Y followed by the reading of word 15. The contents of Register X and Y are added in response to the third instruction and the sum is placed in from Register X to the appropriate channel read/write heads and at the appropriate word time, the data is transferred from the register and recorded on, or 'written to', the drum.

Note that data is recorded by '1' = 'pulse' = 'activate head' = 'magnetize' and 'O' = 'no pulse' = 'not activate' = 'not-magnetize' as shown in Figure 33.

The above examples show the basic principle of drum storage. The use of a magnetic drum as the sole means of internal storage does have some disadvantages. Suppose the drum revolution speed is 3,000 r.p.m., then the time between reading the contents of a location and re-reading (or writing) the contents of that location will be in the region of 20 milliseconds.* Further, the access time for the preceding location (in terms of the direction of rotation) will also be in the

* A millisecond is equal to one thousandth of a second and is usually abbreviated 'ms'.

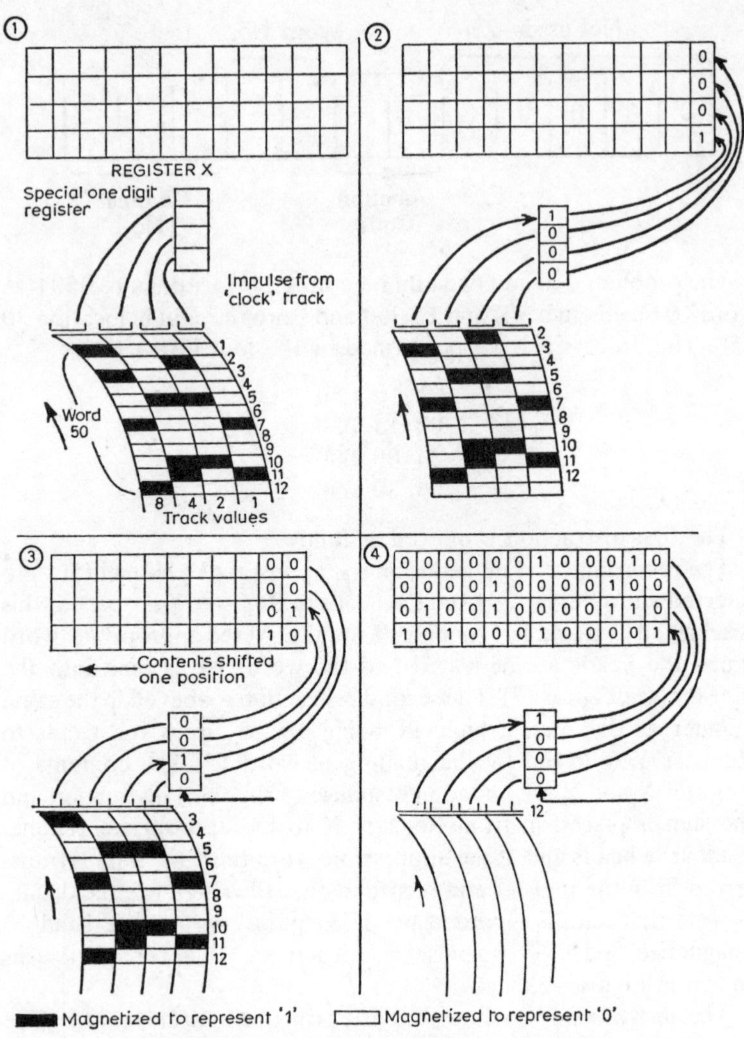

Fig. 33. Example Magnetic Drum Transfer

The number 848,064,900,658 stored in word 50 on channel 30 is transferred to Register X.

region of 20 ms. However, if addition, subtraction or any other operation using only the registers, is affected by means of modern electronic circuits and techniques, then these operations will be performed in a time scale of a few microseconds.* The positioning of the

* A microsecond is equal to one millionth of a second and is usually abbreviated 'μs'.

locations on the drum can be arranged to reduce the time between accesses to adjacent locations; this is called *optimization*. However, in modern computers, drum storage usually proves too slow as the sole means of internal storage or even as supplemental storage.

An alternative system of internal storage is core storage. Core storage comprises a matrix of wires with a torroid or *core* of ferrite at each intersection of the wires; see the example in Figure 34. Ferrite is a form of metal capable of retaining magnetism. Data is stored by magnetizing a core; this is achieved by passing an electric current in one of two directions through a particular core. A current applied in one direction represents '1' and a current passed in the opposite direction represents 'O'. When the current is removed, a core retains a certain amount of magnetism.

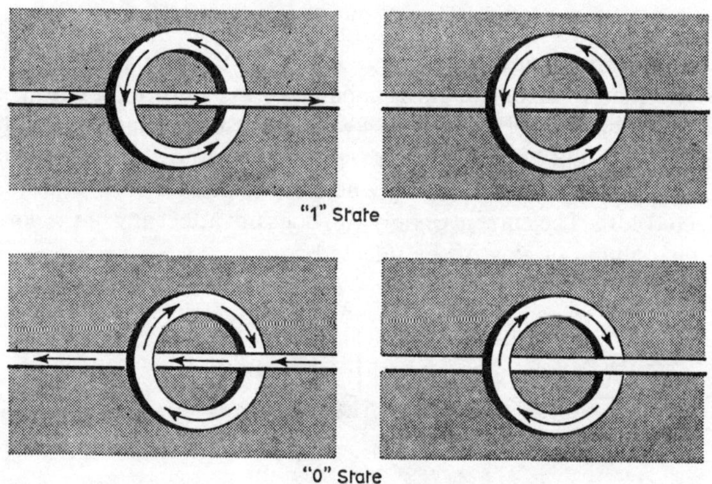

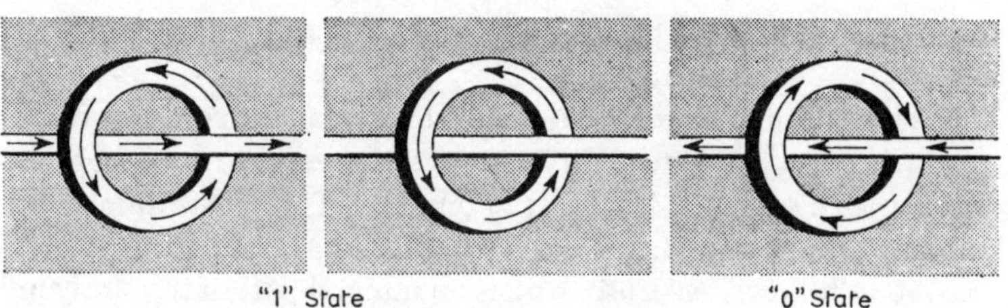

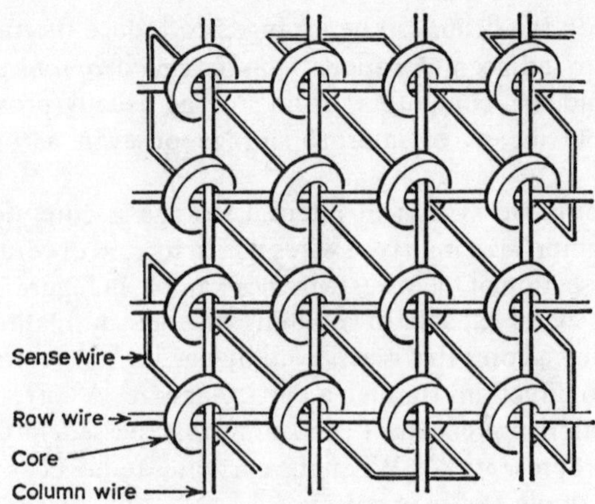

Fig. 34. A Section of Ferrite Core Store (simplified)

As shown in Figure 34 there are two wires through a core. Let us assume that a current of Im is capable of magnetizing a core (i.e. changing the state of a core). A selected core can be magnetized by passing a current of ½Im through a column wire and at the same time ½Im through a row wire, thus giving a combined total of Im in that selected core. The current of only ½Im does not affect any of the cores on the column or row of the selected core.

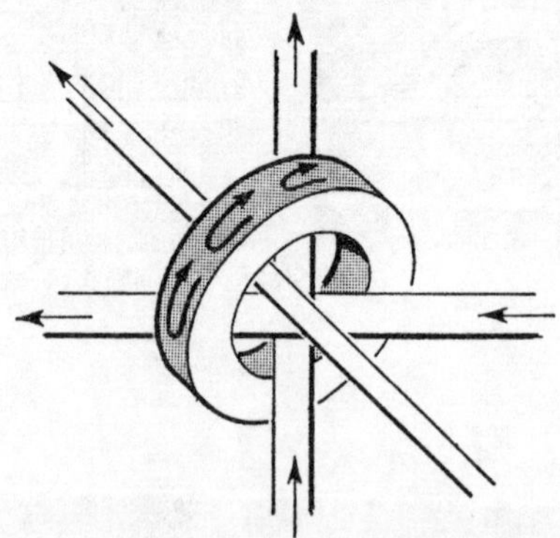

Data is written to store in two stages. Firstly, all the cores representing a word or a character or a byte are set to zero. The appropriate cores are then set to a '1' state; see Figure 35. This illustration shows the recording of one B.C.D. digit (6). Reading data from store is achieved as follows. A 'sense' wire is an integral part of the store and

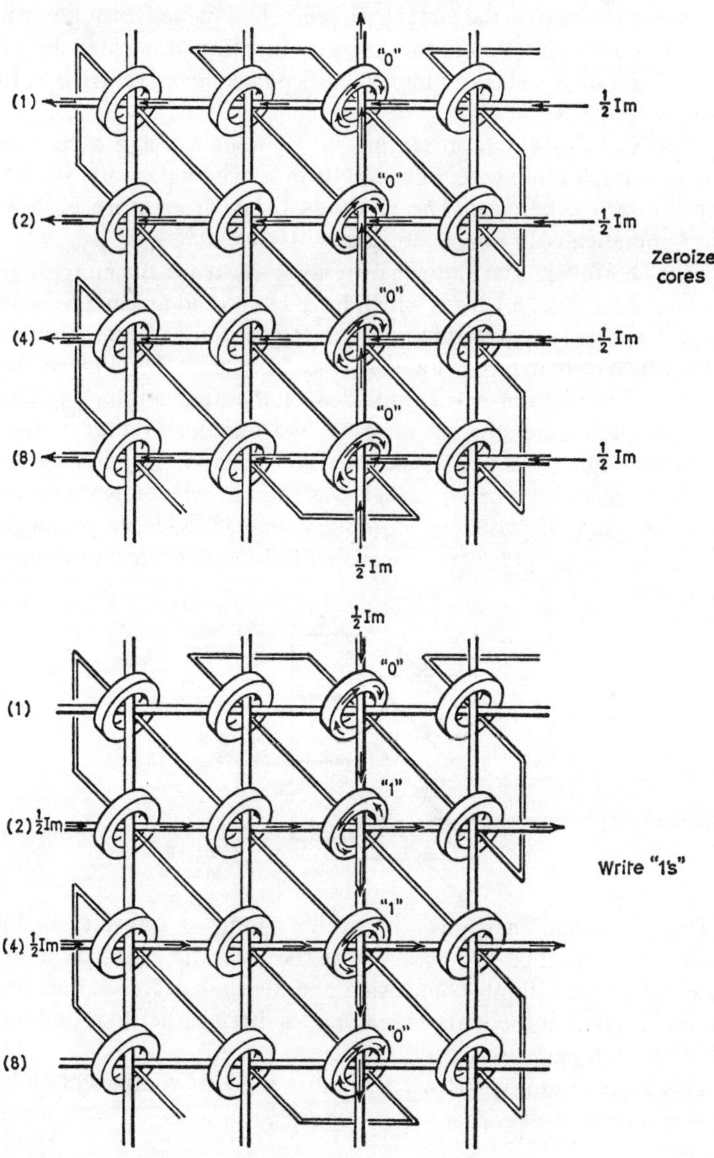

Fig. 35. Writing Data to Core Store

passes through the centre of each core in one plane. The reading technique is based on the fact that if a current is passed through a core in the *opposite* direction to the 'present direction of magnetism', the change of state results in a pulse which is picked up and carried by the same wire.

Thus, if a current representing '0' is input through a row and column wire, a sense wire pulse will be produced if the core is in a '1' state but not otherwise. The reading of data from store is shown diagrammatically in Figure 36, pages 104 to 105.

Note, however, that the act of reading destroys the state of the relevant cores, i.e. all cores which have been read are in a '0' state. Since it is usually required to preserve the contents of core store, the cores which were in the '1' state are reset from '0' to '1'. Thus, reading is effected in two stages – a read phase and a 'regenerate 1' phase.

A complete core store is made up of a number of matrix layers. Although Figures 35 and 36 assumed for explanatory purposes that the cores accessed when one digit was read or written were on one 'layer' or 'plane', it would be more likely that a transfer by reading or writing would be made using cores on different planes as shown in the example below.

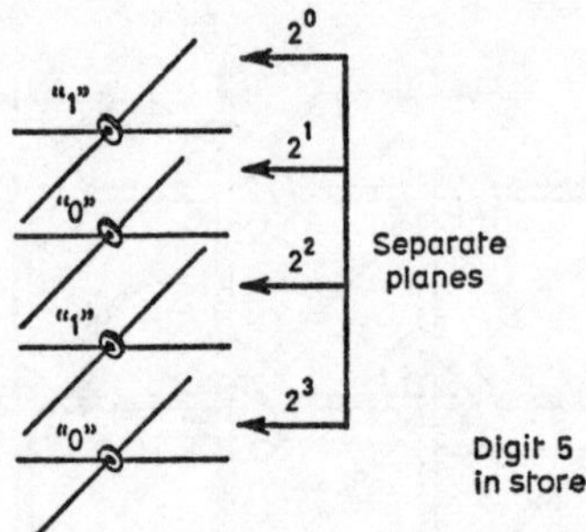

This technique then gives a parallel mode of transfer, all bits comprising one digit are accessed at the same time, rather than a serial mode (i.e. all bits comprising one digit are accessed one after another). Data in the store is read and written rather like finding a location on a map using 'grid references'.

This type of storage is used in most modern computers and is known variously as:

(i) core store
(ii) ferrite core store
(iii) immediate access store (I.A.S.)
(iv) high speed memory (H.S.M.).

The widespread use of ferrite core storage can be examined by reference to four criteria: speed, cost, size and general suitability.

The term ‘immediate access store’ is well suited to core storage. There is no delay, as on a magnetic drum, in accessing the contents of a required location in store; the ‘grid reference’ system permits the accessing of data immediately upon the provision of an address. The access time for one location must be measured in microseconds or even, in some cases, nanoseconds – thousandth millionths of a second. The access time for a store is, roughly, the time that elapses between the moment the command to access a location or area in store is given and the moment when the transfer of data to or from that location can commence.

The transfer time for a modern core store is dependent on the rate at which ‘drive pulses’ are applied to the store input leads of the row column wires. The rate at which drive pulses are generated is called the Pulse Repetition Frequency (the P.R.F.). The transfer time for modern core storage varies according to manufacturer and the circuitry associated with the core store. Generally, however, transfer times are in the region of 8 to 1 μs.

Many early core stores were made by hand and the care required in manufacture meant that their cost was extremely high. The cost of core storage has dropped but it still remains high.

The size of core storage varies as much as the speed; core store varies in size from two hundred locations to half a million locations. The effective size of a computer's core store will largely be determined by cost and the ability of an instruction (and associated circuitry) to address all the locations. Thus, a core store of 100,000 locations, be they words, characters or bytes, will require an address part of five digits, addresses 00000 to 99,999 or of circuitry capable of modifying a four digit address to a five digit address. Even the physical size of core storage may be a limiting factor; the store and its associated circuitry may become so large that access times may drop by virtue of the physical distance that electricity must travel. Similarly, the number of cores on one plane is limited since too many cores may result in excessive ‘noise’ signals. The transfer rate of a store can be developed so that extremely fast (nanosecond) transfers can be affected by generating a P.R.F. of a very high frequency. However, even if ‘drive pulses’ are generated at 100 nanosecond intervals, electricity travels only some six inches along a wire within 100 nanoseconds. Thus, micro-miniaturization of components and logical units becomes significant.

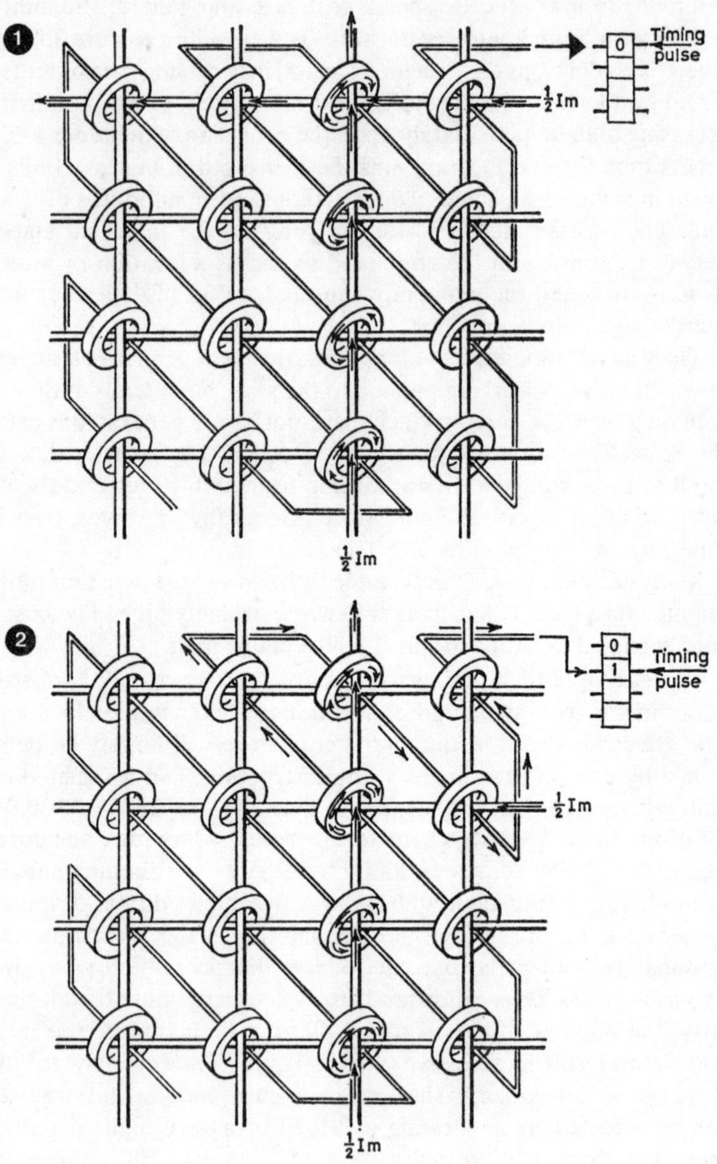

Fig. 36. Reading

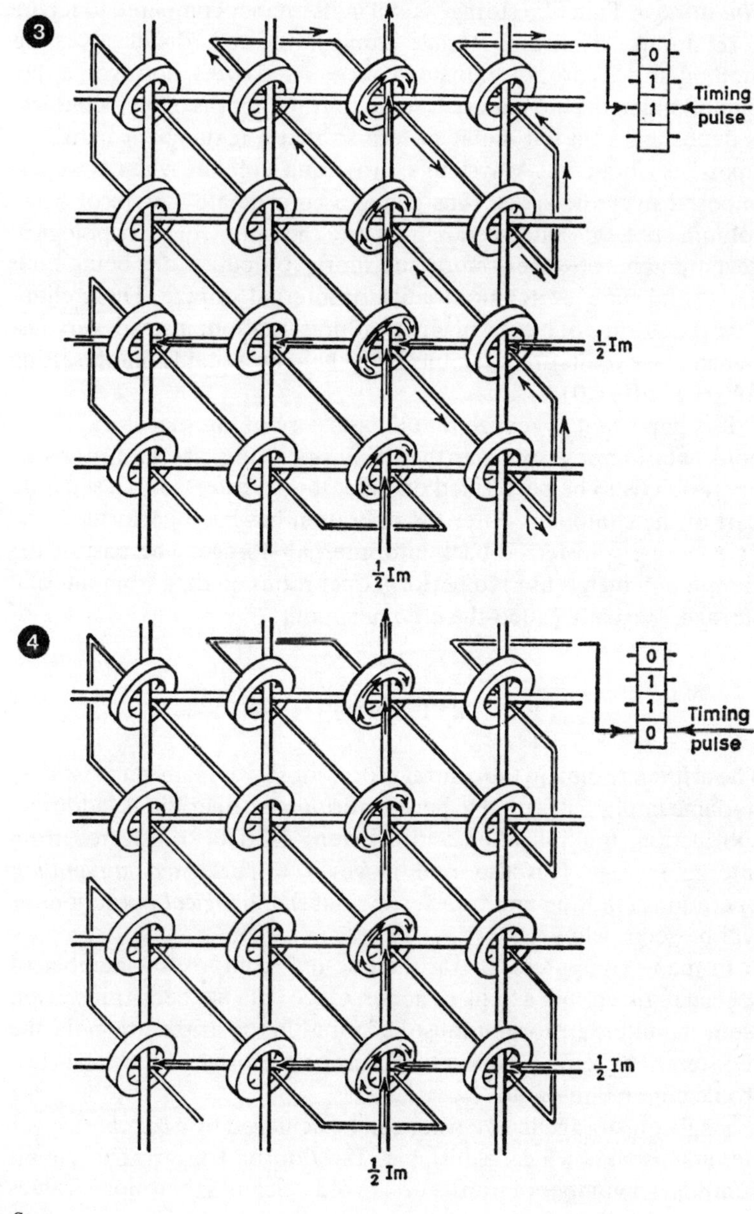

a Core Store

A further alternative is the relatively modern innovation of *thin film storage*. Thin film storage is still in its infancy compared to ferrite core storage. Thin film storage employs the co-ordinate accessing method as in a core store. Instead of threaded cores, however, a thin film of magnetizable material, some four millionths of an inch thick, is deposited on a flat metal surface so that a rectangular matrix of 'spots' is obtained. A system of row and column wires is superimposed over the spots, thus giving a co-ordinate system of 'row-column-spot at intersection'. With the rate of technological development, however, more and more computers are being built with 'solid state' switching circuits for internal storage. These eliminate the storage of bits by magnetic representation; instead, very fast switchable circuits are used, bits being held by a simple on/off setting (on = 1, off = 0).

It is important to realize that the purpose of internal storage is to hold data or programs and that if an operation, say an arithmetic operation, is to be performed on data, it is transferred to a separate part of the computer. After the operation has been performed, the data can be transferred back into internal storage. The part of the computer which is used to perform operations on data from internal storage is usually called the *arithmetic unit*.

THE ARITHMETIC UNIT

The arithmetic unit in the central processor serves many purposes. As its name implies, it is used to perform *arithmetic* operations (addition, subtraction, multiplication and division) on data transferred from internal storage. It is also used, however, to perform *data handling* operations (shifting and transferring data) and *logical* operations as will be seen below.

In many computers, the arithmetic unit comprises a number of special registers and a 'mill' or adder. Once data has been transferred from the internal store, it must be stored in the arithmetic unit, the registers. The required operation must be performed by special electronic circuits, the mill.

Single bit storage in a register can be achieved by a *bistable trigger circuit*, also known as a bistable, flip-flop or trigger. The circuit comprises a number of transistors; in old machines thermionic valves were used. The circuit can be used to retain one bit, i.e. value 0 or value 1. The special circuits which 'manipulate' bits (e.g. adding and bit inversion) are composed of basic 'logical elements'. These elements (or *gates*) consist of a number of transistors which operate on a given input to provide a given output; it should be remembered that the binary system of 1 and 0 is ideally represented by 'pulse' or 'no pulse'. Let us consider two example 'logical' elements; the *and-gate* and the *or-gate*.

The and-gate works on the principle that all available input pulses must be present at the same time to produce an output pulse. Thus, a three input and-gate will produce an output pulse only when all three input pulses are provided:

1, 1, 1 → AND → 1

but not otherwise, e.g.

0, 1, 1 → AND → 0 1, 0, 1 → AND → 0 1, 1, 0 → AND → 0 0, 0, 1 → AND → 0 **etc.**

An or-gate works on the principle that at least one input pulse will produce an output pulse. Thus a two input or-gate will produce an output pulse as follows:

1, 0 → OR → 1 1, 0 → OR → 1 1, 1 → OR → 1

but not when the two input pulses are absent:

0, 0 → OR → 0

This is an *inclusive or*, i.e. a pulse is produced if only one or both input pulses are present. An *exclusive or* works on the principle that only one pulse, not both, produces an output pulse.

0, 1 → OR → 1 1, 0 → OR → 1 0, 0 → OR → 0 1, 1 → OR → 0

Further circuits can perform inversion:

0 → NOT → 1 1 → NOT → 0

These circuits 'and', 'or', and 'not' can be combined to provide various outputs from given inputs. The logical elements or arrangements of gates are composed almost entirely of transistors on plug-in boards (see Figure 37), or on micro-miniaturized chip circuits (see Plate 1). Note that it is not only the arithmetic unit circuits which are constructed in this manner but also most other circuits within the central processor. The operation of the computer's circuits will not be considered here. The basic operations performed within the arithmetic unit will be described in outline using the example arithmetic unit shown in Figure 38. There are three registers, X, Y, and Z, and a mill. There are also two highways, labelled for explanatory purposes 'highway a' and 'highway b'. Note that the only difference between

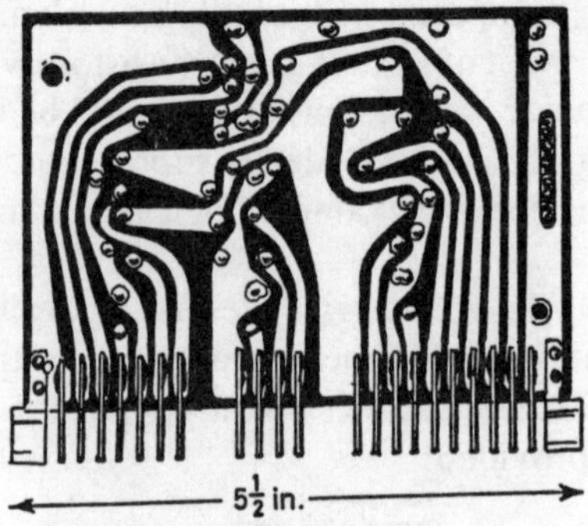

Fig. 37. Printed Wiring

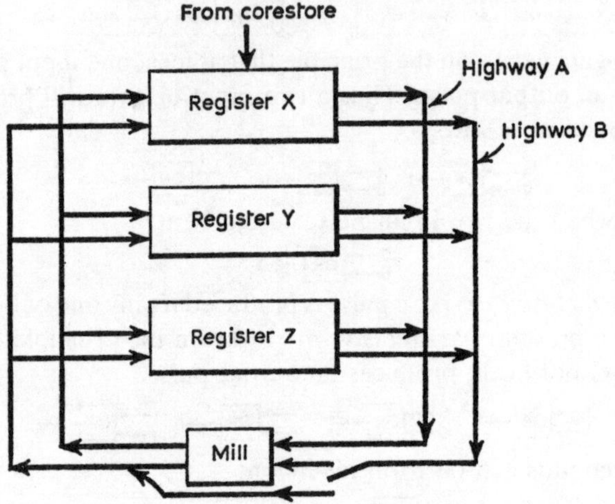

Fig. 38. An Example Arithmetic Unit

these highways is that both pass through the mill but highway b can by-pass the mill. Arithmetic and data handling operations will first be described in general terms and then an example will be given in terms of a pure binary fixed word length of six bits.

Arithmetic Operations

These include addition, subtraction, multiplication and division. The method of addition will depend on how many internal store addresses can be specified in the add instruction. If only one internal store address can be specified, the addition must take place in three stages. Firstly, one addend is transferred to register Y by a 'transfer the contents of an internal store to register Y' instruction. Secondly, the add instruction is given (the location of the other addend being specified in this instruction) and the other addend is placed in register X. The contents of register X and register Y are then transferred (via highway a and highway b respectively) to the mill where they are added together and the sum is written into, say, register Y. Note that the sum overwrites the previous contents of register Y. The sum can then be transferred to internal storage by means of an instruction which transfers the contents of register Y to a specified location in internal storage. Example:

Add the contents of location 100 (11) to the contents of location 101 (14); place the sum in location 200.

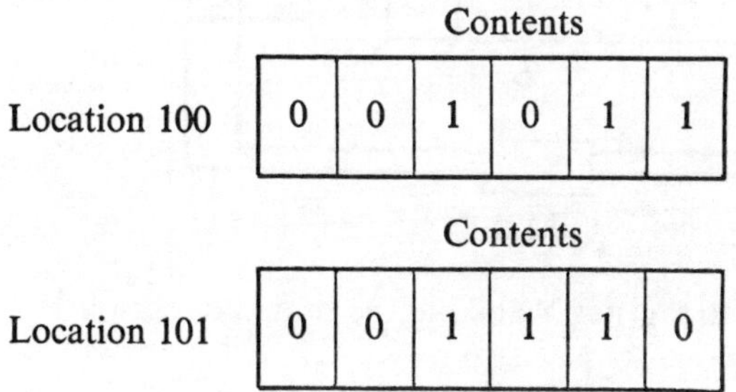

(1) Transfer contents of location 100 to register Y

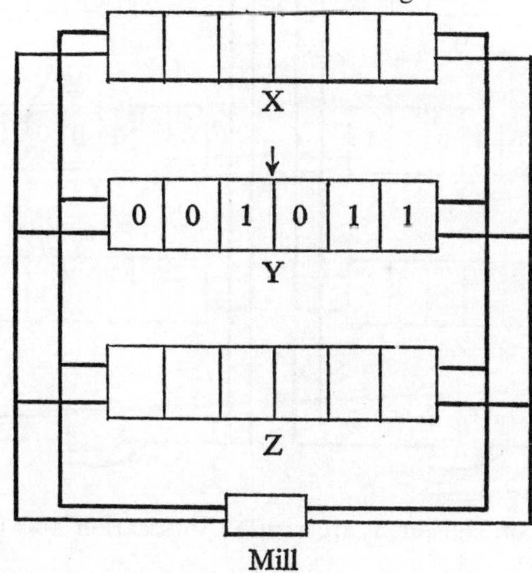

(2) (i) Transfer contents of location 101 to register X

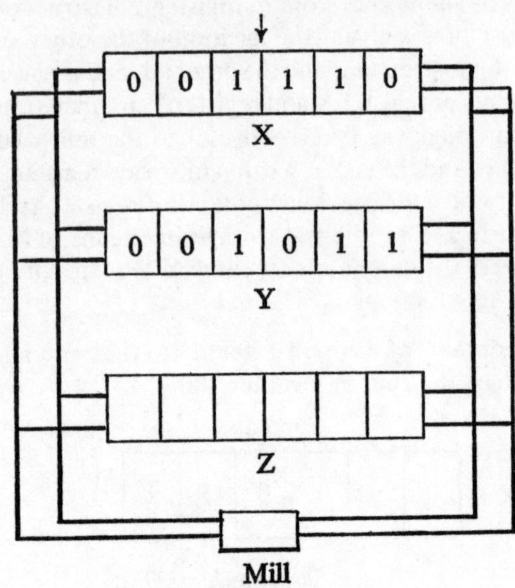

(ii) Add contents of X to register Y and put the sum into register Y

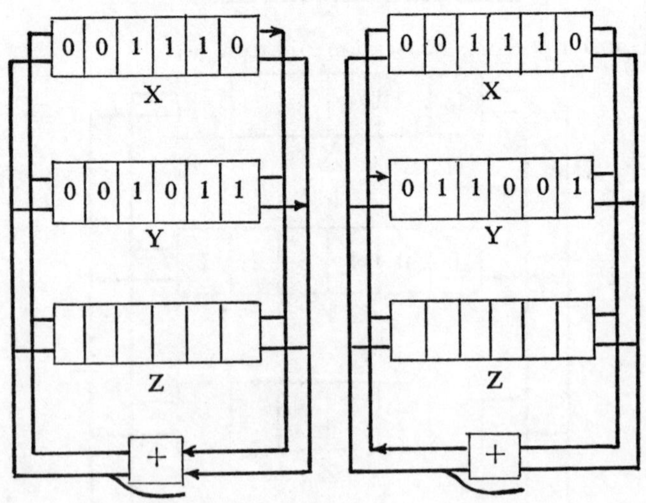

(3) Contents of register Y are written to location 200 in internal storage.

Obviously, if the instruction format permits two internal storage addresses to be specified, then steps 1 and 2 (i) may be performed in one step. Depending on the logic of the computer, the sum may either be left in a register or it may be transferred to a location in internal storage specified in the add instruction, thereby overwriting one of the addends. An instruction which permits three internal storage addresses to be specified can be used to write the sum into any internal store location.

Subtraction, multiplication and division are executed in much the same manner as addition; the circuits in the mill are activated to perform the required operation, transfers to and from the internal storage or between registers being effected via the appropriate highways.

Logical Operations

These are operations which are performed in response to an AND, EXCLUSIVE OR and INCLUSIVE OR instructions. They operate in much the same manner as the 'and' and 'or' circuits described on page 107. Individual bits are matched and the resultant output bit will depend on the logical operation specified. The bit matching processes are:

AND

$0 + 0 = 0$
$0 + 1 = 0$
$1 + 0 = 0$
$1 + 1 = 1$

EXCLUSIVE OR

$0 + 0 = 0$
$0 + 1 = 1$
$1 + 0 = 1$
$1 + 1 = 0$

INCLUSIVE OR

$0 + 0 = 0$
$0 + 1 = 1$
$1 + 0 = 1$
$1 + 1 = 1$

Using the example six bit pure binary word and three register arithmetic unit, an and operation may be shown thus:

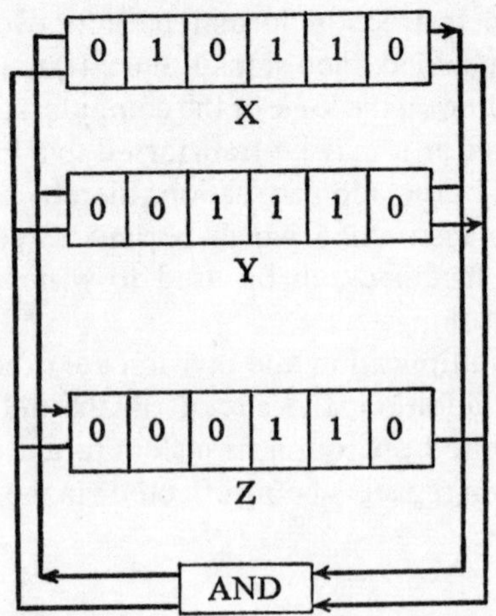

where registers X and Y contain two numbers in six bit form ready to undergo the AND operation and register Z contains the resultant output bit pattern.

The number of steps required to perform this operation will depend on the number of internal storage addresses specified in the AND instruction.

Shifting Operations

These operations are performed on the contents of one word. Thus, in terms of the example arithmetic unit, only one register and highway take place in a shifting operation. The two basic shifting procedures are the right and left cyclic shifts. Diagrammatically, a right cyclic shift may be shown thus:

For example, if the contents

0	0	0	1	1	1

are shifted one position to the right, the contents of the register become

1	0	0	0	1	1

A five position shift will give

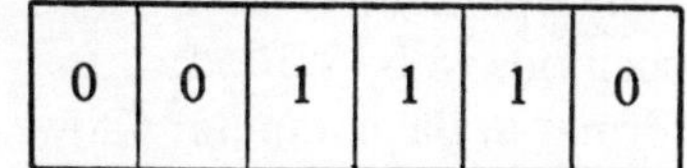

and a six position shift will give

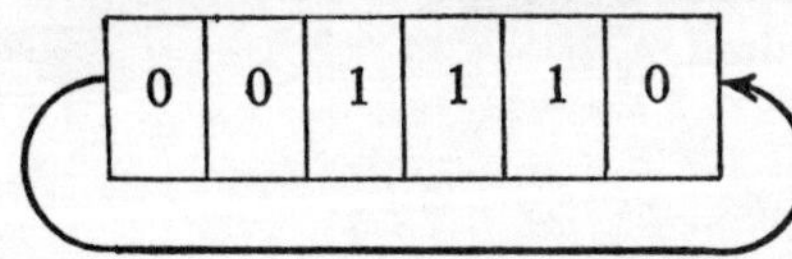

Similarly, a left shift of one position will give

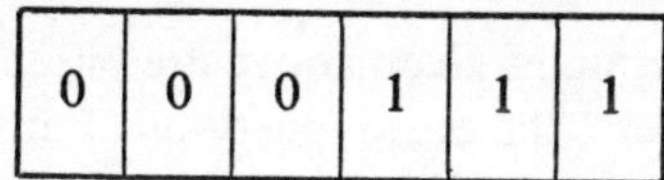

Note that this is equivalent to right shifting five positions.

A simple right shift, but entering zeros, works on the principle of shifting the contents the appropriate number of positions to the right so that the contents 'drop off' the end of the register. Zeros are entered from the left. For example, a right shift of one position of

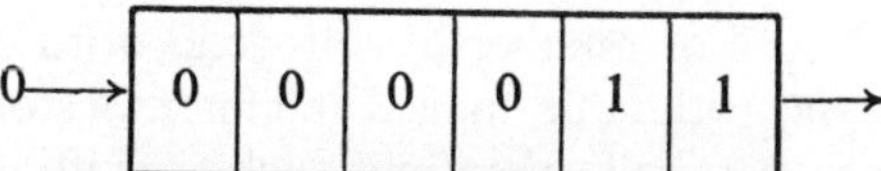

will give

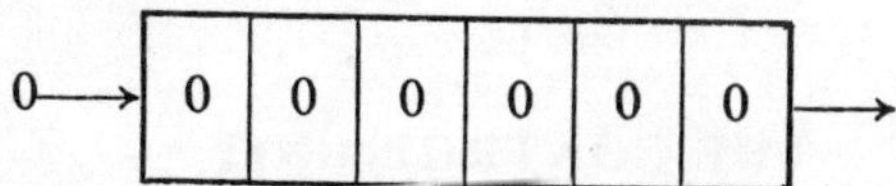

and a three position right shift will give

A left shift will move the contents to the left and insert zeros from the right. For example, a left shift of one position of

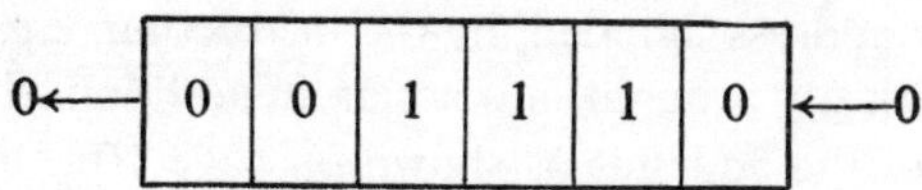

will give

A shift instruction must specify:
(i) the type of shift (by operation code);
(ii) the number of positions to be shifted.

If the instruction format in the computer allows only one internal storage address to be specified, the contents of a word to be shifted must first be positioned in a special register by a separate transfer instruction. In this case, the address part of the shift instruction can contain only the number of positions to be shifted. Alternatively, an instruction with provision for two addresses can specify the address of a word, the contents of which are to be shifted and the number of positions to be shifted.

Transfer Operations

These operations transfer the contents of one cell in internal storage to another cell in internal storage. One register is employed to hold the contents of one cell. Thus, for example, the contents of one cell are transferred from a specified location in internal storage to the register and are then transferred from the register to its destination cell.

Even though the examples given above are based on the presence of three special registers, the basic functions of any arithmetic unit are similar. Two types of operations performed in the arithmetic unit may be summarized as follows. Firstly, there are the operations which involve a complete cell or number of cells (e.g. word or character locations) such as the arithmetic, logical and internal store transfers. Secondly, there are part cell operations such as shifting which are clearly not relevant to character machines.

THE CONTROL UNIT

The basic concept of program instruction execution has been explained in Chapter One and is summarized in Figure 39. The instruction format may now be inspected.

Firstly, there is the *single address* or *one address* system. The basic content of the instruction is an operation or function code and one address of a location in internal core storage. Obviously, there must be another address 'implied' by the instruction, e.g. a register which is automatically brought into action in addition, this register containing one of the addends as shown on page 109. In terms of

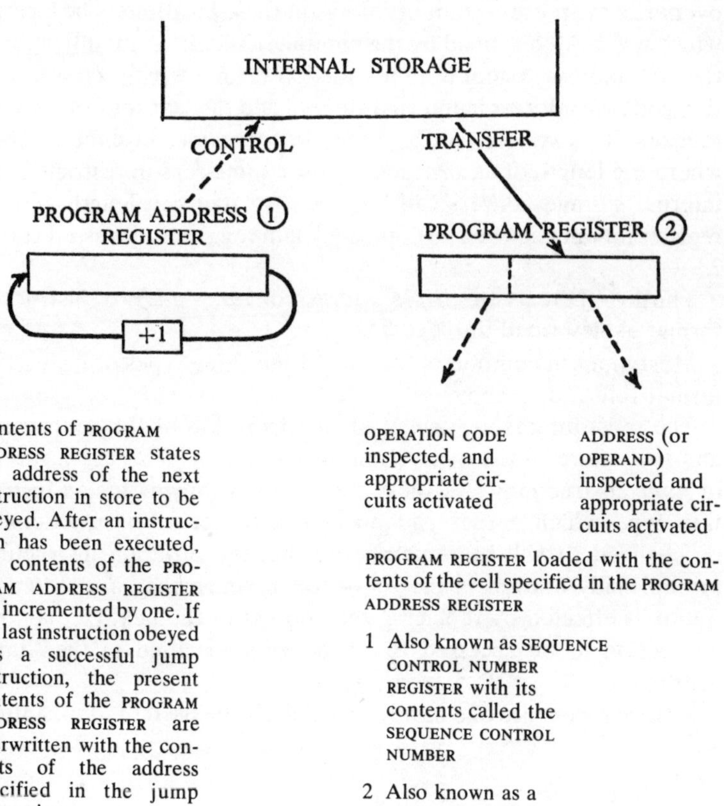

INTERNAL STORAGE
CONTROL
TRANSFER
PROGRAM ADDRESS REGISTER (1)
PROGRAM REGISTER (2)
+1
Contents of PROGRAM ADDRESS REGISTER states the address of the next instruction in store to be obeyed. After an instruction has been executed, the contents of the PROGRAM ADDRESS REGISTER are incremented by one. If the last instruction obeyed was a successful jump instruction, the present contents of the PROGRAM ADDRESS REGISTER are overwritten with the contents of the address specified in the jump instruction.
OPERATION CODE inspected, and appropriate circuits activated
ADDRESS (or OPERAND) inspected and appropriate circuits activated
PROGRAM REGISTER loaded with the contents of the cell specified in the PROGRAM ADDRESS REGISTER
1 Also known as SEQUENCE CONTROL NUMBER REGISTER with its contents called the SEQUENCE CONTROL NUMBER
2 Also known as a CONTROL REGISTER

Fig. 39. Operation of a 'Control Unit'

this example of addition the result will be placed either in a register or the location specified in the instruction; this will be according to the logic (arrangement of circuits) in the computer. Alternatively, the address part of the instruction may be a qualification to the function code; for example the function code may specify 'shift' and the address specifies the number of positions to be shifted.

Secondly, there is the *double address* or *two address* system. The basic content of the instruction is a function code and two addresses capable of addressing any two locations in internal storage. Thus, again using the example of addition, the two locations holding numbers to be added can be specified in the instruction but the sum will overwrite the present contents of one of these locations. The location which will be determined by the computer's logic. A modification of the two address system is an instruction format which states a function code, an address in internal storage and the 'address' of a special register. This system can be used, for example, in circumstances where the length of an instruction is for some reason restricted; the internal storage address can be, say, five digits in length and the register number can be one digit, e.g. eight registers addressed as 0, 1, 2 —— 7.

Thirdly, there is the *triple address* or *three address* instruction format as described on page 55.

Most modern computers use one of the three types of instruction format referred to above.

The most interesting aspect of the operation of the control unit and the nature of the instruction format is that of *decision, branch* or *jump* instructions. All these terms are synonyms for an instruction type which causes the normal sequence of instructions to be changed. It will be remembered that the program instructions are normally obeyed in the sequence in which they are stored. A 'jump' is effected by replacing the address of the next (sequential) instruction to be accessed by an address specified in the 'jump' instruction.

A basic repertoire of conditions which can be used to cause a jump is:

is $x = 0$?
is $x > 0$? (is x positive?)
is $x < 0$? (is x negative?)

Consider the format of jump instructions where the instruction has one address, i.e. the single address system. The function code must specify the 'jump if $x = 0$' action; the address specifies the location of an instruction in storage which is to be obeyed if x does equal zero. How can 'x' be specified? The principle may be illustrated as follows. A register/mill adder system can be employed so that when a number is passed through the mill and that number is equal to zero, an 'electronic switch' is set. When a 'jump if $x = 0$' instruction is obeyed, the 'electronic switch' is tested and, if it is set, the jump is made, i.e. the instruction in the location specified in the jump instruction is accessed and obeyed. If the switch is unset, then no jump is performed. The jump instruction may therefore be read as: 'if the last number through the mill was zero so that the switch is set, then jump to the instruction held in the location specified in the address'. An array of switches may be associated with the mill, each switch being set according to a particular condition.

The format of a jump instruction using the two address system presents two theoretical possibilities. In terms of the instruction 'if x = 0' one address may specify the location of quantity 'x', the other address specifying the location of the instruction to be obeyed if x *does* equal zero. Alternatively, the two addresses in a jump instruction can specify the locations of two instructions, one instruction to be obeyed if x does equal zero and the other if x does *not* equal zero. In the latter case the characteristics of quantity 'x' which form the criteria for the jump must be detected by means similar to that for a single address system as described above.

The format of a jump instruction using the three address system can theoretically specify the location of x, the address of the location which holds the instruction to be obeyed if x does equal zero, and the address of the location which holds the instruction to be obeyed if x does not equal zero. Naturally, an address field can be ignored in a jump instruction and the computer's logic could function as in a two address system.

One special type of jump instruction is an unconditional jump instruction. An unconditional jump instruction will cause an *automatic* interruption to the normal sequence in which instructions are obeyed. Thus, when an unconditional jump instruction is obeyed, the instruction held in the location specified in the jump instruction is accessed and obeyed. The use of the unconditional jump instruction will be discussed later when the function of programming is considered.

Having described the three basic components of a modern central processor, it can now be seen what can be achieved by using internal storage, the arithmetic unit and the program controller. Obviously, provided there is a program held within store and data to be operated on, then any operation utilizing the arithmetic unit and internal storage can be performed. A central processor is therefore worthless if there is no means of inputting data and program or outputting the results of the computation. A basic requirement therefore is that the central processor must be able to receive data and program from its human users and to provide its human users with their required solutions. Input and output is effected by means of 'peripheral units'; the theory and construction of these units are considered in Chapter Three.

COMPUTING POWER

In this chapter we have reviewed the internal workings of the central processor. Perhaps no other component in the computer has been subjected to so much technological change in such a relatively short period of time. For example, the ENIAC computer (Electronic Numerical Integrator and Calculator) developed in the United States in the late 1940s, weighed nearly 30 tons, occupied 1,500 square feet, and its 18,000 vacuum tubes (valves) produced 150 kilowatts of heat. For all its massive physical size, it was by today's standards extremely slow (one addition sum taking, for example, some 20 milliseconds) with a very limited storage capacity (only 20 words of internal storage!). Contrast this with a modern computer with a central processor having some two *million* bytes of storage.* It occupies about 200 square feet and the time to perform one addition is in the order of 20 *micro*seconds!

The processing power of a modern computer is a function of two factors: the amount of core store and the switching speed (P.R.F.) of the central processor.

For a job to be run on the computer, the program instructions must be loaded and held in core store. When the program is executed, data is read into core store, processed (e.g. in the arithmetic unit) and the results held in store. Thus, as a job is executed both program and data must be held in internal storage. The amount of storage available thus defines the size of the program that can be run and the quantity of data that can be processed. The smaller the core store, the smaller and simpler the program must be. Similarly, the more limited the core store capacity, the smaller the quantity of data that can be processed.

Core store capacity thus determines the amount of work the central processor can perform in a given period of time. A small computer may have only 64K bytes of core; a large computer 5M bytes of core. Simply providing more and more core storage will not of itself, however, result in a more powerful computer. It would simply mean that programs could be bigger and greater quantities of data could be held. To produce a more powerful computer, the speed of the central

* The symbol K is used to denote 1,000 core store locations. This could thus be written 2,000K bytes or 2,000 kilobytes of storage. For large machines, the symbol M (mega) is used to denote a million core store locations. This could thus also be written 2M bytes or 2 megabytes of storage.

processor must be increased so that the larger programs and the greater quantity of data can be processed faster.

There is thus a correlation between the size of internal store and the speed of the central processor. Thus a small computer with 64K bytes of storage may have a cycle time of 500 nanoseconds, a medium-sized computer with 524K, a cycle time of 250 nanoseconds, and a large computer with 2M bytes, a cycle time of 100 nanoseconds. Obviously as size and speed increase, so does the cost.

3. The Peripheral Units

THE NATURE OF PERIPHERAL UNITS

Peripheral units may be considered as special devices which surround the central processor. Some devices provide a means of entering 'raw' input to the internal storage in the central processor. Raw input is input originated by human agency; for example, a program is written, coded and then input. Similarly, some peripheral units facilitate the output of information in a form for human inspection, such as printed matter (a tabulation or graph) or a picture projected on a special screen.

A different class of peripheral unit is a 'file' or 'backing' storage device. These devices form an extension to the internal storage of the central processor. Because the internal storage is usually restricted to a practical minimum, peripheral units are used for the mass storage of data.

These three classes of peripheral units are shown diagrammatically in Figure 40.

The problem of inputting raw input is simple: it is necessary to present the basic symbols 0, 1, 2. . . . .9, A, B, C. . . . .Z, '×', '–', '·', '%', '@', '(",")', etc. in a coded form so that they can be held (i.e. as bit patterns) within the computer's internal store.

A basic system for inputting data is the use of an intermediate coding procedure on a special computer input media. There is now a considerable range of input devices which use a specially coded input media, the most important being:

punched cards
punched paper tape
magnetic ink character recognition (M.I.C.R.)
optical character recognition (O.C.R.)

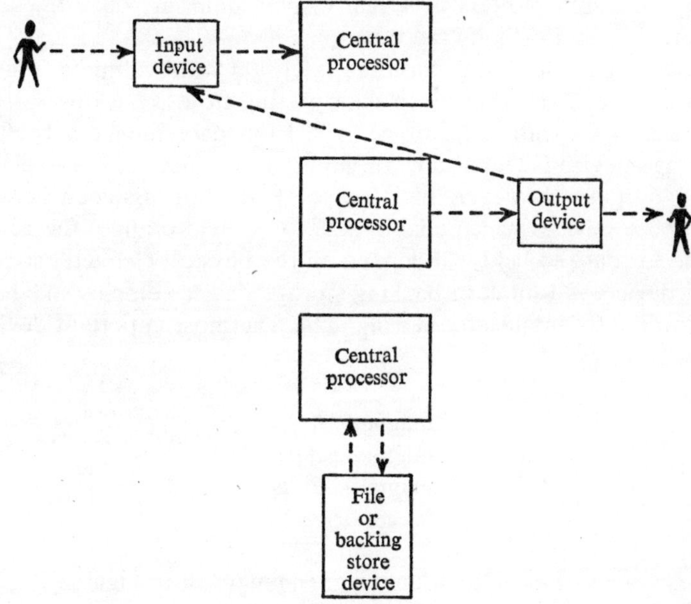

Fig. 40. Classes of Peripheral Units

All the above input media can be prepared manually, i.e. by operators using a special device, from given data represented in common usage symbols 0, 1, 2. . . . .9, A, B. . . . .Z and special symbols as shown above etc. In addition, the media can also be prepared by an output device *on-line* to (that is, a device directly linked to and receiving information from) the central processor. Thus, for example, punched cards and paper tape form a means of inputting raw data, outputting data for re-input to the computer or for processing on another machine.

Some input/output units do not require an 'intermediate medium'. For example, data can be entered directly into the internal storage of the computer as the result of key depressions on a typewriter keyboard. Output can be in the form of a typed message or the display of a message on a cathode ray tube screen, similar to a television screen.

True output devices are those which produce a finished output, e.g. the output of a computation in the form of the characters 0 to 9, A to Z, and special punctuation and mathematical symbols. Such output is produced on a high speed printer. Alternatively, the output devices may be graph plotters or visual display units in which lines are projected on a cathode ray tube.

Backing or file storage forms an extension to the computer's internal storage. Note that, since data passing from a backing storage device to the internal storage is strictly 'data input', a backing storage device is technically an 'input/output' device. For explanatory purposes however, file storage devices are assumed here to be those devices which enable data to be held on-line; the access time for data so held will depend on the physical characteristics of the device. All modern backing storage devices employ magnetic recording techniques for storing data. The most important devices are:

magnetic drums
magnetic tape
magnetic discs
magnetic cards

These types of peripheral units are summarized in Figure 42.

COMMON PERIPHERAL UNITS

Each of the peripheral units shown in Figure 42 will be described in the following pages. Methods of performing peripheral transfers are then described.

Punched Cards

Punched cards have been used as a means of input from the earliest days of computers, and before that, for input to conventional tabulators and calculators. A punched card is a piece of high quality card stock of uniform length, width and thickness. The card comprises a number of vertical *columns* and a number of horizontal *punching positions*; see Figure 41. The most common 'sizes' of punched cards, where 'size' is measured in columnar capacity, are:

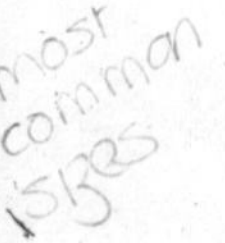

40 column – physical size of approximately $4\frac{11}{16}'' \times 2\frac{1}{16}'' \times \cdot 007''$
80 column (see Figure 41) – physical size of approximately $7\frac{3}{8}'' \times 3\frac{1}{4}'' \times \cdot 007''$

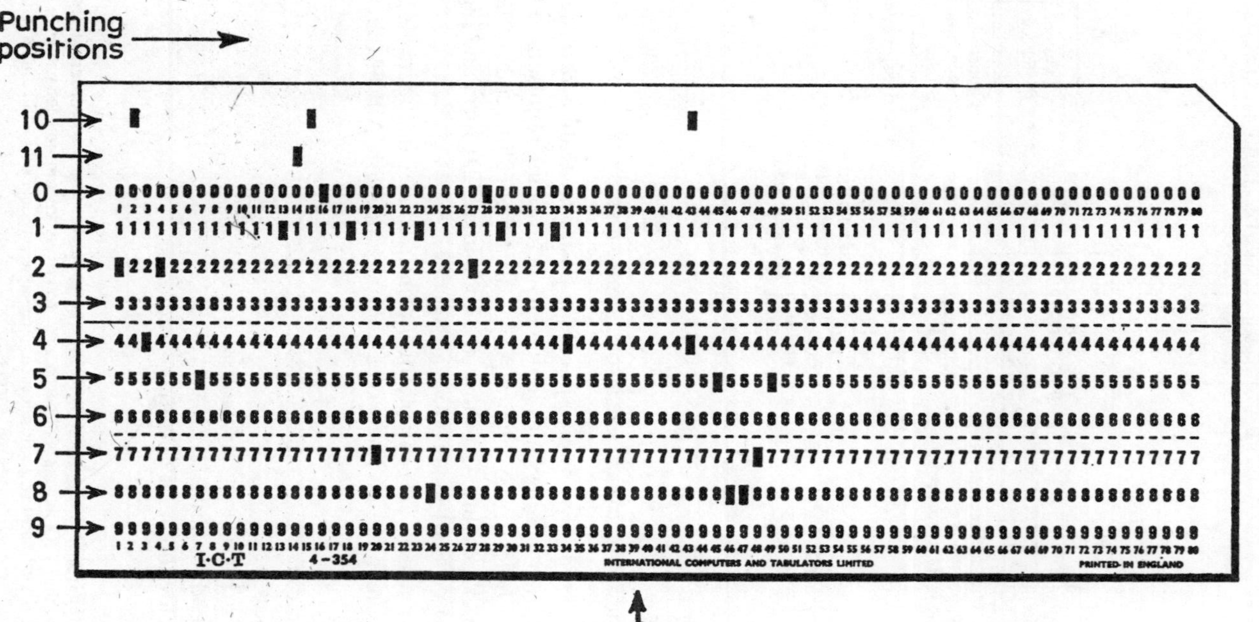

Fig. 41. An 80-Column Punched Card

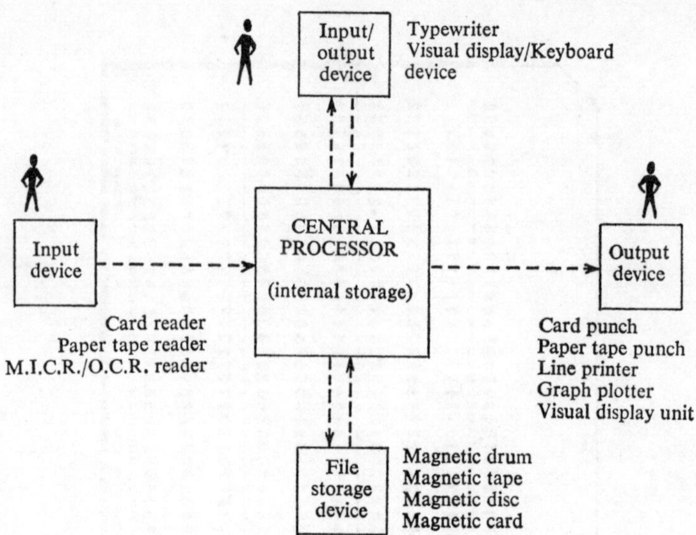

Fig. 42. Types of Peripheral Units

90 column* – physical size also of approximately $7\frac{3}{8}'' \times 3\frac{1}{4}'' \times \cdot 007''$

All these cards have twelve punching positions. Data is recorded in the card by punching holes in it, a character being represented by a pattern of holes in one column. A typical card punching code is shown in Figure 43; Figure 43a shows the code in tabular form and Figure 43b shows a card punched with the code.

Card readers, an example of which is shown in Figure 44, are devices which are on-line to the central processor. All card readers have:

(i) a stacker
(ii) a hopper
(iii) a card transport mechanism
(iv) a reading unit
(v) a 'clocking' and encoding system.

* 90 column and 80 column cards are the same size but with different spacing between columns. Other sizes of cards, now relatively uncommon for use with computers, are 65, 130 and 160 column cards (the same physical side as 80 and 90 column cards) and 21 column cards measuring $2\frac{3}{4}'' \times 2'' \times \cdot 007''$.

Column	Character Description	Printed Symbol
1	Ampersand	&
2	Minus	–
3	Zero	0
4	One	1
5	Two	2
6	Three	3
7	Four	4
8	Five	5
9	Six	6
10	Seven	7
11	Eight	8
12	Nine	9
13	A	A
14	B	B
15	C	C
16	D	D
17	E	E
18	F	F
19	G	G
20	H	H
21	I	I
22	J	J
23	K	K
24	L	L
25	M	M
26	N	N
27	O	O
28	P	P
29	Q	Q
30	R	R
31	S	S
32	T	T
33	U	U
34	V	V
35	W	W
36	X	X
37	Y	Y
38	Z	Z
39	Quarter	¼
40	At the rate of	@
41	Open Parenthesis	(
42	Close Parenthesis	)
43	Equals	=
44	Colon	:
45	Semicolon	;
46	Apostrophe	'
47	Ampersand	&
48	Period	.
49	Pound	£
50	Asterisk	*
51	Plus	+
52	Minus	–
53	Oblique	/
54	Half	½
55	Comma	,
56	Per cent	%

(a)

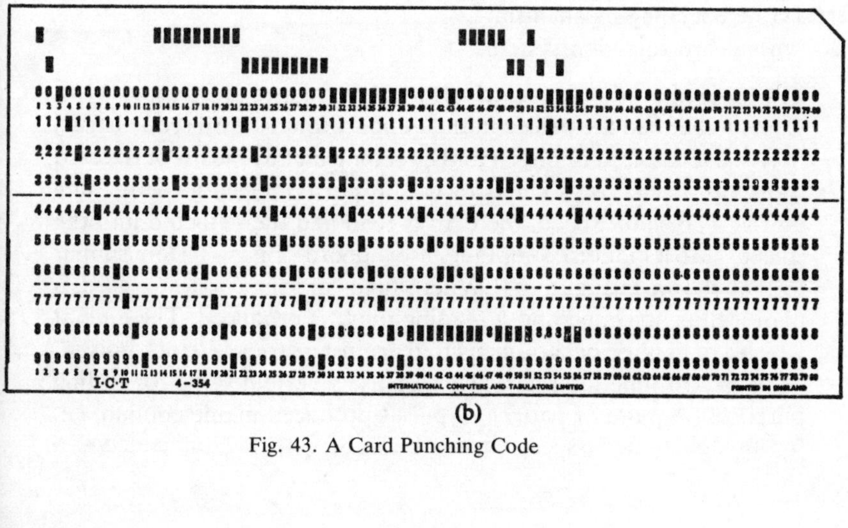

(b)

Fig. 43. A Card Punching Code

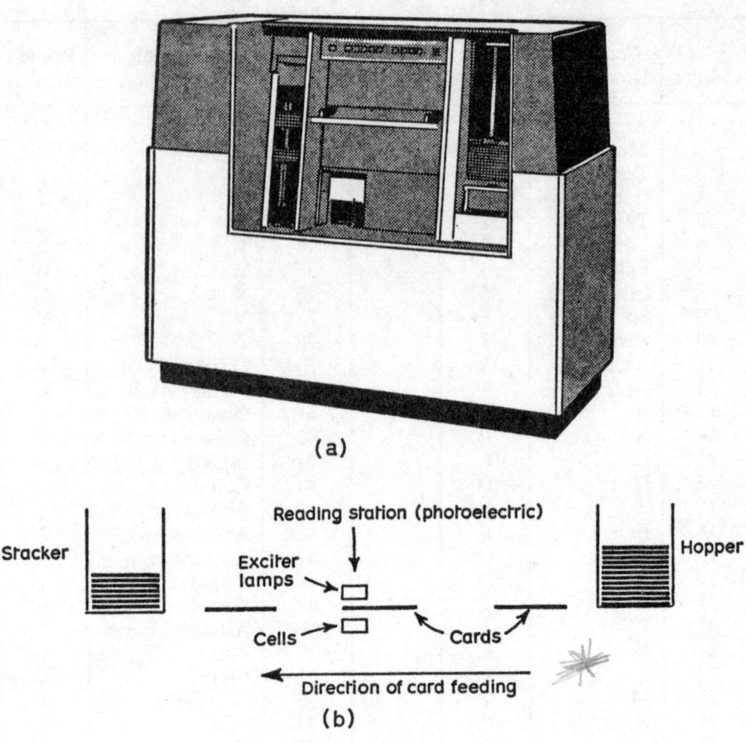

Fig. 44. A Card Reader

In addition most, but not all, card readers have:

(vi) a checking mechanism
(vii) a card rejection system.

The basic operation of a card reader is as follows (see Figure 44b). Cards to be read are placed in the hopper; when a card read instruction is given, a card is moved to the reading unit by means of the card transport mechanism. The card is transported beneath the reading unit at a constant speed, the card is read and then ejected into the stacker. Most modern computers use a photo-sensing system similar to that shown in Figure 44. Where holes are punched in a card, a photocell is activated and a reading pulse is produced. The *time* at which a read pulse occurs, measured against a series of 'clock pulses', i.e. standard time intervals, gives a pulse a certain value for coding purposes. A pulse or pattern of pulses produced in one column, i.e. for an alphabetic or special symbol, can be detected and coded as a particular character. The coding system generates an appropriate code for entry into the central processor's internal store. For example, the card code shown in Figure 43 can produce any of the following: a six bit character code for entry into part of a pure binary word (Figure 29); a six bit character code (plus parity bit) in a character machine (Figure 32); a two digit code for entry into a B.C.D. word or a byte (Figure 31). The card feeding system shown in Figure 44 employs a parallel reading system, whereby one punching position is read at a time in *all* columns. An alternative system is the serial reading method which requires the card to be fed 'endwise' with all punching positions in only one column being read at one time. The card may be fed with either column 1 or, say, column 80 leading.

Checking systems vary considerably. Firstly, there is the 'lamp testing' procedure; as the leading edge of the card approaches and passes the reading unit, a check is made that a 'pulse' and then 'no pulse' is produced. Secondly, a double reading system may be used, such that a second reading station is positioned behind, in terms of the card feed direction, the normal reading station; the two readings produced are then compared. The check can be made either by storing the readings in two registers within the card reader and making the comparison within the card reader or the comparison may be made by using registers within the central processor. Alternatively, a simple 'hole count' check may be made inside the card reader. Where the readings do not agree, the error card is either channelled into a special reject stacker or it is 'offset' in the normal stacker.

With the present rate of development in peripheral technology, it is difficult to quote card reading speeds. Generally however, card readers on commercial computers operate at speeds in the region of 600 to 2,000 cards per minute.

The two most common ways of preparing punched cards for computer input are by manually operated key punches and by on-line computer controlled card punches.

Manually operated key punches have a key board linked to a punching unit which usually consists of twelve *punch knives*, one punch knife being positioned over each punching position. Information keyed in on the key board activates the punch knives over the appropriate column and the required data is punched. The key punch may either be a simple mechanical hand punch with the keys marked to represent punching positions or an electrically driven machine with the key board closely resembling that of a typewriter (see Plate

2). The automatic punch usually has provision for 'skipping' columns and automatically ejecting a card to the hopper when the last required column has been punched. In addition, there is often the facility for 'ganging' data, i.e. the facility for punching data in a card from the previous card. Thus a field of standard information, such as the current date, may be punched into one card and this field can be punched automatically into the following cards.

A computer card punch usually resembles a card reader as described on page 124, the reading device being replaced by a punching device. Cards are fed from a hopper to the punching station which comprises a number of punch knives operated under the control of the computer. When a card has been punched, it is ejected to the stacker. The actual operation of punching can be performed by one of three methods.

Firstly, the cards may be punched column by column. Cards are fed serially, e.g. column 1 or column 80 leading, to the punching station which consists of twelve punch knives. As each column is positioned beneath the knives, the character to be punched into that column is inspected and the appropriate punch knives are activated; see the example in Figure 45.

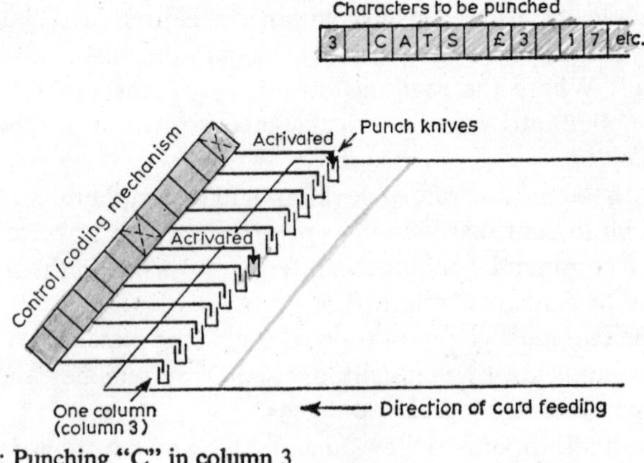

Example: Punching "C" in column 3

Fig. 45. Serial Punching

Secondly, the cards may be punched punching position by punching position. Cards are transported to the punching station by means of parallel feeding, e.g. punching position 10 or punching position 9 leading. The punching station comprises eighty punch knives, one

4. Switch Panel Console

5. Three general purpose Digital Computer configurations:
(a) Small—International Computers Limited (ICL) 1900 computer. (b) Medium—International Business Machines (IBM) System 370/145 comprising (*rows left to right, units top to bottom*) row 1: five magnetic tape drives; row 2: VDU (on table), card reader, card punch; row 3: CPU/console, line printer; row 4: eight exchangeable disc-drives in cabinet, CPU. (c) Large—UNIVAC 1108 computers at the NASA Manned Spacecraft Centre in Houston.

knife being positioned over each card column. As each punching position is beneath the punching station, the data to be punched is inspected and the appropriate punch knives are activated; see the example in Figure 46.

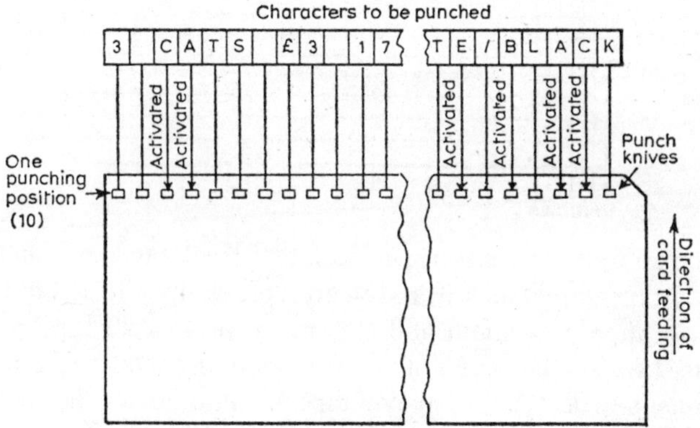

Example: Holes punched when punching position 10 is beneath punch knives

Fig. 46. Parallel Punching

Finally, there is the block punching method. The punching station comprises one punch knife for each punching position in each column of the card. For example, the block punching station in an 80 column card comprises 12 × 80 = 960 punch knives. A card is positioned beneath the punch knives, the data to be punched is inspected, and *all* the appropriate punch knives are activated at the same time.

Punched data can be checked by means of a check reading station, thus, giving a 'read-after-punch' check by comparison. Alternatively, an 'echo-checking' system can be employed. The operation of the punch knives is monitored by a special device and the actual movement of a punch knife is correlated to the data presented for punching. Thus, if a character presented to the card punch required a certain punch knife to be activated and it did not in fact move through the card, this will be detected by the monitoring device and the appropriate error mechanism activated.

Punched Paper Tape

Punched paper tape is a continuous strip of paper. Data is recorded by punching holes to represent a character *across* the tape; a number of characters can be recorded serially *along* the tape. A vertical position across the tape is called a *row* or *frame* and a punching position along the tape is called a *track*. Diagrammatically, a frame and a track can be shown thus:

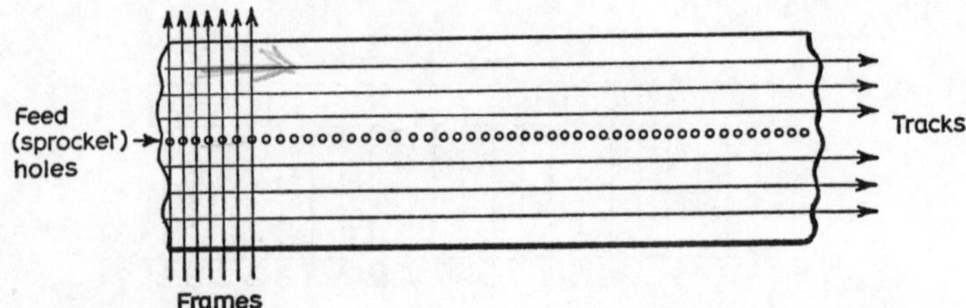

The example shown is a specimen of 6 track tape; the small holes located between tracks 3 and 4 are sprocket or feed holes which facilitate tape movement and alignment on a paper tape reader or punch. Just as the 'size' of a card is denoted by the number of columns, so the 'size' of paper tape is denoted by the number of tracks. The most common sizes of paper tape are:

5 track	—	$\frac{11}{16}''$ wide
6 track		
7 track	}	1″ wide
8 track		

The tracks on 5 track tape enable thirty-two combinations of code holes to be punched. However, a character set of approximately sixty characters is required for normal commercial work. A special 'shift' code can be employed and this shift code can be associated with a character represented in another frame. For example, a 'letter shift' code can denote that the contents of the succeeding frame(s) are alphabetic or special symbol characters. A 'figure shift' code can denote that the contents of the succeeding frame(s) are numbers. An example of a 5 track paper tape code is shown in Figure 47(a) (see page 131), and a specimen of punched tape is shown in Figure 47(b). Note that once a shift is established, a shift code is punched only when the shift is changed.

There are sixty-four combinations of punched hole codes possible on 6 track tape. The tape tracks are numbered thus:

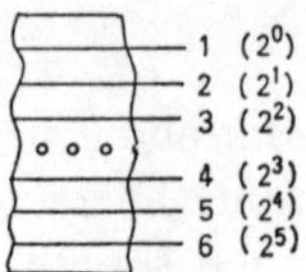

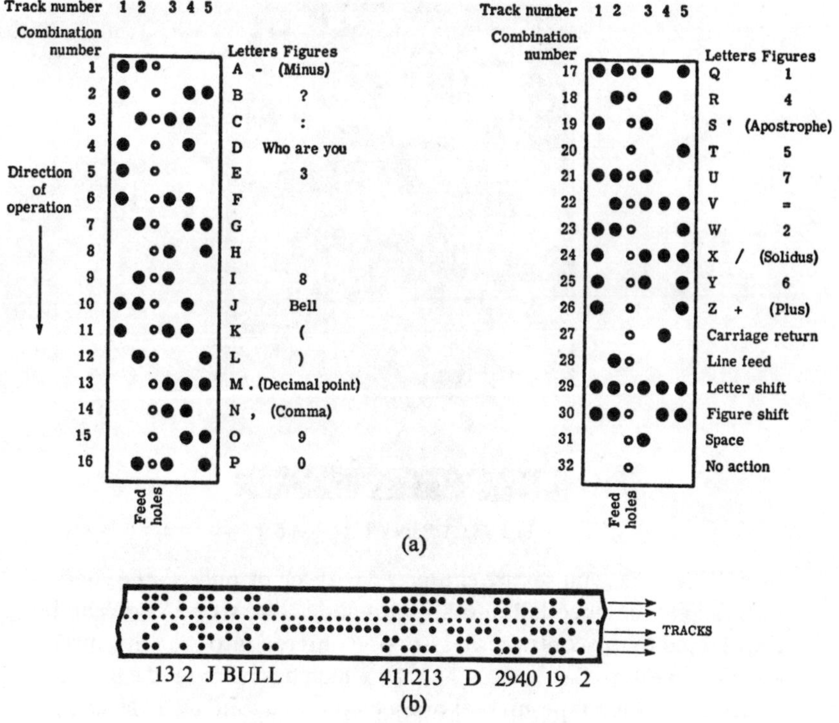

Fig. 47. Five-track Paper Tape

The allocation of a 'bit value' indicates that a punching position may have a 'value' such that a hole represents '1' and no hole '0'. The tape punching code has a direct correlation to the six bit code used inside the computer's internal storage; see Figure 32. The additional track in 7 track tape can be used to punch a parity hole which serves the same purpose as a parity bit described on page 93.

Eight track tape permits a greater number of punched hole code combinations; more control codes, special symbols and lower case characters may be punched. However, the lower case alphabetic characters are of little use since, as we shall see, computer printers have only upper case alphabetic characters in their repertoire.

A paper tape reader (see Figure 48) comprises a tape transport mechanism and a reading station. The reading station usually consists of a number of photo-electric cells and corresponding exciter lamps; one cell is associated with each track. The tape is transported past the reading station and pulses are generated where a hole is present in the

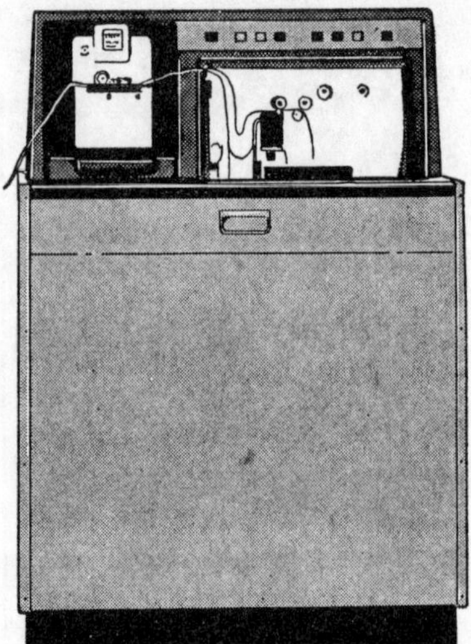

Fig. 48. A Paper Tape Reader

tape. When these pulses are compared with 'clock pulses', the character read can be encoded into a six bit code. The six bit code can be transferred to the central processor and entered into the appropriate location in internal storage. The tape which has been read can either be collected on a tape-up reel or ejected into a 'bin' as is the case in Figure 48. The tape in the bin may later be wound onto a spool as required. Reading speeds are usually in the order of 1,000 characters per second.

Paper tape can be prepared by many methods. As with punched cards, punched paper tape can be prepared by a manually operated keyboard device or on on-line computer controlled paper tape punch. In addition however, paper tape can be punched as a by-product of a machine performing some other operation, such as an accounting machine. Similarly, paper tape can be used in a data transmission system. The tape can be prepared by means of a keyboard device, and the tape read by means of a special device which transmits the contents of the tape over telegraphic lines, the tape being recreated at the receiving station. Alternatively, the tape may be created at the receiving station as a result of key depressions at the transmitting station. Similarly, the paper tape prepared by an on-line paper tape punch may be input to a transmission system and punch tape created at a remote terminal. The punched paper tape produced by the computer may be used to operate a machine which is not a data processing one. For example, some modern machine tools may be operated by instructions read from paper tape; the tape controls a complex system of cams and microswitches.

For the moment, however, the preparation of tape by key punches and computer tape punches only will be considered.

A manually operated key punch consists basically of a keyboard, resembling a typewriter keyboard, a punching station with one punch knife per tape track and a tape loading/take-up and transport mechanism. The punch knives are activated according to the character key depressed on the keyboard. Tape movement can also be controlled from the keyboard. Blank unpunched tape is usually loaded in spooled form; the punched tape can either be received on a take-up spool or it can be ejected into a 'bin'. If the take-up spool operates on a simple winding basis similar to a film projector or tape recorder, then the tape must be rewound before being input to the computer. Some key punches, however, have a 'reverse' spooling mechanism such that as the tape is taken up after punching it is spooled ready for input to the paper tape reader.

Computer controlled paper tape punches are similar in construction to paper tape readers previously described, the reading unit being replaced by a punching mechanism. The punch knives are activated under the control of data presented to the punch from the computer. The punched data is usually checked by means of an odd or even parity check.

Magnetic Tape Input

Originally, magnetic tape and magnetic discs were developed as file or backing storage units as will be described later in this chapter. For more than fifty years, punched cards and paper tape provided the main means of computer input. In the middle-to-late 1960s, however, there was a major change in input technology which has become increasingly popular throughout the 1970s.

Input media based on stationery stock (such as punched cards and paper tape) suffers from three major disadvantages. The first is that punched cards and the like are 'one-time' media; having been punched as input, they cannot be used again. Further, the cost of raw material stock has been increasing dramatically over the years. The second disadvantage lies in the speed of preparation. During the punching operation the card or tape is stationary as the knives descend and literally cut-out the holes. This mechanical process limits the speed with which the media can be prepared in response to key depressions made on the keyboard by the operator. The last disadvantage is the speed with which the prepared media can be read by the computer input device. Card and paper tape reading speeds equate to some 800 to 2,500 characters per second. Compare this to magnetic tape reading speeds (as will be explained later) which are in the order of 40,000 to 100,000 characters per second.

These three disadvantages led to the use of magnetic tape as the input media as opposed to the traditionally popular punched cards and paper tape. The device, a magnetic tape encoder, has a keyboard operated by the data preparation operator. Key depressions made by the operator result in the data being recorded magnetically on the tape (as will be shown in Figure 59). Note that because the 'blips' of magnetism on the tape are not visible to the unaided eye of the operator, a small display screen must be provided to enable the operator to see what has been keyed onto the tape.

This solves the three problems of conventional stationery media, i.e.

(i) the tape can be reused by over-recording it with new data;
(ii) the keying operation can be speeded-up because the media preparation process is now one of continuous magnetic recording as opposed to mechanical punching;
(iii) the prepared tape can be read at high computer input speeds.

Magnetic tape encoders did, however, present operational problems. The next development was that of *key-to-disc* systems. A number of keyboards are attached to a 'mini-computer' with a magnetic disc storage device. Data entered from the key stations is encoded on the disc. When a batch of data is assembled on the disc, it is transferred to a magnetic tape which is then loaded on the computer:

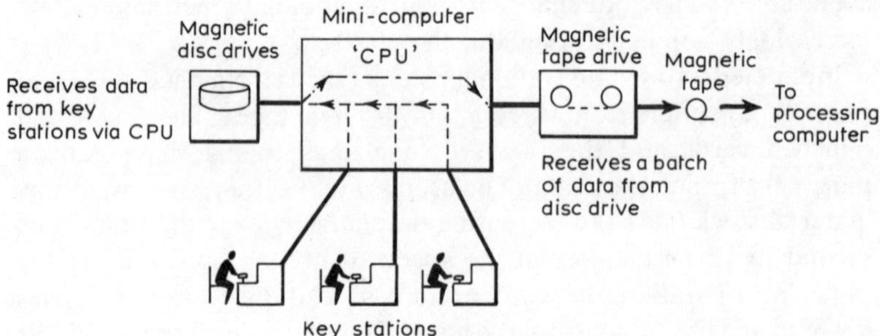

The future of keyboard input preparation thus lies in the development and refinement of magnetic recording techniques. Note, however, that all the input techniques described so far are based on a manual *data preparation process*. Data to be input to the computer is written on documents which are then transcribed by an operator (using a keyboard) on to the input media, be it punched cards, paper tape or magnetic tape. This can be a very time consuming, labour intensive process which is consequently very expensive. An alternative approach is to eliminate the keyboard data preparation process altogether by making the source document directly readable by a machine.

Magnetic Ink Character Recognition

Magnetic ink character recognition, abbreviated to M.I.C.R., employs a system of printed characters which are easily decipherable by human as well as machine readers. A special printing fount is used to represent characters; two examples are shown in Figure 49. In the C.M.C. 7 fount, each character comprises a number of vertical lines. The characters are printed in special ink which contains a magnetizable material. Before a character is to be read, it is passed beneath a device which creates a magnetic field. The magnetizable material in the ink retains the magnetism. When a character is subsequently read, it passes beneath a reading head, the magnetism in the printed character induces a current in the circuit and an output signal is derived. In terms of the C.M.C. 7 fount, a 'wide' gap between two vertical magnetized bars can be given value '1' and a narrow gap can be given value '0'. With the aid of clocking pulses, a six bit character code may be originated as shown in Figure 50. Similarly, the *shape* of an E 13 B coded character can produce a unique signal pattern as shown in Figure 51. The output signal can be used to produce a six bit code for the character read.

In its simplest form, data can be input to the computer by reading, say, one line encoded in magnetic ink characters on a document. For this, documents are stacked in a hopper and transported past the 'magnetizing' and reading stations. Documents are carefully aligned so that the line of encoded characters passes beneath the two stations. The magnetizing and reading heads are activated as the line of characters on one document passes beneath them.

ENLARGED

1234567890

ABCDEFGHIJKLMNOPQRSTUVWXYZ

ACTUAL SIZE

C.M.C. 7 FOUNT

(a)

ENLARGED

1234567890

ACTUAL SIZE

E 13 B FOUNT

(b)

Fig. 49. Example M.I.C.R. Founts

Optical Character Recognition

Optical character recognition, abbreviated to O.C.R., like M.I.C.R., employs a system of printed characters which are easily decipherable by both human and machine readers. Characters are encoded in a special printed fount, an example of which is shown in Figure 52.

Machine reading of these characters is by a light scanning technique in which each character is illuminated by a light source and the reflected image of the character is analysed in terms of the 'light/dark' pattern produced. A unique signal pattern is produced for each character; the signal may be analysed and a six bit input code originated for each character.

Keyboard devices are being developed to give the required print quality; plate or computer printing is generally used.

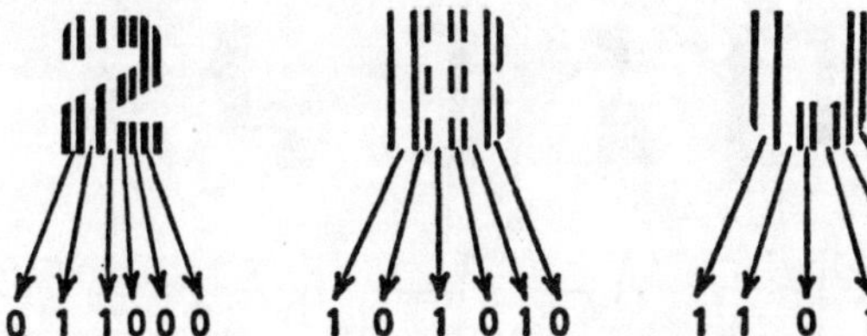

Character	Code
0	0 0 1 1 0 0
1	1 0 0 0 1 0
2	0 1 1 0 0 0
3	1 0 1 0 0 0
4	1 0 0 1 0 0
5	0 0 0 1 1 0
6	0 0 1 0 1 0
7	1 1 0 0 0 0
8	0 1 0 0 1 0
9	0 1 0 1 0 0
control symbol 1	1 0 0 0 0 1
control symbol 2	0 1 0 0 0 1
control symbol 3	0 0 1 0 0 1
control symbol 4	0 0 0 1 0 1
control symbol 5	0 0 0 0 1 1
A	0 1 0 0 0 0
B	1 0 1 0 1 0
C	0 0 0 1 1 1
D	1 0 0 1 1 0
E	1 0 1 1 0 0
F	0 0 1 0 1 1
G	1 0 0 0 1 1
H	0 0 0 1 0 0
I	0 0 0 0 0 1
J	0 0 1 0 0 0
K	0 1 1 0 1 0
L	0 0 0 0 1 0
M	0 0 1 1 1 0
N	0 1 1 1 0 0
O	1 0 0 0 0 0
P	0 1 0 1 1 0
Q	1 1 1 0 0 0
R	1 0 1 0 0 1
S	1 0 0 1 0 1
T	0 1 0 0 1 1
U	1 1 0 1 0 0
V	1 1 0 0 0 1
W	0 1 0 1 0 1
X	1 1 0 0 1 0
Y	0 1 1 0 0 1
Z	0 0 1 1 0 1

Fig. 50. C.M.C. 7 Six Bit Character Code

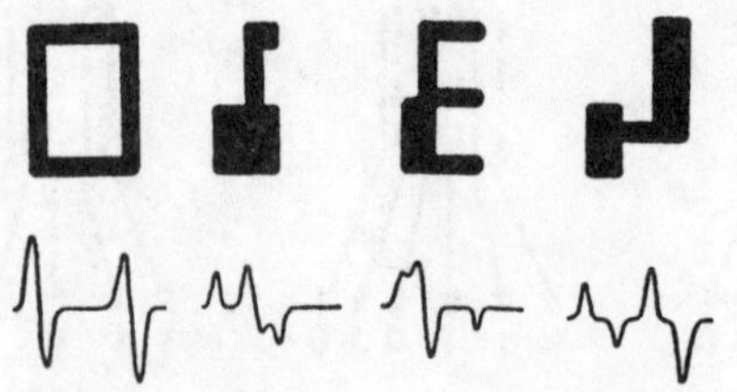

Fig. 51. Output Signals From E 13 B Coded Characters

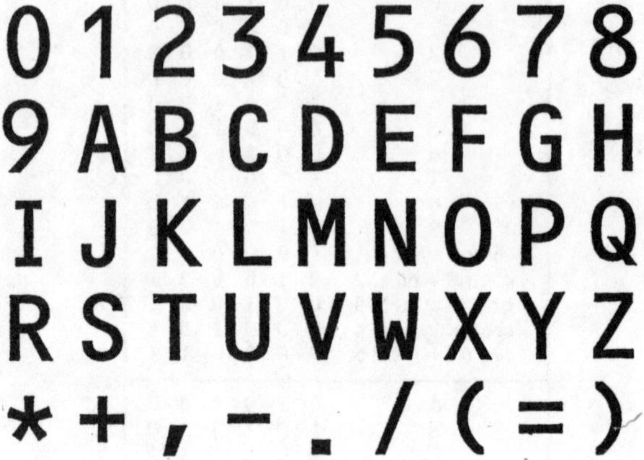

0 1 2 3 4 5 6 7 8
9 A B C D E F G H
I J K L M N O P Q
R S T U V W X Y Z
* + , - . / (=)

Fig. 52. An O.C.R. Fount

Typewriters

Typewriters (see the example in Figure 53) can be used to input data into a computer and, in some cases, to output data from the computer. The operator depresses keys on a typewriter keyboard (see Figure 54), a character code is generated for each character key depression and this code is directly input to the computer's internal storage. The need for an intermediate coded media is thus obviated. To illustrate the working of a typewriter linked to a computer, an example procedure for inputting a message and subsequently outputting a reply message in response is described. The typewriter shown in Figure 54 is being used to 'interrogate' a file held in backing storage device.

When the operator wishes to type in a message, say a request for the present state of a customer's account, the 'request type-in' key is pressed. This causes a special code to be input to the central processor signifying that a message is to be input. When the computer is ready

Fig. 53. An Input/Output Typewriter

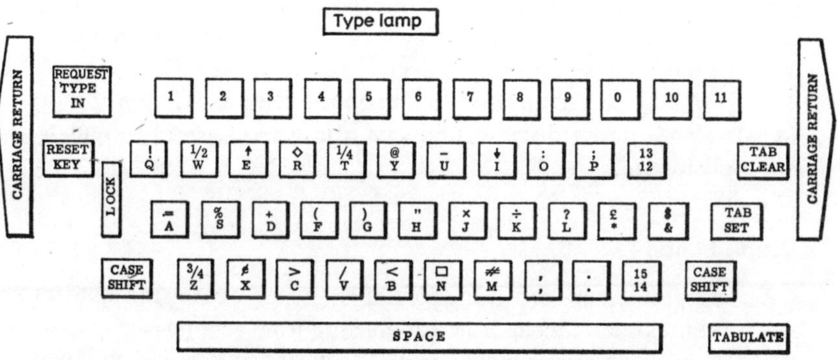

Fig. 54. An Input/Output Typewriter Keyboard

to accept the message, the 'type' lamp is illuminated and the keyboard is 'unlocked'. Note that the keyboard remains 'locked' unless the computer is ready to accept an input message. The operator types in the required message; the format of the input message is carefully controlled in accordance with the user program, i.e. the format of an input message must be in accordance with a strict specification of the number of data characters and spaces, and the grouping of characters within a field etc. As the message is typed-in, it appears in printed form on the paper in the carriage mechanism. The message is also stored in a six bit coded form in a special register. If the message has been typed correctly, an 'accept' character key is pressed and the contents of the register are transferred to internal storage under the control of the input program. If the message has not been typed correctly, then a 'cancel' character key can be pressed and the contents of the register are not transferred to internal storage.

The input message is 'inspected' by program and the appropriate action is taken. When the results are available and a response message is to be typed, the keyboard will be locked. The program to print the response message causes it to be transferred to the print unit of the typewriter and be printed.

Visual Display/Keyboard Devices

These devices usually consist of a cathode ray tube and sometimes, a small keyboard (see Figure 55). The keyboard can be used to input data to the computer's internal storage in much the same manner as an input/output typewriter.

Output messages transferred from the computer's internal store can be displayed on the cathode ray tube (CRT) screen. Some visual display units are also capable of receiving data via the CRT screen. A 'light pen' may be used to trace a line on the screen and appropriate signals representing discrete digits can be generated and input to internal storage.

Graph Plotters

The usual structure of a graph plotter is a paper feeding mechanism and a pen holder mechanism capable of transversing the paper. Program instructions can be given which control paper and pen movement and graphs can be drawn from a pattern of discrete digits held in internal storage.

Printers

Most computer printers are *line* printers, i.e. devices in which one line of data is printed at a time. The data must usually be held in character form within internal storage prior to a print instruction

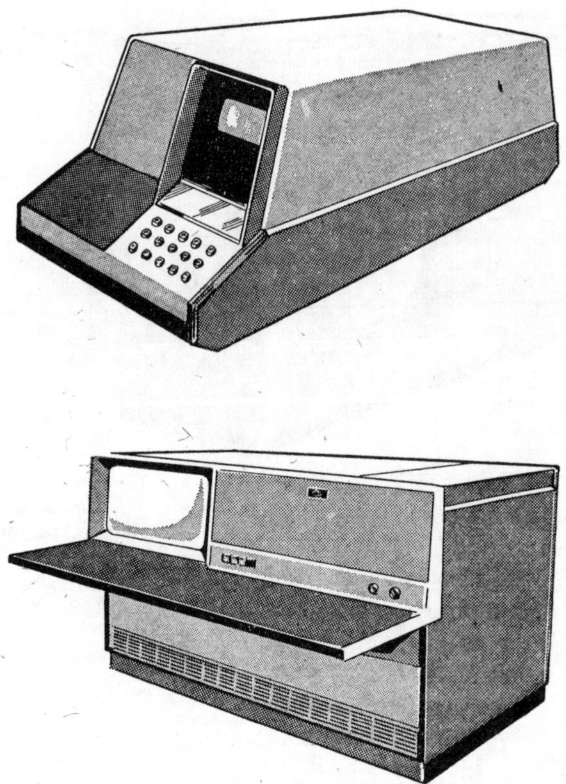

Fig. 55. Visual Display Devices

being given. Data is arranged in store in character form which includes spaces, punctuation symbols, special symbols, etc. Three types of printer are described below: barrel printers, chain printers and optical printers. Although it is difficult to generalize, barrel printers appear to be the most popular type of printer at this time. This can be attributed to its mechanical reliability and speed related to reasonable cost. Most of the description below, therefore, relates to barrel printers.

The basic components of a modern high speed barrel printer are shown in Figure 56. The print barrel revolves at high speed; the complete character set of the computer is embossed on its periphery, with one character symbol per line. Opposite each 'character position' on the barrel there is a print hammer; to print a character, the hammer is fired when the required character is in alignment with

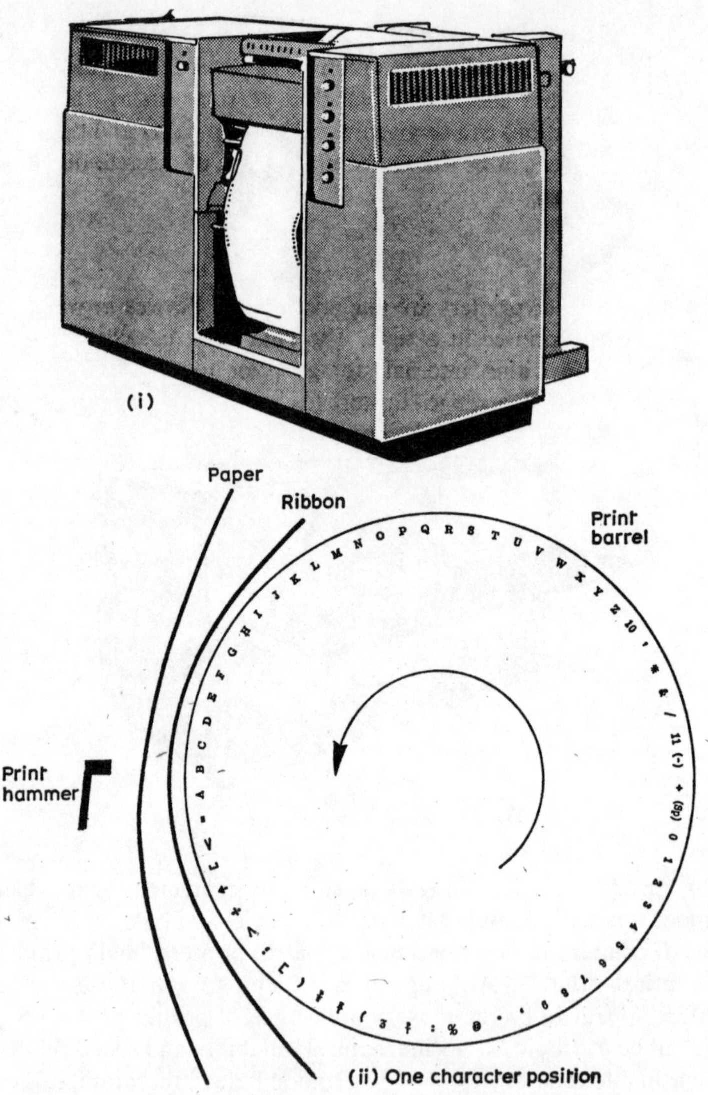

Fig. 56. Components of a Barrel Printer

the hammer. The 'firing' of the hammer causes the paper to make contact with the embossed character through the ink ribbon. The speed at which the barrel revolves and the time for which the hammer forces the paper into contact with the barrel is carefully controlled to avoid smudging, etc. With this basic appreciation of the method of operation, the procedure for printing one line may now be examined.

To print one line, one character (which may be a space) held in store is associated with one 'print position' on the printer, a print position being defined by the presence of a print hammer. Thus, in a printer with 120 print positions, 120 characters in internal storage are associated with the 120 print positions. The time at which a hammer is fired (or, in the case of a space, not fired) in relation to the character on the barrel which is opposite the hammer, determines the character to be printed. Diagrammatically, the process of printing may be shown as in Figure 57. The characters to be printed may either be held in storage or in a special register. As each character on the barrel is opposite the hammers, the 120 characters representing one line of print are inspected. Where there is coincidence between the character to be printed and the character *available* to be printed, the appropriate hammers are fired.

Line spacing can be by program instruction; i.e. the number of line spaces required can be specified *in* the program instruction. Alternatively, spacing may be by a 'tape loop'. A pre-punched piece of tape is loaded on a special reading device which is an integral part of the printer. The tape is usually read by means of the 'brush sensing' or photo-electric sensing unit; there are usually between eight and twelve tracks on the tape. Tape movement is synchronized with paper movement. Holes are punched in the tape which correspond to lines on the paper at which paper movement is to be arrested. A space instruction addresses one track on the tape loop and the instruction can be read as 'move the paper until a hole is detected in track x'. Since tape loop movement corresponds to the paper movement, the paper moves the required amount.

The speeds of modern barrel printers are in the region of 600 to 1,300 lines per minute.

Finally, a few words may be devoted to 'chain printers' and 'optical printers'. The chain printer works on the principle of print hammer, paper and embossed character contact. The characters are embossed in metal and linked together in the form of a chain which traverses the printer in a horizontal direction. As a character to be printed passes a print hammer, the hammer is fired.

Optical printers usually work on the following principle. A character to be printed is displayed on a cathode ray tube screen and is 'projected' onto the surface of a drum which is continuously rotating. The surface of the drum is light sensitive and, when a suitable powder

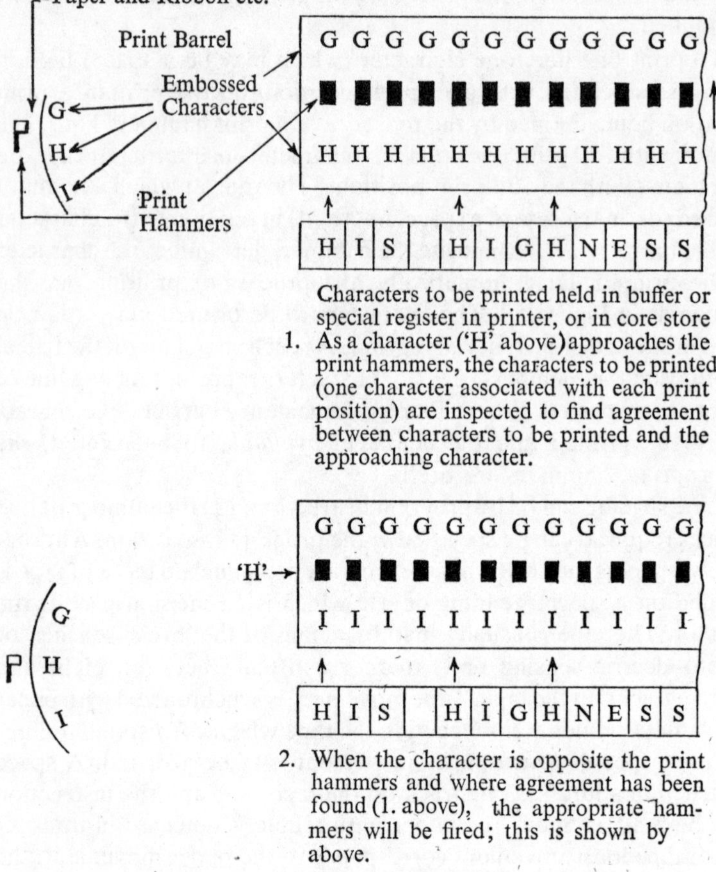
Paper and Ribbon etc.
Print Barrel
Embossed Characters
Print Hammers
G G G G G G G G G G G G
H H H H H H H H H H H H
H I S H I G H N E S S
Characters to be printed held in buffer or special register in printer, or in core store
1. As a character ('H' above) approaches the print hammers, the characters to be printed (one character associated with each print position) are inspected to find agreement between characters to be printed and the approaching character.
'H'
I I I I I I I I I I I I
2. When the character is opposite the print hammers and where agreement has been found (1. above), the appropriate hammers will be fired; this is shown by above.
This example shows the printing of character 'H' (where required) on a limited section of the print barrel.

Fig. 57. Operation of a Barrel Printer

is sprinkled on the surface, it adheres to the pattern of the projected image of the character. A continuous sheet of paper makes contact with the drum at one point. The pattern of the characters traced in the powder on the drum surface is transferred to the paper giving a permanent image on the paper. The drum is 'wiped' clean for the next character, or characters, to be projected and printed.

Horizontal and vertical lines can be 'projected' by means of separate optical devices and a 'form' with appropriate content can be printed at the same time.

Magnetic Drum Storage

The principle of storing information on a magnetic drum has been explained previously on page 95. As shown there the drum forms an integral part of the central processor. Alternatively, the drum or even a number of drums, may be attached to the central processor as 'true' peripheral units. The magnetic drum acts as an extension to the central processor's internal storage. Although the magnetic drum provides for an interchange of data between drum store and internal store, all data written on the drum emanates from the internal storage. Naturally, data written on the drum from internal storage can be input to the internal store by punched cards, paper tape, etc. as shown in Figure 41.

Magnetic Tape Storage

Magnetic tape is a continuous strip of material between 1,000 and 3,600 feet in length and between a quarter of an inch and one inch in width. It comprises a thin plastic base some 0·0015 inch thick which is coated on one side with minute particles of a magnetizable material, usually an oxide of iron. This magnetizable material is capable of receiving and retaining (almost indefinitely) spots of magnetism of either of two polarities. The tape is spooled on a reel. For data to be recorded (or 'written') on magnetic tape, a reel is loaded on a magnetic tape deck as shown in Figure 58. The basic components of a traditional magnetic tape deck are shown in Figure 59a.

A reel of magnetic tape, the 'feed' reel, is loaded on one reel holder and a plastic leader is threaded along the appropriate tape path to the 'take up' reel. The tape passes through a 'reservoir', past the read/write heads, through another reservoir and on to the take up reel. To write data to tape, the tape deck operates as follows. The tape is transported past the read/write heads at high speed. Data is transferred from internal storage to the tape deck and the read/write heads are activated according to the data presented and the appropriate data codes are recorded on tape. In most cases, the tape is transported past the read/write heads by a pinch roller system. The tape is fed from the 'feed reel' to the tape reservoir by a separate tape movement mechanism; the tape is 'removed' from the reservoir by

Fig. 58. A Magnetic Tape Deck

the pinch roller system at the read/write heads as required. The reservoir associated with the take-up reel 'receives' the tape from the read/write heads; the tape from the reservoir is wound on to the take-up reel by the rotation of the reel. The reservoir system ensures constant and even tape movement at high speed. As we shall see, the tape will be subjected to considerable strain when stopping and starting.

Data recorded on tape is encoded as a special code employing the binary system. Part of an example magnetic tape code is shown in Figure 59(b). Note that this corresponds to the seven bit character code shown in Figure 32 in Chapter Two. This code comprises seven 'tracks', and a character is recorded in a 'frame'. A code such as this can be recorded by means of seven read/write heads positioned over the tape, one head per track. The data read or written can be checked by:

(i) writing and checking a system of parity bits by means of a 'read-after-write' check;

(ii) an 'echo check' operating on the same principle as described on page 129;

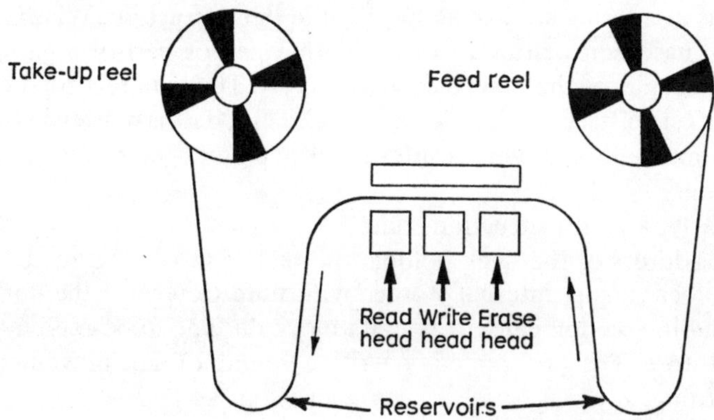

Note: (i) The erase head may not be required depending on the tape system.
(ii) A 'dual purpose' head used for reading and writing may be fitted.

(a)

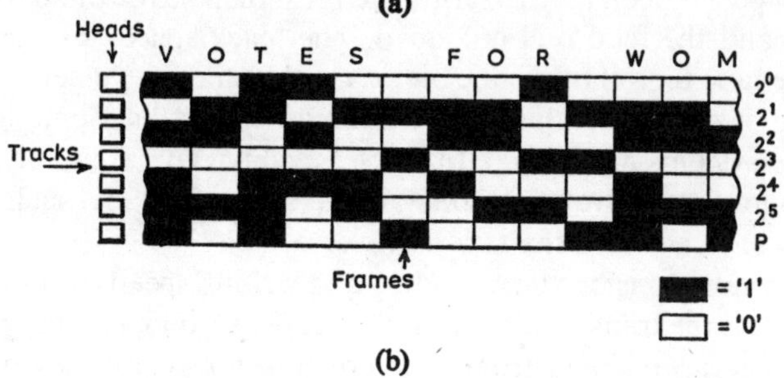

(b)

Fig. 59. Components of a Magnetic Tape Deck

(iii) 'dual recording', i.e. recording a character twice across the tape and reading both characters for checking purposes.

The basic mechanics of reading and writing described above can now be related to the program instructions employed. Firstly, there are the read and write instructions. The write instruction states:

(i) the location of the data to be written in internal store,
(ii) the tape deck which holds the reel of tape which is to receive the data.

Several tape decks may be linked to the central processor and each deck is identified by a unique number or 'address' as is the case with an internal store cell. When a write instruction is given, the tape begins to move. The writing of data must take place only when the tape reaches the required constant speed. From the time the tape begins to move to the time when the write heads are activated to record data, a 'gap' is created. The data is transferred from the locations in internal storage as specified in the instruction. When all the data has been written to tape, another gap or part of a gap is created, usually as the tape is brought to rest. The data recorded by means of one instruction is called a 'block'. Thus, data is written in the form of 'inter-block gap/block/inter-block gap/block/inter-block gap' and so on.

Similarly, a read instruction states:
(i) the address of the deck holding the reel of tape to be read,
(ii) the locations in internal storage which are to receive the data.
One read instruction causes one data block on tape to be read into internal store. The gap created on writing is used for tape movement as in writing.

Other magnetic tape instructions include 'rewind', 'backspace' and 'read reverse' instructions. The take-up reel is usually fixed and once a reel of tape has been read or written, it must then be rewound to the feed reel and the feed reel unloaded. The 'back space' instruction causes the tape to 'roll back' one block, i.e. the tape is reversed to the beginning of the block which just been read or written. Some magnetic tape systems have a 'read reverse' facility. This is merely the provision for tape movement from take-up reel to feed reel such that data may be read from the tape in reverse.

We may now consider tape reading and writing speeds. Of major importance is the transfer rate in characters per second, i.e. the speed at which characters read from tape are transferred to the central processor and the speed at which the data is transferred from the central processor and written to tape. The transfer rate can be calculated from:
(i) the speed of tape movement in inches per second
(ii) the packing density in characters per inch.
Some example transfer rates are shown in Figure 60. Note that the transfer rate is expressed as *kch/s* – thousands of characters per second. The use of magnetic tape as 'backing' or 'file' storage will be discussed later.

Magnetic Disc Storage – Fixed Discs

This type of magnetic disc storage device consists of a number of large metal discs mounted on a central spindle. The surfaces of the discs are coated with a magnetizable substance. Positioned opposite the surfaces are a number of read/write heads. The spindle is driven by a powerful motor and the discs rotate at high speed. Data is

Tape Speed (Inches/Sec)	Packing Density (Characters/Inch)	Transfer Rate (kch/s)
37½	200	7·5
	556	20·8
75	200	15
	556	41·7
	800	60
120	200	24
	556	66·7
	800	96

Example Inter-Block Gap Sizes = 0·75″ and 0·56″

Fig. 60. Example Magnetic Tape Transfer Rates

recorded on the magnetizable surfaces by means of the read/write heads. Data is recorded in six or eight bit character form (plus appropriate check or parity bits). The area of the disc surface transcribed by a read/write head is called a *track*.

The device shown in Plate 3 is a *fixed head* device. Opposite the recording surface of one disc side there are 150 read/write heads. There are thus 150 tracks. In this device a disc surface consists of the 150 tracks, each track segmented into a number of *sectors* or *blocks*; there are 96 blocks per track. Each block is a fixed length area capable of holding 100 characters (encoded in binary form). There are thus 100 × 96 = 9,600 characters per track. Because there are 150 tracks per disc surface, the capacity of the recording surface is 150 × 9,600 = 1,440,000 characters. There are 4 discs per unit, thus giving 8 recording surfaces; both the surfaces are used on each disc for recording. This means that one unit can be used to hold in excess of ten million characters. Data is written to the device by specifying, in effect,

the surface (1 to 8)
the track (1 to 50)
the part of the track (i.e. a block or sector, 1 to 96).

The total recording area is thus segmented into separate storage compartments, each compartment having a unique address. Similarly, data can be selectively retrieved from the unit by specifying a

sector on a specific track on a specific surface. To get any one item of data from a selected sector will take an average of approximately 20 ms. The data transfer rate is in the order of 232,000 characters per second. This type of device has a very fast access time (i.e. a minimal time delay to get to a selected item of data before reading/writing takes place). However, fixed head (one-head-per-track) devices are generally very expensive. This is because of the large number of read/write heads required to cover the available storage surface.

An alternative device is shown in Figure 61. This is a moveable arm device. In this case there are four read/write heads per disc surface,

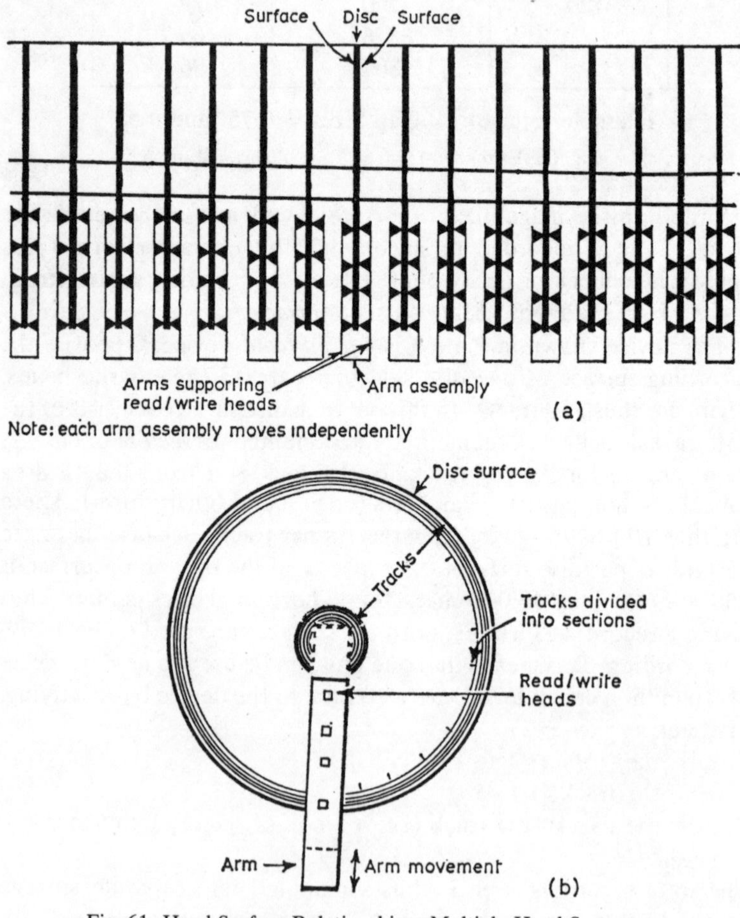

Fig. 61. Head Surface Relationship – Multiple Head System (diagrammatic representation)

each group of four heads mounted on a moveable arm. A quarter of the tracks on each disc surface is serviced by one read/write head. Data is accessed by moving a read/write head so that it is positioned over the appropriate track. This method of arranging the heads reduces the number of read/write heads required, but it increases the access time because of the mechanical movement of the head-carrying arms.

The transfer rate will depend on the packing density and on the disc rotation speed. The access time for a selection item of data will depend on:

(i) arm movement time, i.e. the time required to position the read/write head over the required track – if the head is already positioned over the appropriate track, no head movement is required.

(ii) sector location time, i.e. the time required to position the appropriate sector beneath the read/write head – the positioning of the sector may require either almost a full disc revolution or the sector may be immediately available.

In the above examples, a track was shown divided into a number of fixed length blocks or sectors. These are hardware divisions. An alternative method which is becoming more and more popular, is the variable track format. Rather than dividing a track into fixed hardware sectors, data is recorded in a continuous stream. Records are separated by special marker codes which can be detected by program. This approach is used on, for example, IBM disc devices.

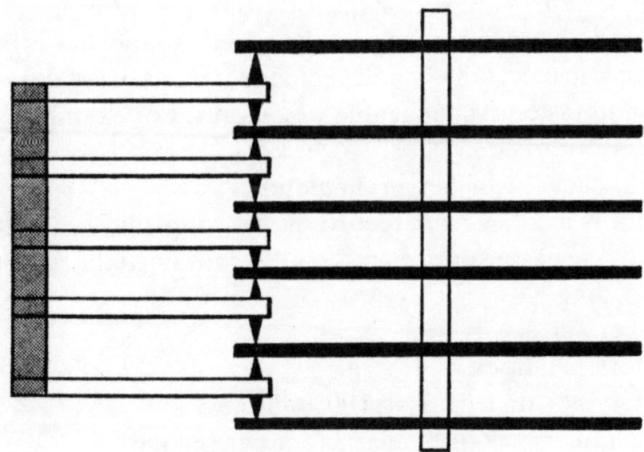

Fig. 62. Head Surface Relationship – Single Head System (diagrammatic representation)

Exchangeable Disc Stores

Exchangeable disc store devices (an example is shown in Figure 63) have, to a large extent, the same physical characteristics as the fixed disc store devices described above. The main difference in construction is that the discs can be removed and replaced as required. The discs are in the form of a 'cartridge' or 'disc pack'. Thus, a cartridge or disc pack may be loaded and unloaded in much the same manner as a reel of magnetic tape. Generally, discs in exchangeable disc store devices are smaller than permanently fixed discs, thus making for compactness and portability. A result of this is that the storage capacity in terms of characters per disc, is less than the storage capacity of the fixed disc. The one head per surface method is generally used (see Figure 62).

A small disc pack consists of six discs, arranged as follows:

6 discs, each 14 inches in diameter

10 surfaces used for recording (i.e. top surface of top disc and bottom surface of bottom disc are not used for recording)

tracks per surface = 200 (i.e. there are two hundred head positions)

characters per track = 3,650

characters per disc pack = 7·25 million

transfer rate = 156,000 characters per second

arm movement: 25 ms to move the heads from one track to the adjacent track
135 ms to move the heads over all the tracks

rotational delay (i.e. sector location time) = 12·5 ms

Perhaps in no other area of peripheral technology have there been the advances in electromechanical engineering as in the development of larger and faster exchangeable disc stores. For example, a typical large disc store of today has:

11 discs, each 14 inches in diameter

19 surfaces available for recording, i.e., top surface, bottom surface and one extra surface (reserved for timing data, etc.) not used for recording

tracks per surface = 400

characters per track = 13,500

characters per disc pack = 100 million

transfer rate = 806,000 characters per second

arm movement: 10 ms to move head from one track to the adjacent track

55 ms to move heads over all tracks
rotational delay = 8·25 ms

With discs of this capacity and speed, and with a portability similar to that of magnetic tape, it is not surprising that EDS devices are being used more and more in preference to either magnetic tape or fixed discs.

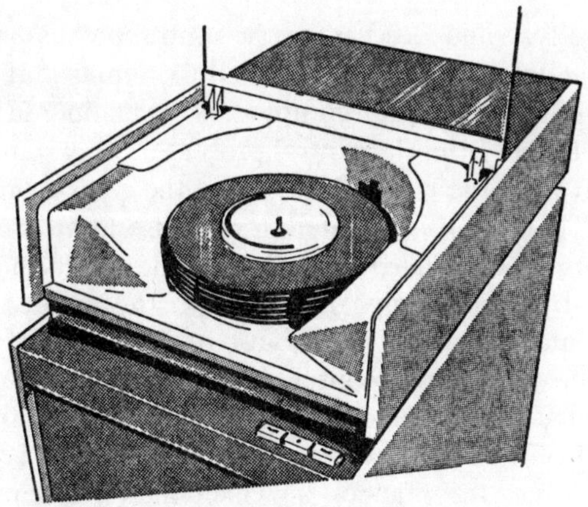

Fig. 63. An Exchangeable Disc Storage Device

Magnetic Cards

The magnetic drum and disc devices previously described had a continuous magnetic surface rotating at high speed beneath read/write heads which may be fixed or moveable. Magnetic card devices on the other hand have a single magnetic surface broken into convenient sections. A number of flat plastic cards coated with a magnetizable substance are housed in a magazine. Any one card may be pulled from a magazine and transported to a drum or capstan. The card is wrapped around the capstan which rotates at high speed. A number of read/write heads are positioned opposite the capstan. Data is recorded along the card in longitudinal tracks. Data is read and written by selecting a card, extracting it, transporting it to the capstan and activating the read/write heads positioned over the appropriate track. When the card has been read, it is released from the capstan and returned to the magazine. The access time for the device will be determined by the total time required to select and extract a card from a magazine, transport it to the read/write unit, and position the read/write heads over the required track. The transfer time will depend on the packing density and card rotation speed on the capstan.

PERIPHERAL TRANSFERS

Thus far, the type and structure of the central processor and a range of peripheral units have been described. An important factor in the operation of a modern digital computer is the manner in which data is transferred to and from the central processor. Any transfer of information to or from the internal storage of the central processor from or to a peripheral unit is initiated in response to an input or output program instruction. There are three considerations in investigating the method by which peripheral transfers are initiated. Firstly, the amount of data transferred in response to one program instruction is important. Secondly, the content and format of an input/output program instruction, i.e. an instruction which initiates the transfer of data to or from the required peripheral unit, must be considered. Thirdly and last, the manner in which the peripheral transfer is actually effected must be considered.

The amount of data transferred in response to an input/output instruction will depend on the characteristics of the hardware, i.e. its physical structure. Basically, it is true to say that the amount of data transferred as a result of an input/output instruction being given will be:

(1) a fixed sized unit of data determined by the characteristics of the peripheral device,

or,

(2) a variable size unit of data determined by the computer *user*.

Examples of the former case are:

(i) the reading (or punching) of one punched card,
(ii) the reading (or punching) of one character in paper tape,
(iii) the printing of one line of print on a line printer.

In each of the above instances, a fixed number of characters will be input or output; in example (ii) this is in fact one character. Similarly, in example (iii) one hundred and twenty characters are output to a one hundred and twenty print position line printer in response to a 'print' instruction.

The alternative method of effecting peripheral transfers requires that the user must specify the amount of data to be input or output.

For example, magnetic tape is processed serially, and one *block* of data is read or written in response to a read or write tape instruction. For writing data to tape, there are two possibilities. The data can be arranged in internal storage in consecutive locations and the write instruction can be read as 'write the contents of location x and the contents of the subsequent y locations to tape'. Thus, the operation code must specify the operation – write to tape, the address of the location 'x' and the number of locations 'y' holding data to be written to tape. An alternative system can use an 'end of block marker' in store. In this case, the read instruction causes one block to be written automatically and the transfer terminates when the end of block marker is detected. The end of block marker can be a special character stored in the normal way. When data is to be read from magnetic tape and into the internal storage, the read instruction states the address in internal storage which is to receive the first unit of data from the tape. Data will continue to be read from the tape into subsequent locations of internal storage. The transfer will terminate when the inter-block gap and/or the end of block marker is detected.

The information that must be available for a peripheral transfer to be initiated is:

(i) an appropriate operation code;
(ii) the address of a location which is to receive the first 'unit' of data *from* a peripheral device on input, or the address of a location which contains the first 'unit' of data which is to be transferred *to* a peripheral device on output.

The transfer is terminated by:

(i) the physical characteristics of the peripheral device,
(ii) a fixed number of characters having been transferred,
(iii) a special 'marker' being detected during the transfer.

One further factor must be considered. The peripheral devices so far cited in this discussion on peripheral transfers have been *serial* devices. When file storage devices, such as magnetic drums, magnetic discs and magnetic cards are considered, the address of data held on the device involved in a perhipheral transfer must be specified. For example, suppose data is to be transferred between internal storage and a magnetic drum. In addition to the internal storage address, the address of the locations involved in the transfer on the drum must also be stated.

It is not strictly true to say that serial devices such as card and paper tape readers and punches and magnetic tape decks are not 'addressed'. For example, if there are eight magnetic tape decks on-line, a read or write tape must be related to one particular tape deck. The *address*, i.e. the identifying physical unit number of the deck which is to be employed in a peripheral transfer, must be stated in the read or write instruction.

ENSURING DATA ACCURACY

All but a very few systems have people generating and processing input; the human error factor is thus always present.

A basic principle of computer operations is GIGO – 'Garbage In Garbage Out'. The accuracy of output is limited by the quality of the input. Over the years, therefore, much time and attention has been devoted to developing techniques which ensure accurate input data.

These techniques can be illustrated by describing the two major types of input systems: off-line batch data preparation and on-line data entry.

Off-line Batch Data Preparation

This type of system has a production line of several activities. Typically these are as follows:

Data Capture: Some event happens and a user completes a document with details of the event. For example, a customer places an order and a salesman completes an order form; a delivery is made and a warehouseman completed a goods inwards docket.

Manual Check: The documents are scrutinized to ensure that they are legible, properly completed and authentic.

Data Preparation: The documents are transcribed by a keyboard process on to the computer input medium such as punched cards or paper tape.

Computer Validation: This is the first program which processes the data. The input data is read by the program and checked. Data that passes these checks is written on to an 'O.K.' data file on magnetic tape or disc. Data which fails the checks is printed on an error listing. A further procedure allows for the re-submission of the corrected data. The error free data can now be passed on to and processed by the other programs in the system.

Note that the name for this type of system is derived as follows:

Off-line: in that there is no *direct* link between data capture and the processing computer, or between data preparation and the computer.

Batch: in that the forms (called source documents), completed by the user in the data capture function, are accumulated and processed through the system together on a pre-set cycle (each day, each week, etc.).

Data Preparation: in that the data is transcribed on to the computer input medium by a keying process.

Bearing in mind the GIGO principle, how can garbage reach the computer?

It can happen in many ways at several stages. The user, in completing the source document, may make an error, such as transposing two digits in a quantity field (91 is written instead of 19). A document may be lost between data capture and data preparation, a punched card may be mislaid between data preparation and computer validation. During the data preparation stage, the keyboard operator may turn over two pages in error. The operator may mis-read a character, transpose figures or press the wrong key at random.

Ensuring data accuracy starts with the design of good source documents. This means that the forms are designed so that they can be completed easily by the user and thus minimize the incidence of error. Similarly, the forms must be designed so that the keyboard operator in data preparation can easily transcribe them in an error-free manner. Even with the best designed documents, however, we must assume that errors can and will occur.

Error detection methods can be divided into three broad classes: batching, verification and field validation.

Batching is the control of a group of documents as a whole. This is done by the use of control totals. The simplest form is the batch record count. Users submit their documents with a batch control form which states the number of documents in the batch. This is checked on receipt in the computer centre. The records (e.g. punched cards) produced at the data preparation stage are counted and checked against the number of documents. Similarly, the validation program counts the number of records read and this can be compared with the previous totals. Erroneous omissions and insertions can thus be detected.

An extension of batching is the calculation and re-calculation of field control totals. The control can be by quantity or hash totals. A quantity control total is the sum of fields such as monetary amount or quantity of goods ordered on *all* documents in a batch. A hash total is the sum of a particular code field on all the documents in a batch. For example, a hash total in an order processing system could be the sum of product codes in a batch. The answer is, of course, a meaningless figure, but if it is re-calculated at each state it forms the basis of a check for accuracy of transcription, omissions or additions.

Verification is a way of ensuring the accuracy of keyboard transcription in data preparation. In essence, it is the keying of the data by two operators working independently. For example, verification using punched cards works as follows:

(a) Operator 1 loads blank cards on the keypunch and proceeds to key the data from the source documents on to the cards.
(b) The punched cards and the source documents are passed to Operator 2.
(c) Operator 2 loads the punched cards on to a verifying machine. This is similar to a keypunch but has a reading unit instead of a punching unit. Operator 2 proceeds to key the data from the source documents. The key depressions are compared (by the reading unit) to the characters actually punched into the cards by the previous operator. If a mis-match is detected, an error is signalled.

Similar facilities are available with paper tape and magnetic tape transcription.

The whole basis of verification is: what are the chances of two operators, working independently, making the identical keying error on the same field? The answer is, of course, very low. The problem is that the two processes are *not* completely independent. The two operators are working from the *same* source document. Thus a badly hand-written '2' may be read as a 'Z' – erroneously – by both operators.

There are many validation checks that can be made by a computer program. Examples of the checks are given below:

Range Checks: The program checks that the value in an input field is within certain limits. Note that the check may signal a positive error or provide a warning that the value is unusual (though not specifically wrong) and should be checked. For example:

hours worked in a week = 171
(must be wrong)
hours worked in a week = 83
(unusual warning)
day, date = 41
(must be wrong)

quantity of very expensive articles
ordered = 172
(unusual warning)

Format Check: The program checks that the characters in a field are of a particular type: that there is the appropriate pattern of alphabetic, numeric, spaces, special characters. For example:

product code must consist of two alpha characters followed by four numerics; errors detected:

B74132
DF3Z98
A7512

customer number must consist of five characters: three alpha, followed by an oblique '/', followed by a numeric; errors detected:

ABF2
2CD/7
GHK/Z

quantity field, three characters, all numeric; errors detected:

12Z
S 5
F79

Master Check: The program checks codes against a list or file of valid codes. Any input code not present on the master list is an error.

Check Digits: A check digit is used to form a self-checking number. The principle of this check is that code numbers, such as employee numbers and customer account codes, must have a special check digit appended to them. The check digit is normally assigned by the computer when the code is initially allocated. Subsequently, the input code is checked by the validation program.

An example of the check digit validation process is given below. The technical name for this particular method is 'modulus 11 check with serial weighting'. The example code used is 3174.

(a) Check digit calculation when code is allocated by computer: Computer 'weights' each digit in the code by a pre-set series; in this example, 5, 4, 3, 2, 1. The code digits are multiplied by weighing

$$\begin{array}{rrrrr} & 3 & 1 & 7 & 4 \\ \times & 5 & 4 & 3 & 2 \\ \hline & 15 & 4 & 21 & 8 \end{array}$$

The products are summed 15 + 4 + 21 + 8 = 48.
Program calculates that value which when added to the sum, raises it to the next highest value completely divisible by '11'; i.e. 7 when added to 48 = 55 which is completely divisible by 11. The value '7' is allocated as the check digit.

(b) Whenever the code is quoted it must be quoted as a five digit figure, i.e. including the check digit: 31747.

(c) Check digit calculation when code is input to validation programs:
Computer weights each digit in the code by a pre-set series; in this example 5, 4, 3, 2, 1. The code digits are multiplied by the weighting and the products are summed:

$$\begin{array}{rccccc} & 3 & 1 & 7 & 4 & 7 \\ \times & 5 & 4 & 3 & 2 & 1 \\ \hline \end{array}$$

$$15+4+21+8+7 = 55.$$

The sum is divided by 11; if the remainder is zero then the code is taken as being correct:

$$55 \div 11 = 5, \text{ remainder } 0; \text{ code is valid.}$$

(d) Example of invalid code: first two digits are transposed:

$$\begin{array}{rccccc} & 1 & 3 & 7 & 4 & 7 \\ \times & 5 & 4 & 3 & 2 & 1 \\ \hline \end{array}$$

$$5+12+21+8+7$$

$$53 \div 11 = 4, \text{ remainder } 9; \text{ code is invalid.}$$

On-line Data Entry

An on-line data entry system is one in which data is keyed directly into a computer via a terminal, such as a visual display unit. The terminals may be located in user departments and operated by user staff; for example, sales clerks in an office entering orders directly into a computer via visual display units. Alternatively, the terminals may be operated by data preparation operators (the equivalent of keypunch operators). A common technique is to connect the terminals to a small ('mini') computer. This mini computer produces an output magnetic tape which can then be input, as required, to the main processing computer.

On-line data entry systems make extensive use of the type of validation checks as described above, with one major advantage over batch systems. This is that the validation program checks each item of data as it is keyed. Errors are detected instantly and an error message is displayed on the visual display screen. The data can then be corrected immediately by the operator.

On-line data preparation (i.e., full time operators transcribing from user-prepared documents) can use the batching techniques described previously. The combination of batching and validating techniques can thus eliminate the need for verification.

9. Programming

THE NATURE OF A PROGRAM

So far in this book, the individual instruction types and physical units of a modern digital computer have been discussed. What must now be considered is how a program, i.e. an organized group of instructions, can be written, prepared for input to the computer and finally, input to and obeyed by the computer.

A program can initially be considered as a series of instructions so organized that a required operation is performed by the computer. Inside the computer's internal storage, the instructions are arrayed in numeric form prior to being obeyed. Depending on the nature of an internal storage cell (that is whether the cell is a word or a character and in the former instance, the word length), one instruction is stored per cell, per part of a cell or per number of cells. The instructions are obeyed in the sequence in which they are stored, unless a jump or branch instruction is given and a new sequence is established by program.

The fundamental problem is how to interpret the operation to be performed in terms of the string of numeric instructions. Once the required action has been interpreted in the light of how the particular computer can perform that action, the actual instructions must be prepared. The program can be prepared by listing out the instructions in numeric form in the sequence in which they are to be obeyed. This is usually called *machine code* programming. The programmer must be aware of the action initiated by each machine instruction and the precise format of each instruction. Once a problem or operation has been defined in terms of how the computer is to solve the problem or perform the required operation, the programmer selects the appropriate machine code instruction types from the computer's complete repertoire, or *order code*, and builds up the required program. Thus, given a repertoire of instructions which includes:

Arithmetic Instructions
Input/Output Instructions
Data Handling Instructions
Logical Instruction
Jump or Branch Instructions

these instructions can be assembled in the required sequence to perform a defined operation.

Machine code programming requires that the operation code must be in numeric form so that, when stored within the computer, it can be inspected and obeyed. This is not a complicated or difficult aspect of machine code programming since an order code listing of: operation code number – action initiated – operand or address format and content, can be to hand for quick reference purposes. A far greater problem is that of interpreting the items of data in terms of the numeric internal store addresses. For example, an operation such as 'multiply quantity by price to get cost' may appear in machine code when using a two address fixed word length system, as:

Operation Code	Address A	Address B
10	1251	0090
29	1049	0090

The first instruction with operation code 10, is a transfer instruction: transfer the contents of location 1251 to location 0090. The second instruction, operation code 29, is a multiply instruction: multiply the contents of 1049 by the contents of location 0090 and put the product in location 0090. If location 1251 holds the quantity and location 1049 holds the cost, then after obeying these two instructions the price is stored in location 0090 with the quantity and cost preserved in their original locations. What the programmer is faced with therefore, is the identification of 'quantity' with 'address 1251', 'cost' with 'address 1049' and 'price' with 'address 0090'. As the number of items of data increases and the number of times an item of data is transferred from one location to another increases, so the mass of numbers representing the items of data increases. Further, not only must the internal storage locations holding data be known but, in addition, the addresses of all instructions must be known. For example, if a jump is to be made to a particular instruction on a specific condition, the address of the instruction to which control is to be passed must be stated in the jump instruction and must therefore be known. In many modern computers, the *hardware*, the physical electronic circuits and mechanics of a computer, which is related to the structure and use of program instructions is so complex that machine code programming would be time consuming, not to say difficult.

A more convenient means of program coding is provided by *programming languages*. As will be seen later in this chapter, programming languages enable a program to be written, or more properly *coded* in a more comprehensible form. The manner in which the program is coded is biased towards the programmer rather than the machine.

Before considering the problems and methods of program coding, it is first necessary to place the function of coding clearly in perspective by considering the various stages in preparing a program.

PREPARING A PROGRAM

The basic stages in preparing a program are:
(1) problem analysis
(2) outline or macro-flowcharting
(3) detailed or micro-flowcharting
(4) coding
(5) input preparation
(6) testing and for programming languages – compilation or assembly.

The list given above states the basic functions in a simple chronological sequence. Some of the above functions may overlap and each function is followed by careful checking of the work completed. The functions or stages listed above may now be briefly investigated.

Problem Analysis and Outline Flowcharting

A program is written to solve a particular problem or to enable one operation or a group of specific operations to be performed. The type of problem to be solved or the operation to be performed will be determined by the particular application. For example, the problem requiring a program may be the calculation of results from a given formula and input. Alternatively, the problem may be to perform one complex operation which is, say, the preparation of printed invoices with a given content and format, from the sales orders also with a given content and format.

The distinction between the types of problem is not important at this stage, although it may be observed that the programmer may also be the person originating the problem, or a 'problem specification' may be prepared by a specialist originator and handed to a specialist programmer. It is essential to realize however, that the problem must be clearly defined and stated before the 'programming' function can be performed. The statement of the problem can be, for example, a list or range of values that can be assumed by variables in a given formula to calculate the required results. Alternatively, the problem may be the definition of format and content of

(i) an input sales orders file
(ii) an output 'invoices' file
(iii) a customer file to be updated

and so on.

The specified problem must now be analysed in terms of 'how can a program be written so that the selected computer can be employed to solve this problem?' The considerations in the initial problem analysis, which usually runs concurrently with outline flowcharting, can best be examined by investigating the content of the resultant outline flowchart.

The outline flowchart represents, in diagrammatic form, the basic logic and structure of the required program. For explanatory purposes, the following flowcharting symbols and conventions are used in this book.

(1) Flowcharts are drawn from top to bottom of a page.
(2) The 'flow' is assumed to be down and to the right unless shown otherwise by means of arrowheads.
(3) The symbol

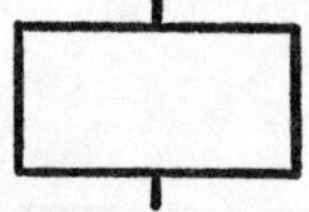

represents any kind of *processing* function

(4) The symbol

represents an *input/output* operation

(5) The symbol

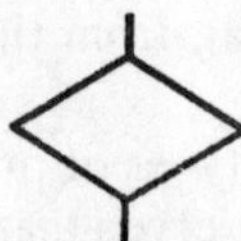

represents a *decision* and shows the branches of a program according to the condition specified. Only one branch is selected on each occasion of passing through the symbol. The basis for the decision is stated in the symbol and each branch is labelled with the appropriate reason for taking this exit; e.g.

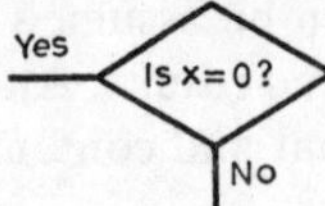

Where more than three branches are to be shown, the symbol is modified thus:

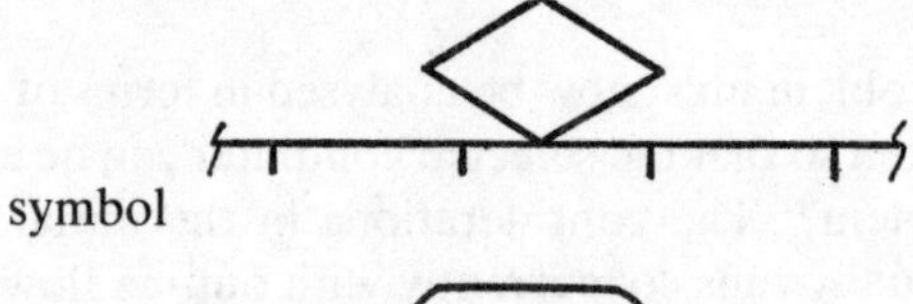

(6) The symbol

represents a terminal point such as the start or end of a flowchart.

(7) The symbol

is a 'connector' symbol and is used to show the exit to, or entry from, another point in the same flowchart. It can be used for indicating the flow in place of a flow line where this is inconvenient (or impossible to draw), i.e. when the flowchart is continued on another page. An identifying reference is written in the symbol.

(8) The symbol

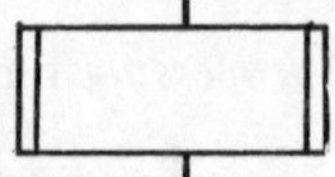

represents a predefined process. The symbol contains a name and the process is defined by a separate flowchart identified by that name.

(9) The symbol

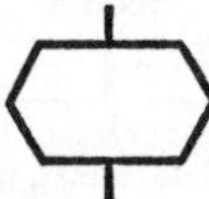

represents a 'preparation' procedure in which an instruction or group of instructions are to be modified. This will become clear when some examples are considered later in this chapter.

Two example outline flowcharts are shown in Figures 64 and 65. Note that the purpose of these flowcharts is to show the overall structure of the required program in terms of its 'logical elements'. The two flowcharts represent the programs to solve the following problems.

The program shown in flowchart form in Figure 64 is a problem in a commercial company. The company maintains a 'customer file' which is held on a file storage device. The customer file comprises a number of records, one record holding the details of one customer. Each customer record comprises, amongst other items of data:

(i) a customer account number
(ii) sales region number
(iii) the customer's credit status
(iv) details and value of all orders placed by that customer in the past six months
(v) details and value of those orders placed in the past six months for which payment has not been made.

The credit status (iii) is determined for each individual customer by the regional sales staff and in some cases by head office sales staff.

The computer configuration to be used includes, in addition to the file storage device, a number of remote typewriter terminals. The terminals comprise one or more input/output typewriters in each regional sales office and in some head office sales establishments. Three types of message can be input via the typewriters by the sales staff: two messages request the credit status as output and one message inputs a revised credit status of a specified customer. The three messages, each identified by a message type code number, which can be input are:

Message Type 1 Request Credit Status: this message gives as output the details (i) to (v) above for the customer specified in the message by customer account number.

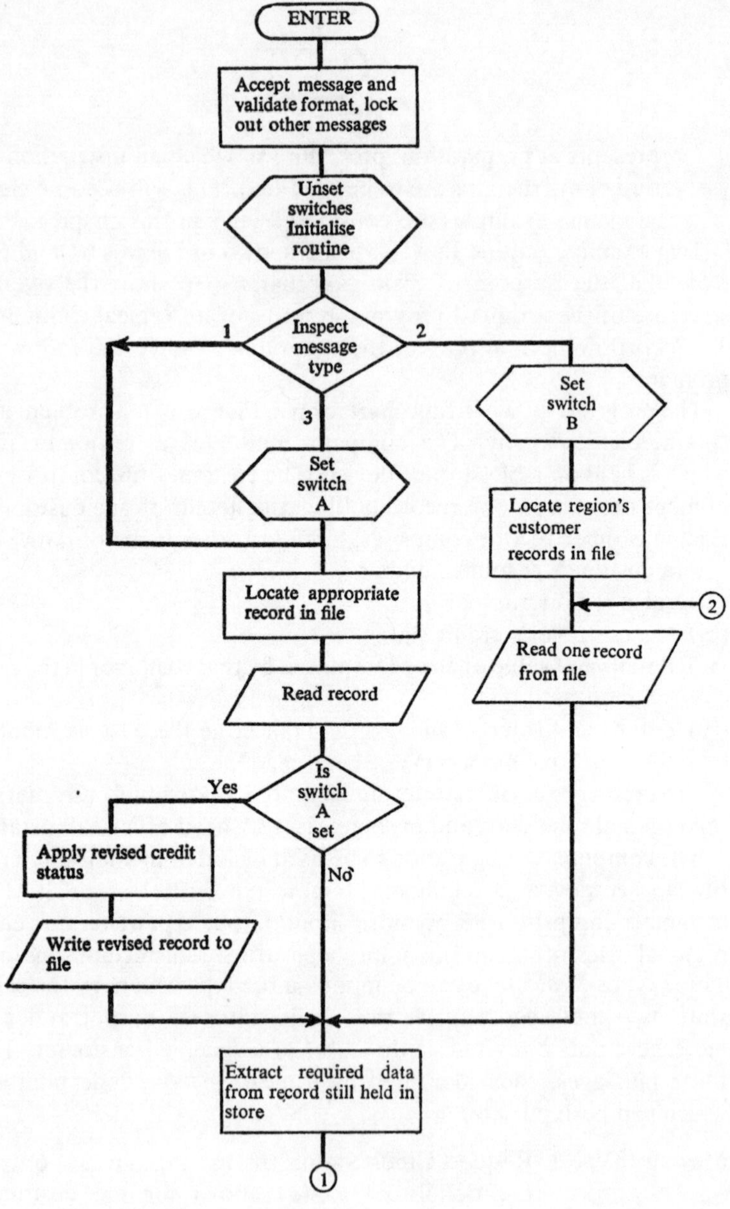

Fig. 64. Outline Flowchart I: Commercial File Interrogation

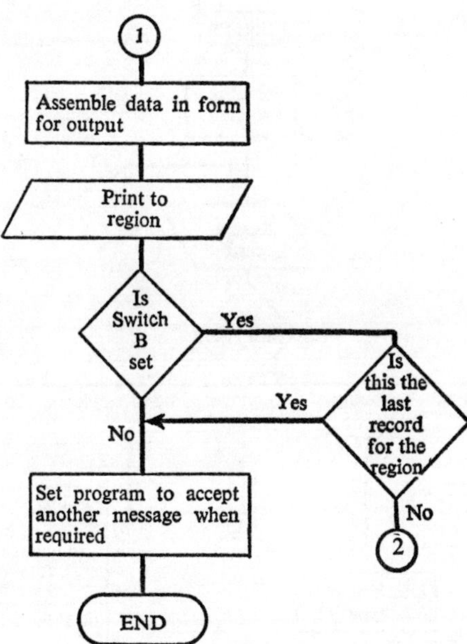

Fig. 64. – *continued*

Message Type 2 Request Regional Credit Status: this message gives as output the details (i) to (v) above for all customers in the region stated in the input message.

Message Type 3 Revise Credit Status: this message updates the customer's credit status in a specified customer record. The customer account number and new credit status must be stated in the message. As a check, the details (i) to (v) with new credit status are output to the appropriate terminal which requested the revision.

The structure of the program is quite straightforward as shown in Figure 64. The only aspect of this flowchart which requires additional explanation is the use of 'Switch A' and 'Switch B'. It would be possible to make three separate strings of instructions to perform the required operation in response to each message type. This would clearly be wasteful since the series of instructions for message types 1, 2 and 3 would be essentially the same, the only difference being the revision of the credit status in response to message type 3. In effect, the setting of Switch A, which occurs only when a message type 3 is received, notes the type of message which has been input for later

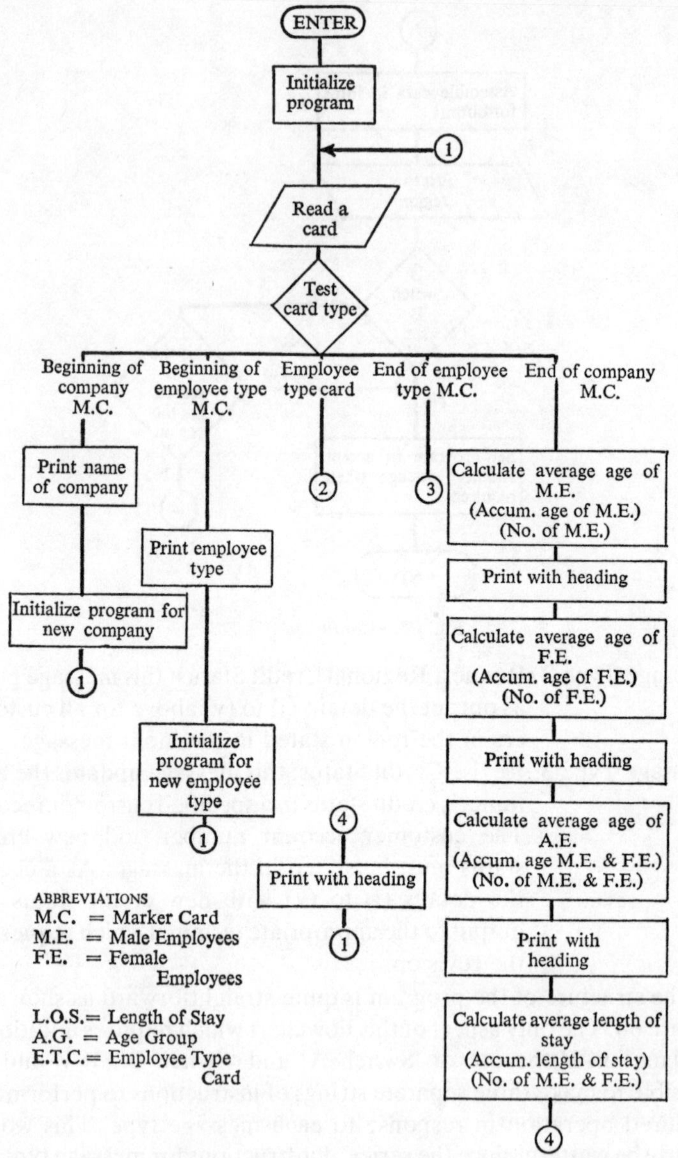

Fig. 65. Outline Flowchart II: Employee Analysis

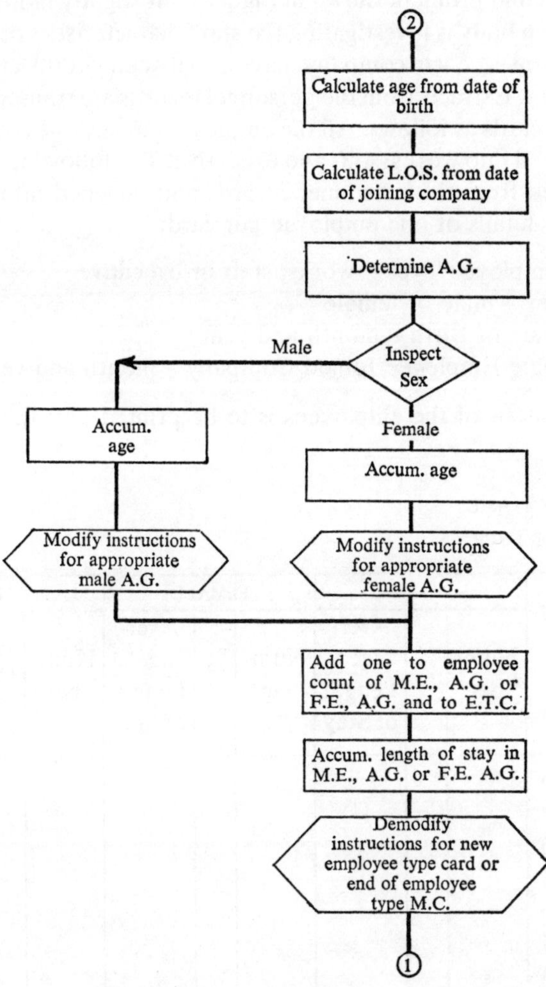

Fig. 65. – *continued*

reference in the program. For example, the setting of Switch A can be the simple addition of '1' into a specified location in internal store. When the switch is tested, the '1' signifies that the switch is set and '0' signifies that it is unset. In practice, a simple 'is x zero?' instruction can be given and a jump can be made if the switch is unset (x = 0) and no jump can be made if the switch is set (x = 1). Note that before another input message is processed, the switch must be unset, e.g. '1' subtracted from 'x' thus giving the unset '0'.

The second problem shown in Figure 65 is slightly more complex. A research body is investigating the staff characteristics of a number of companies, each company having between 5,000 and 40,000 employees. Extracts from the personnel records are transcribed on to punched cards as follows. All the employees in any one company are categorized into works, staff and executive. The following details are abstracted from the personnel records and punched into the cards with the details of one employee per card:

Employee Type – works, staff or executive
Sex – male or female
Date of Birth – month and year
Date Employee Joined Company – month and year.

An analysis of the employees is to be printed out; this is shown below.

COMPANY NAME:
EMPLOYEE TYPE:

AGE GROUP	MALE			FEMALE			TOTAL		
	Number	%	Average* Length of Stay	Number	%	Average* Length of Stay	Number	%	Average* Length of Stay
15 to 20									
21 to 25									
26 to 30									
31 to 35									
36 to 40									
41 to 45									
46 to 50									
51 to 55									
56 to 60									
61 to 65									
TOTALS									

The above summary is provided for the works, staff and executive classifications. Finally, an overall summary on a company is given thus:

Average age of all employees*
Average age of male employees*
Average of female employees*
Average length of stay of all employees*

The cards for each employee type are grouped together and the pack of cards for one company are assembled thus:

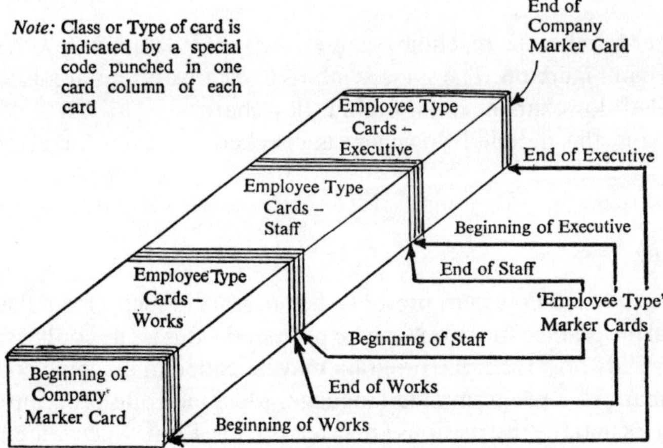

Different action is initiated according to the type of card read. Note that extensive use is made of instruction modification in the accumulation and processing of data within the age groups.

These two examples indicate the level of detail and structure of an outline flowchart. The correctness of the flowchart as regards logic can be checked by 'dry running' on test data. This can establish that the overall logic of the program is correct, e.g. that jump instructions create the required exits, that the appropriate instructions, and only those instructions, are modified and demodified as necessary. The detailed flowchart is developed from the outline flowchart.

Detailed Flowcharting

The detailed flowchart, which is prepared as the next stage in the development of a program, is used to show the program in sufficient detail preparatory to coding. Many, if not all, of the statements on the outline flowchart must be shown in more detail before coding can

* In years and months.

commence. A basic procedure step in an outline flowchart must be shown in terms of the machine's capabilities.
For example, a procedure statement such as:

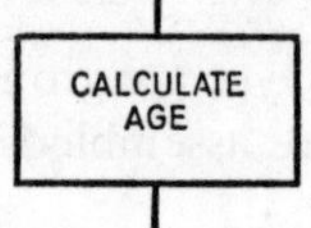

can be stated in the machine oriented steps of a detailed flowchart as shown in Figure 66. The same symbols and conventions are used in a detailed flowchart as in an outline flowchart.

Again, the detailed flowchart is checked carefully for errors in logic.

Coding

The detailed flowchart presents the program in such a form that the actual program instructions can be prepared – this is the coding stage. As already observed, the program may be coded in machine code or by means of a programming language. Machine code programming requires that the instructions are listed out in a form which is identical to, or closely resembles, the format of the instructions as held in the internal store. The requirements for preparing a program in machine code have been described previously.

For example, we have seen that all operations must be specified by a machine code, usually numeric, and an operation code; more important, the address of each constant, item of data and instruction must be noted. Many operations must be related to an address in internal storage (as for example, the operands in an arithmetic instruction) and this includes the addresses of instructions which must be specified in a jump instruction. Naturally therefore, this method of programming is biased towards the machine rather than towards the programmer and his problem.

When a program is coded in a programming language, it is written in a relatively simple form biased towards the programmer rather than the machine. The bridge between the programming language program and the required machine code program as obeyed by the machine, is provided by means of a special processor program.

Because machine code programming is not today of much consequence, the following discussion on coding will be confined almost exclusively to the purpose and use of programming languages.

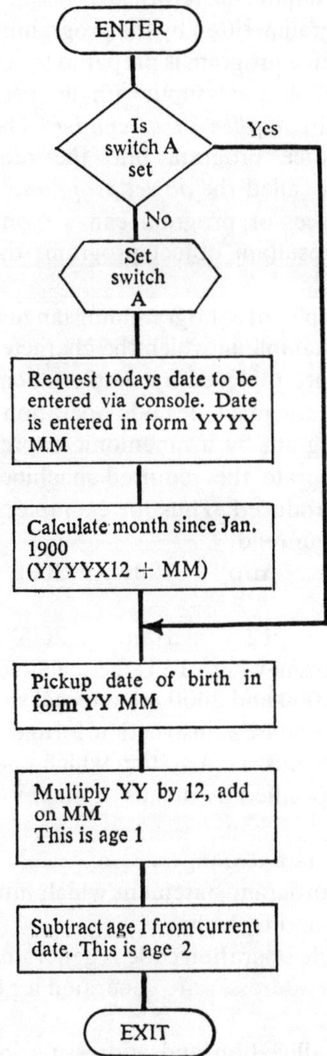

Fig. 66. Example Detailed Flowchart

Notes: 1. YYYY MM: Y = Year: M = Month (e.g. 1966 12 is December 1966).
2. Switch A is unset when the program is initially entered. Thus, the current data is only requested once.
3. It is assumed that no employee was born before 1st January 1900.

Let us first examine the basic concept of a programming language and define some important terms.

The initial program written by the programmer is called the *source program*. The source program is prepared for input, e.g. it is punched in cards or paper tape, and is input with the special processor program which is called a *compiler* or *assembler*. The processor program converts the source program into the required machine code program which is called the *object program*. There are many ways in which the processor program can act on the source program to produce the resultant object program; these will be discussed later.

The basic principles of a programming language may be considered by means of an example in which the characteristics of the machine code instruction are replaced by simple mnemonic expressions.

Firstly, the numeric machine code operation code can be replaced in the source program by a mnemonic expression. The processor program will generate the required machine code when the object program is produced. Thus for example, one statement in the source program can read:

```
ADD    1000    2000
```

and this produces

```
12     1000    2000
```

in the object program, where 12 is the machine code operation code for addition and 1000 and 2000 are internal storage addresses of the operands in a two address instruction format.

Secondly, there must be a system which enables the operands or addresses to be specified by means of mnemonic expressions. Thus for example,

```
ADD RECEIPTS BALANCE
```

may be a source program statement which must generate an object program instruction in which:

(i) a machine code operation code is generated as described above;
(ii) machine code addresses are generated for the operands RECEIPTS and BALANCE.

Internal storage allocation and addressing in the object program from mnemonic data operands in the source program presents a number of problems. There are two instances in which an area of internal store is allocated to hold data. The first, when data is input from a peripheral device, the destination addresses of the data in store must be specified in the input or read instruction. The second is as a result of:

(i) transferring data from its initial input location in internal storage to a new location;

(ii) generating or producing new data as a result of a calculation procedure.

This may be illustrated by a simple example.

Three quantities A, B and C are input on a punched card. Quantities A and B are to be multiplied together; another quantity, AB, has thus been produced. Quantity C is to be added to quantity AB and five quantities are to be output: A, B, C, AB and AB + C. Initially, three areas of store must be allocated to hold A, B and C on input; two further areas must be allocated to hold AB and AB + C during the calculation stage of the program. Given a machine with an order code as shown in Figure 67a and a card format as shown in Figure 67b, a machine code program to perform the above operation is shown in Figure 67c. Equivalent source program statements in a programming language are shown in Figure 68. When the source program is acted upon by the processor program, the resultant object program will be similar to the machine code program shown in Figure 67c. The action of the processor program can be considered in the two stages of operation code conversion and storage allocation.

The operation code conversion can be the simplest inspection of the source program mnemonic and the generation of the appropriate machine code, e.g.

READ	=	06
TRANS	=	10
MULT	=	11
TRANS	=	10
ADD	=	12
PRINT	=	07

and so on.

The allocation of internal storage to data is slightly more complex. The READ instruction operates as follows. When the object program is obeyed, the operation code 06 will cause one card to be read and the contents to be transferred into internal storage. The processor program allocates an area of internal storage to receive the input data and the appropriate address is inserted in the generated instruction. In this case the address is the location which is to receive the contents of the first column. Let us assume that the processor program allocates the location 0100 to the card read instruction. In terms of the example twelve digit B.C.D. word, the contents of columns 1 to 6 containing A, are stored in location 0100; the remainder of the card is

FORMAT OF COMPUTER'S MACHINE CODE INSTRUCTIONS

Operation Code	Operands	Action
06	Address A: The location in store which is to receive the first six columns. Address B: Zero.	One card will be read and the contents will be placed in the location specified in Address A and subsequent locations. Thus, in this program, the read instruction results in: A | B | Blank | C | Blank 100 | 101 | 102–103 | 104 | 105–113 Words
07	Address A: The location of one word in store, the contents of which are to be printed. Address B: Zero.	The contents of the location specified in Address A are printed. *Notes* A twelve print position printer assumed to be employed. Each digit position in a word is associated with one print position (i.e. there is no zone/numeric coding) and only numeric data can be printed. This assumption has been made for explanatory purposes only.
10	Address A: The location of one word in store, the contents of which are to be transferred. Address B: The location of one word in store which is to receive the transferred data.	The contents of the word specified in Address A is transferred to the word specified in Address B.
11	Address A: The location of one addend. Address B: The location of the other addend.	The contents of the location specified in the A and B Addresses are added and the sum is entered in the location specified in Address B.
12	Address A: The location of the multiplicand. Address B: The location of the multiplier.	The contents of the location specified in Address A will be multiplied by the contents of the location specified in Address B; the product is put in the location specified in Address B.

(a)

Fig. 67. A Mac

FORMATS

Card Format

Card Columns	*Contents*
1 to 6	A
7 to 12	B
13 to 24	Blank
25 to 30	C
31 to 80	Blank

Format in Store
Input format in a word

Z x	Z x+1	Z x+2	Z x+3	Z x+4
Z x+5	N x	N x+1	N x+2	N x+3

N x+4	N x+5

where Z = Zone
N = Numeric
x to x_5 = six columns

Machine Code

Character	Zone	Number
0	0	0
1	0	1
2	0	2
3	0	3
4	0	4
5	0	5
6	0	6
7	0	7
8	0	8
9	0	9

(b)

MACHINE CODE PROGRAM

Operation Code	Operands	
	Address A	Address B
06	0100	0000
10	0101	0114
12	0100	0114
10	0114	0115
11	0104	0115
07	0100	0000
07	0101	0000
07	0104	0000
07	0114	0000
07	0115	0000

Note: The above instructions will perform AB + C; for simplicity, instructions to perform AB + C the required number of times (i.e. a looping procedure) have been omitted.

(c)

rogram

read into subsequent locations. Thus, when the card is read, the contents of the relevant locations will be:

Location	Content
100	A (columns 1 to 6)
101	B (columns 7 to 12)
102	NOT SIGNIFICANT – BLANK
103	columns 13 to 24)
104	C (columns 25 to 30)
105	NOT SIGNIFICANT – BLANK
113	(columns 31 to 80)

Now, the operand of the READ statement defines the *contents* of the input area, locations 100 to 113, by giving names to certain locations. The defining of data areas by a 'data name' is achieved by listing out, by name, the fields in the card. Fields are listed out from left to right i.e. column 1 to column 80. Thus,

READ A(6), B(6), X(12), C(6)

defines the first six columns by the name A (this is location 100) and the second six columns by the name B (this is location 101). The next twelve columns are called X (these are locations 102 and 103) and the next six columns are called C (this is location 104); the defining of the twelve columns called X is necessary to define C in terms of the correct columns. The addresses of the locations of A, B and C which are deduced as shown above, can be placed in the appropriate instructions. After the operation code conversion and the allocation and definition of the store for input data, the resultant object program can be visualized as follows:

06	0100	—
10	0101	xxxx
11	0100	xxxx
10	xxxx	xxxx
12	0104	xxxx
07	0100	—
07	0101	—
07	0104	—
07	xxxx	—
07	xxxx	—

The 'gaps', xxxx, in the object program must be filled by allocating internal storage locations to AB and AB + C. In the context of the simple programming language used here, we can assume that the processor program will allocate a sufficient area of store to accept the transferred data. For example, AB is allocated one word of internal storage to accept B in the transfer. Briefly, the processor program allocates an area of store and defines that area by the given name; the allocation and definition of storage occurs only on the first occasion that a data name is detected. Subsequent reference to that data name will cause the previously defined address to be generated in the instruction. Thus, if the processor program allocates location 114 to the name AB, the object program can be shown as follows:

06	0100	—
10	0101	0114
11	0100	0114
10	0114	xxxx
12	0104	xxxx
07	0100	—
07	0101	—
07	0104	—
07	0114	—
07	xxxx	—

Similarly, when the data name AB + C is detected for the first time, the processor program allocates one location in internal storage and whenever AB + C is referred to in a source program statement, the address allocated initially is generated in the appropriate machine code instruction. If the processor program allocates the address 115 to the data name AB + C, then the object program is as follows:

06	0100	—
10	0101	0114
11	0100	0114
10	0114	0115
12	0104	0115
07	0100	—
07	0101	—
07	0104	—
07	0114	—
07	0115	—

Although the above explanation implies that each process of operation code conversion and storage allocation executed by the processor program occurs serially, it is usually the case that each source statement is inspected and the operation code and address generated. The result of this source program statement inspection is the generation of the required machine code instruction with the appropriate operation code and machine code address.

Our simple programming language can now be extended and three more facilities can be introduced, namely:

(i) the storage and addressing of constants;
(ii) the generation of machine code jump instructions;
(iii) the provision for simple *macro* instructions.

Constants can be dealt with in our example programming language by making a rule that all data names must have an alphabetical character as the first character. If a numeric character is detected as the first character of an operand field, that field is taken to be a constant. For example,

ADD 1310 OHMS

does *not* result in an area of store being allocated and being identified by the data name '1310'. What it does mean however is 'add the number 1310 to the contents of the location identified by the data name OHMS'. The processor program stores 1310 in one location and notes the address. The operation code is converted in the normal way and the actual internal storage address is inserted for the data name 'OHMS'. The address of the location holding the constant, in this case 1310, is also substituted.

Provision for jump instructions can be made by modifying the existing format of the source program statements. At present, the format of the source program is:

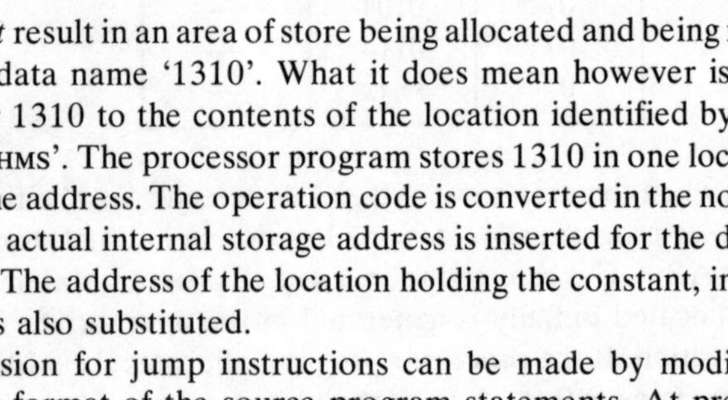

	Operation	Operands
→		
→		
Statements →		
→		

(The term 'statement' is used in preference to the term 'instruction' to avoid confusion between the contents of the source program and the contents of the object program.) The operands, if more than one, must be specified in a statement, and are in this example language terminated by commas, with the last field terminated by a full stop. To enable jump instructions to be specified in the source program, an additional field is required in the format of the source program. This can be called the LABEL field thus

	Label	Operation	Operands
→			
→			
Statements →			
→			
→			

Those statements that represent instructions to which a jump is to be made are given labels. For example, if a conditional or unconditional jump is to be made to the instruction:

READ A(6), (B6), X(12), (C6)

then a label must be specified, say INPUT, thus:

Label	Operation	Operands
INPUT	READ	A(6), B(6), X(12), C(6).

A jump statement of the format

OPERATION : UNCON
OPERAND : Label of statement to which a jump is to be made,

and the content

Label	Operation	Operands
	UNCON	INPUT

will cause a jump to the instruction generated from the READ statement labelled INPUT. The processor program builds up a list of labels and the machine code address of the instructions generated from the statement identified by the label. The machine code addresses of the appropriate instructions can then be inserted in the generated jump instructions.

Finally, the use of 'macro' instructions or statements may be introduced. So far, the example programming language has been based on a 'one source statement equals one machine code instruction' system. It is possible, however, for the processor program to generate a number of machine code instructions from one source program statement. For example, in the two address system described previously, the addition of two quantities so that the addends and sum are preserved requires a transfer followed by addition, e.g.

```
TRANS      B, AB.
ADD        A, AB.
```

However, the statement

```
TRADD      A, B, AB.
(TRANS/ADD)
```

could be used and the processor program could be so arranged that the contents of B are transferred to AB and the contents of A and AB are added and the sum placed in AB. The processor program could generate *two* instructions; a machine code transfer instruction and a machine code add instruction.

By way of a summary, a complete source program incorporating some of the facilities described above is shown in Figure 69. The general operation of the processor program is shown in flowchart form in Figure 70.

This example programming language has been useful to illustrate the concept and use of a simple language. Some limitations in the language structure and alternative methods of operation may now be pointed out.

The method of allocating storage in the example programming language does have limitations. The allocation of storage for a data name not defined in an input statement imposed the limitation that the amount of store allocated was equal to the amount of store allocated to the related data name, i.e. if the contents of A are to be transferred to X and X is as yet undefined, an area of storage will be allocated equal in size to the area allocated to A. An alternative system is to define the data areas and constants by means of a special statement. This type of statement, which may be called a *directive*,

Operation	Operands
READ	A (6) , B (6) , X (12) , C (6) .
TRANS	B , AB .
MULT	A , AB .
TRANS	AB , AB + C .
ADD	C , AB + C
PRINT	A .
PRINT	B .
PRINT	C .
PRINT	AB
PRINT	AB + C .

⊔ = One character position, the contents can be punched into one column (punched cards) or one row (punched paper tape).

Fig. 68. An Example Programming Language Program – I

Label	Op. Code	Operands	Narrative
	TRANS	1000, C.	Set C = 1000 by transferring constant
	ZERO	Y1.	Zeroize an area called Y1
Y GREAT	TRANS	Y1, Y.	Transfer the contents of Y1 to an area called Y
	READ	X(6).	Read X
	SUBTCT	X, Y.	Subtract X from Y and put result in Y
	JUMNEG	Y, X GREAT.	If Y is negative (X > Y) a jump is made to X
	UNCON	COUNT.	GREAT and if X < Y, a jump is made to COUNT
X GREAT	TRANS	X, Y1.	Transfer X to Y1
COUNT	SUBTCT	1, C.	Subtract 1 from C (1 is a constant)
	JUMZER	C, PRINT Y.	If C is zero jump to PRINT Y, if not jump
	UNCON	Y GREAT.	to Y GREAT
PRINT Y	PRINT	Y1.	Print Y1
	FINISH		Finish

This program calculates and prints the largest of 1000 numbers as shown in the flowchart.

Note that separate areas Y1 and Y are used since the contents of Y are destroyed when Y—X is formed

Fig. 69. An Example Programming Language Program – II

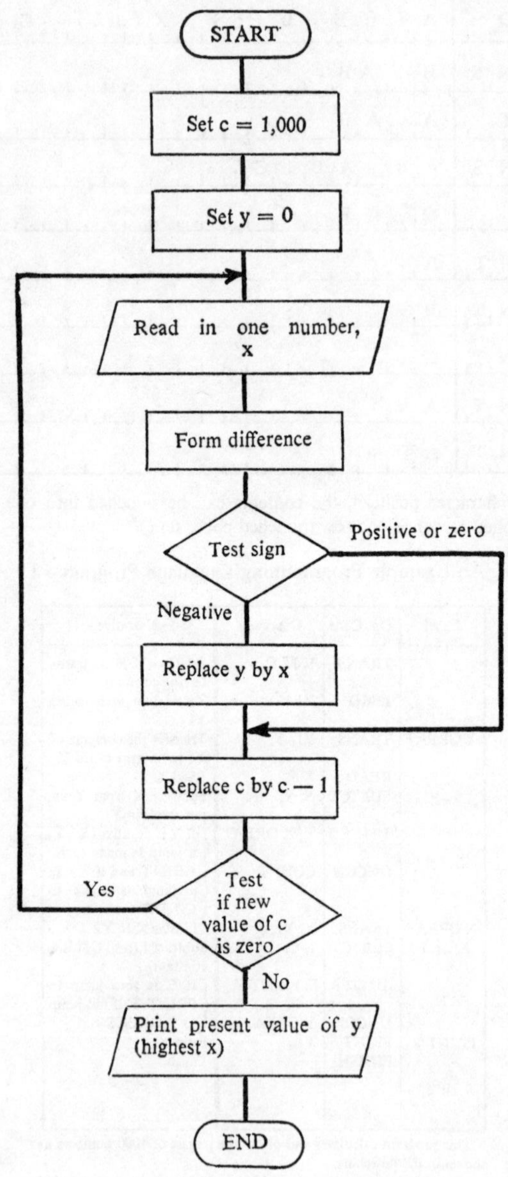

Fig. 69b. – *continued*

Phase 1

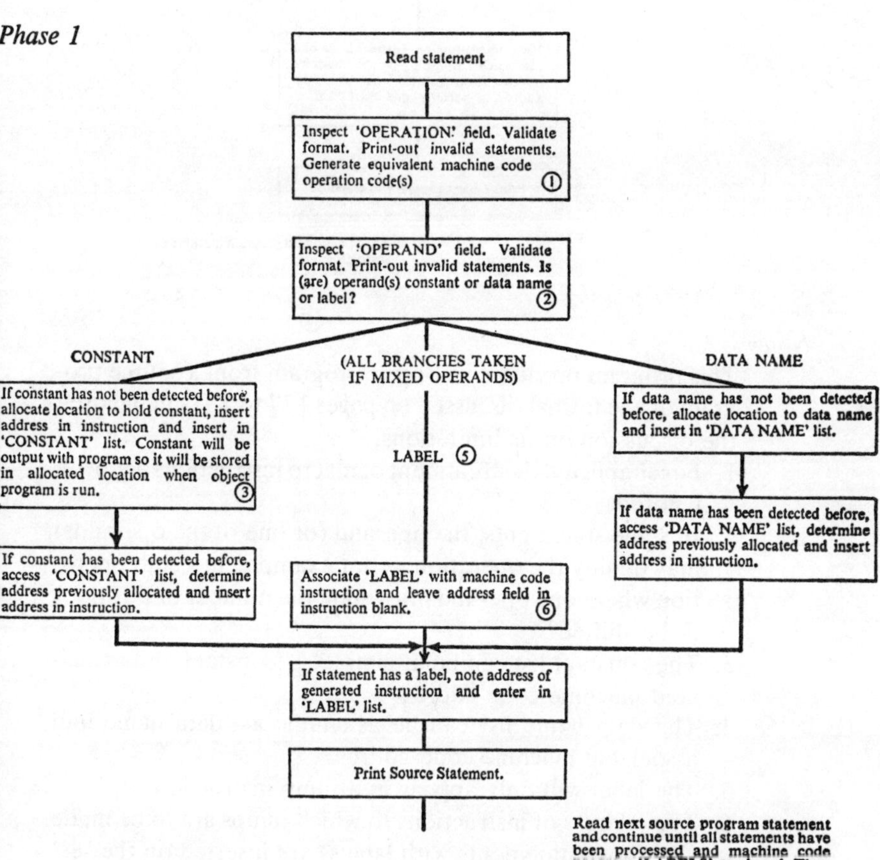

Fig. 70. Operation of an Example Processor Program

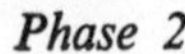
Phase 2

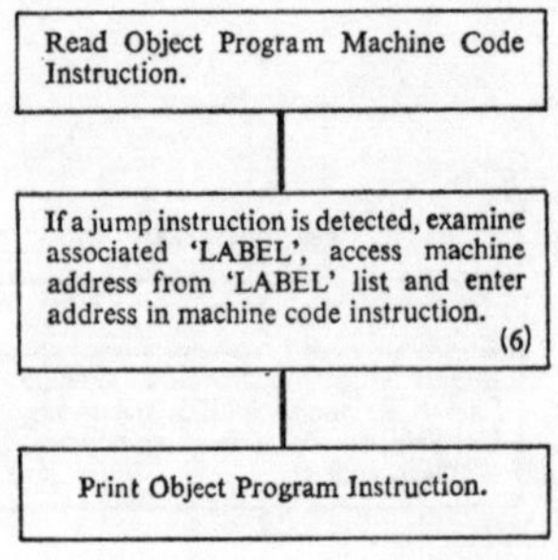
Read Object Program Machine Code Instruction.
If a jump instruction is detected, examine associated 'LABEL', access machine address from 'LABEL' list and enter address in machine code instruction. (6)
Print Object Program Instruction.

Read next object program machine code instruction etc.

Notes:

This program produces an object program from a source program of the format discussed on pages 177 to 184 and ignores the discussion on its limitations.

1. For simplicity, the treatment of macro instructions has been ignored.
2. In some statements, the operand (or one of the operands) may qualify the operation as, for example, in a shift operation where one operand must state the number of positions to be shifted.
3. The constant list can be as simple as 'constant and associated machine code address'.
4. The data name list can be as simple as 'data name and associated machine code address'.
5. The label will only appear in a jump instruction.
6. The address of instructions to which jumps are to be made (i.e. those statements with labels) are inserted on the second pass. This is necessary since jumps may be made *forward*, i.e. to a statement which has not yet been processed.

Fig. 70. – *continued*

does not produce any machine coded instructions *in* the object program. A directive is used only to specify certain conditions and requirements to the processor program. A directive can be used at the beginning of the source program to define certain data names such that the processor program can allocate internal storage to these names. For example, the operation DEFINE can be used by the programmer to specify the areas of internal storage and their data names. Thus,

Label	Operation	Operand
	DEFINE	TOTAL, DESCR (10) TAXT (2), QTY.

will specify to the processor program that:

(i) one 'cell' must be reserved and this will be called TOTAL in the source program.
(ii) ten 'cells' must be reserved and these will be called DESCR (description) in the source program;
(iii) two 'cells' must be reserved and these will be called TAXT in the source program;
(iv) one 'cell' must be reserved and this will be called QTY in the source program.

Similarly, constants may be defined by name rather than the actual constants having to be specified in a statement. The LABEL can be used to name constants listed as operands.
For example:

Label	Operation	Operand
	DEFINE	TOTAL, DESCR (10), TAXT (2), QTY.
CONS 1		172431.
CONS 2		HEAD _ _.

defines the four data names as described previously but, in addition, two words, in terms of the B.C.D. 12 digit word machine, are allocated. One word is loaded with say 172431 and the other is loaded with HEAD _ _, the line _ indicating a space. The former word is called CONS 1 and the latter CONS 2. Thus

Label	Operation	Operand
	ADD	CONS 1, TOTAL.

would add the number 172431 to the contents of the word called TOTAL. The machine code instruction generated by the processor program for this statement would contain the machine code operation code and address of the name TOTAL. In addition, the processor program would enter the address of the word allocated to, and called, CONS 1.

Having now described the 'mechanics' of one example programming language to illustrate the relationship between source program, processor program and object program, we now survey the types and characteristics of the programming language available.

There are three significant factors which must be considered when investigating programming languages. Firstly, there is the manner and time at which the object program is prepared. Secondly, there is the 'level' of the programming language. Thirdly, there is the format and general structure of the source program.

When the object program is produced as a result of the processor program acting on the source program, there are three courses of action. The most common is that the complete object program is produced and output. The object program can then be input with the required data as a separate operation. This is shown diagrammatically in Figure 71a. Another method of producing and using an object program is shown in Figure 71b. This is the 'load and go' principle in which the object program is not output but as soon as it is complete, it is entered and obeyed. Thus, because no object program is produced as output, the source program must be converted to the required object program every time the program is to be run (see Figure 71c). The processor program which performs the conversion of source to object program is commonly known as an *interpreter* or *generator*.

The 'level' of a programming language may be determined by the basic structure of the program prepared by the programmer. Initially, this may be considered as the 'bias' in the method of coding, i.e. the degree to which the method of coding is biased towards the machine or towards the programmer and his 'problem'. Machine code programming is of course the 'lowest' level in coding techniques since this is biased towards the machine. The example programming language described previously can be called an 'intermediate' level language. Although it is biased towards the programmer and his problem, it still reflects the format and structure of the machine code instruction. We saw, for example, that the computer employed a two address system and that with the exception of a limited number of 'macro' instructions, a source program statement generated one

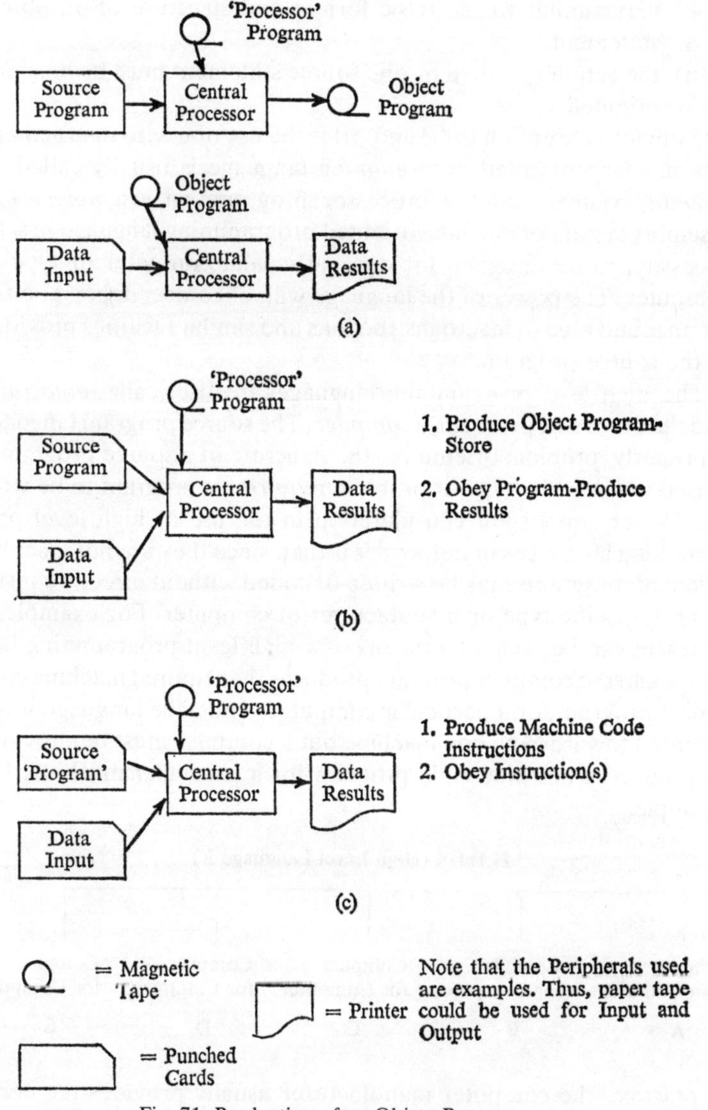

Fig. 71. Production of an Object Program

machine code instruction. This 'one for one' relationship between source program statement and object program instruction usually results in the restriction that

(i) the basic format and structure of a source statement must be very similar to the basic format and structure of an object statement:

(ii) the action specified by one source statement must be machine oriented;

The obvious exception to (i) and (ii) is the use of macro instructions. The machine oriented programming language is usually called an *assembly system* and the processor program, an *assembler*. The assembly system or machine oriented programming language has, by necessity, to be designed for one particualar computer or type of computer. The power of the language will, of course, depend on the number and type of macro instructions and similar facilities provided in the source program.

The 'high' level programming languages are often called *autocodes* and the processor program, a *compiler*. The source program language is primarily 'problem oriented' – the structure of a source program is biased towards the type of problem requiring a program to be written. A very important consideration in the use of high level programming languages or autocodes is that, since they are not machine oriented, programs may be written or coded without directly considering a specific type or manufacturer of computer. For example, a program can be coded by means of a high level programming language and the compiler program produces the required machine code object program for a particular computer. Thus, the language is not oriented towards any one machine but a compiler must be provided to produce a machine code program for a particular machine. For example,

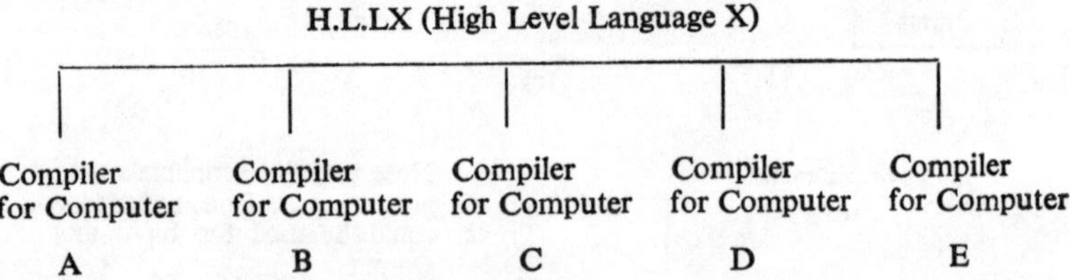

In practice, the computer manufacturer usually provides the compiler for a particular type of computer; this practice will be considered later (page 203). In terms of the example given above, the object program produced by the compiler for a computer A may be a series of two address type instructions for use in a character or byte machine. The object program produced by the compiler for computer B may be a series of single address type instructions for use in a

B.C.D. fixed word length machine; computer D may be a two address B.C.D. fixed word length machine and computer E may be a three address pure (serial) binary fixed word length computer and so on.

In practice, the production and use of high level languages does not provide universal programming languages, giving facilities for direct program interchangeability between machines is seldom, if ever, achieved. Computer manufacturers implement say, a COBOL compiler, as described below, from an outline language specification of a standard-defining authority. In the implementation of the compilers by various manufacturers, the structure of the language and many facilities are the same. However, the policy of a computer manufacturer, its resources, the characteristics of the hardware made and many other minor contributing factors, tends to lead to manufacturer-specialized versions of a language. However, universal languages need not necessarily be an ideal goal. If a job is to be run on a computer of a different type, the data may be handled on a peripheral unit which requires it to be held in a different form. Some form of program modification must thus be made. Similarly, it is not very difficult for programmers versed in one manufacturer's version of a high level language to learn another manufacturer's version. The programmer would probably have to re-orient his thinking for a new internal storage system or range of peripheral devices anyway.

Two high level programming languages which can be used here as examples to illustrate the structure and purpose of autocodes are COBOL (*C*ommon *B*usiness *O*riented *L*anguage) and FORTRAN (*For*mular *Tran*slation).

COBOL is a language which is biased towards commercial problems and is for general purpose use. The source program is prepared in four divisions: identification, environment, data and procedure. An example COBOL source program to perform the task shown in flowchart form in Figure 69b is shown in Figure 72. The identification division is very brief and serves only to label the program, i.e. name of program, name of programmer, date program written and so on. The environment division is used to relate the source program to the required object computer and its compiler. In fact two computer configurations must be described: the source computer to be used for compilation, and the object computer to be used when the compiled object program is run. The environment division is used to relate the source program to the hardware of the particular computers to be employed. The data division is used to define files, working storage and constants. The areas of storage (and their contents) are defined

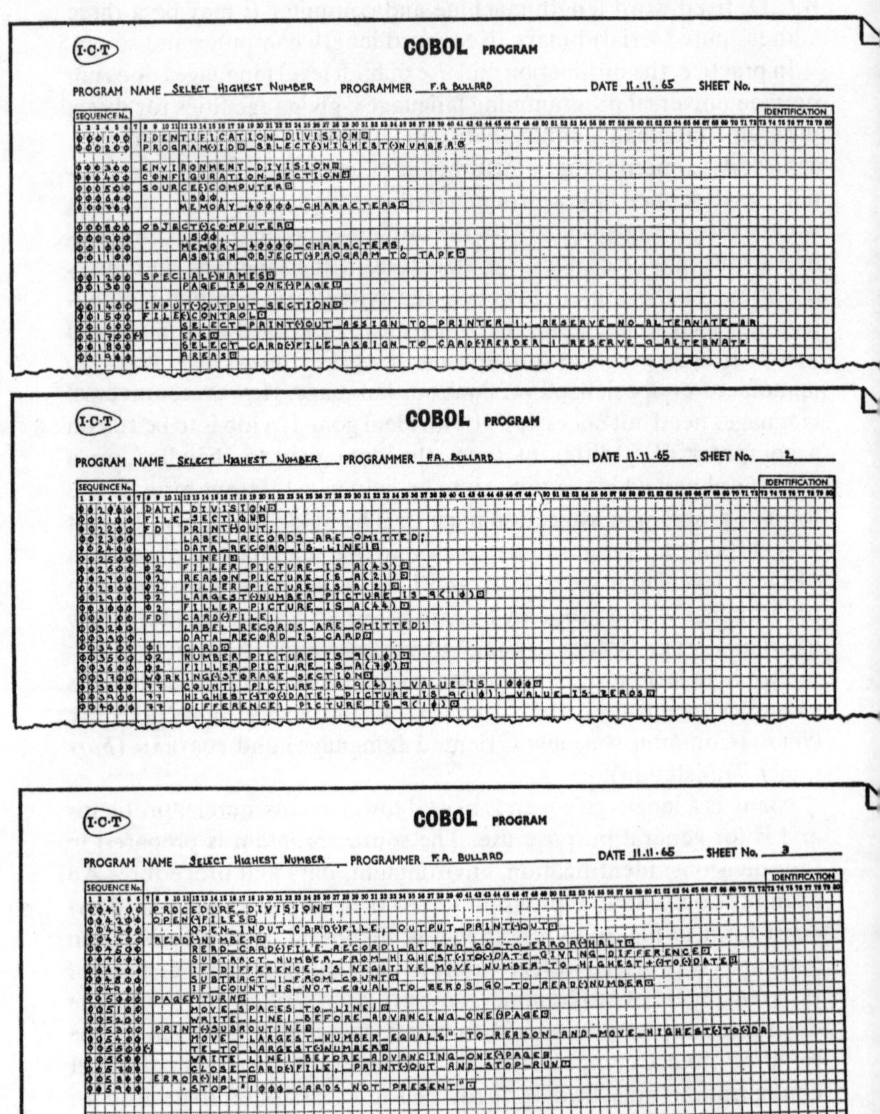

I·C·T COBOL PROGRAM

PROGRAM NAME Select Highest Number PROGRAMMER F.A. BULLARD DATE 11.11.65 SHEET No.

```
000100 IDENTIFICATION DIVISION.
000200 PROGRAM-ID. SELECT-HIGHEST-NUMBER.

000300 ENVIRONMENT DIVISION.
000400 CONFIGURATION SECTION.
000500 SOURCE-COMPUTER.
000600     1500,
000700     MEMORY 40000 CHARACTERS.

000800 OBJECT-COMPUTER.
000900     1500,
001000     MEMORY 40000 CHARACTERS,
001100     ASSIGN OBJECT-PROGRAM TO TAPE.

001200 SPECIAL-NAMES.
001300     PAGE IS ONE-PAGE.

001400 INPUT-OUTPUT SECTION.
001500 FILE-CONTROL.
001600     SELECT PRINT-OUT ASSIGN TO PRINTER 1, RESERVE NO ALTERNATE AR
001700-    EAS.
001800     SELECT CARD-FILE ASSIGN TO CARD-READER 1 RESERVE 9 ALTERNATE
001900     AREAS.
```

I·C·T COBOL PROGRAM

PROGRAM NAME Select Highest Number PROGRAMMER F.A. BULLARD DATE 11.11.65 SHEET No. 2

```
002000 DATA DIVISION.
002100 FILE SECTION.
002200 FD  PRINT-OUT;
002300     LABEL RECORDS ARE OMITTED;
002400     DATA RECORD IS LINE1.
002500 01  LINE1.
002600 02  FILLER PICTURE IS A(43).
002700 02  REASON PICTURE IS A(21).
002800 02  FILLER PICTURE IS A(2).
002900 02  LARGEST-NUMBER PICTURE IS 9(10).
003000 02  FILLER PICTURE IS A(44).
003100 FD  CARD-FILE;
003200     LABEL RECORDS ARE OMITTED;
003300     DATA RECORD IS CARD.
003400 01  CARD.
003500 02  NUMBER PICTURE IS 9(10).
003600 02  FILLER PICTURE IS A(70).
003700 WORKING-STORAGE SECTION.
003800 77  COUNT1 PICTURE IS 9(4); VALUE IS 1000.
003900 77  HIGHEST-TO-DATE; PICTURE IS 9(10); VALUE IS ZEROS.
004000 77  DIFFERENCE1 PICTURE IS 9(10).
```

I·C·T COBOL PROGRAM

PROGRAM NAME Select Highest Number PROGRAMMER F.A. BULLARD DATE 11.11.65 SHEET No. 3

```
004100 PROCEDURE DIVISION.
004200 OPEN-FILES.
004300     OPEN INPUT CARD-FILE, OUTPUT PRINT-OUT.
004400 READ-NUMBER.
004500     READ CARD-FILE RECORD; AT END GO TO ERROR-HALT.
004600     SUBTRACT NUMBER FROM HIGHEST-TO-DATE GIVING DIFFERENCE.
004700     IF DIFFERENCE IS NEGATIVE MOVE NUMBER TO HIGHEST+-TO-DATE.
004800     SUBTRACT 1 FROM COUNT.
004900     IF COUNT IS NOT EQUAL TO ZEROS GO TO READ-NUMBER.
005000 PAGE-TURN.
005100     MOVE SPACES TO LINE1.
005200     WRITE LINE1 BEFORE ADVANCING ONE-PAGE.
005300 PRINT-SUBROUTINE.
005400     MOVE "LARGEST NUMBER EQUALS" TO REASON AND MOVE HIGHEST-TO-DA
005500-    TE TO LARGEST-NUMBER.
005600     WRITE LINE1 BEFORE ADVANCING ONE-PAGE.
005700     CLOSE CARD-FILE, PRINT-OUT AND STOP RUN.
005800 ERROR-HALT.
005900     STOP "1000 CARDS NOT PRESENT".
```

Fig. 72. A COBOL Program

in terms of name, size and class (e.g. alphanumeric, alphabetic or numeric). Of primary importance is the procedure divisions. As shown in Figure 72, the statements in the procedure division are written in reasonably intelligible English. Each statement comprises groups of words; they are usually verbs and operands. A verb is equivalent to an operation code while the operands are usually names taken from the data and environment divisions. As can be seen in Figure 72, COBOL's procedure division is composed of a number of English phrased statements which will usually make for easy programming. However, such a narrative statement form can be disadvantageous if a program has to be prepared to solve mathematical problems. For the mathematician and scientist, the source program statements must be oriented towards mathematical statements rather than the English 'narrative' statements. Such a source program statement format is offered by FORTRAN. An example FORTRAN source program is shown in Figure 73; the program will perform the operation as shown in flowchart form in Figure 69b. Note that the entire structure of the source program is different from the COBOL source program and is based on a mathematical notation.

TITLE SELECT HIGHEST NUMBER — I.C.T. FORTRAN CODING SHEET — SHEET 1 / 1

PROGRAMMER A.N. ØTHER — DATE 18/11 /65

```
C STATEMENT NUMBER | CONT. | FORTRAN STATEMENT | IDENTIFICATION AND SEQUENCE No.

      MASTER SELECTHINØ
C     TØ PRINT THE LARGEST ØF 1000 PØSITIVE NUMBERS READ IN ØNE BY ØNE
      PERIPHERAL (1,CRO),(2,LPO)
100   FØRMAT(F6.0)
      Y=0
      DØ 102  J=1,1000
      READ(1,100)X
      IF(Y-X)101,102,102
101   Y=X
102   CØNTINUE
103   FØRMAT(13HHIGHEST NUMBER = ,F6.0)
      WRITE(2,103)Y
      STØP
      END
      FINISH
```

FORM 1/542 (8.64)

Fig. 73. A FORTRAN Program

Basic operations are specified by means of a symbol thus

Addition	+
Subtraction	–
Multiplication	*
Division	/
Exponentation	**

The basic statement in a FORTRAN source program is an *expression*. An expression comprises one or more variables, constants or functions, or combinations of these, with the appropriate punctuation, e.g. parentheses and commas. There are certain basic rules in formulating and writing an expression. Some examples of FORTRAN expressions are given below.

Mathematical Notation	Fortran Expression
AB	A * B
$A + B$	A + B
$-(A + B)$	−(A + B)
A^2	A **
$\frac{AB}{CD}$	A * B/(C * D)
$\left(\frac{A + B}{C}\right)^{5.5}$	((A + B)/C)**5·5

Storage allocation may be by an input READ statement or by means of an *array*; jumps may be specified by IF and GO TO statements as shown in the example source program.

To summarize, the coding stage is the preparation of the program statements. The method of coding may be ascribed to a 'level' thus:

Low Level – machine code

Intermediate Level – assembly systems or languages, i.e. machine oriented programming languages:

High Level – autocodes, i.e. problem oriented programming languages:

Commercial/General Purpose	Mathematical/Scientific
e.g. COBOL	e.g. FORTRAN and ALGOL

where the 'level' is determined by the degree of bias towards the machine, and is thus also dependent on:

(i) the ease with which the source program can be written,

(ii) the number of machine code instructions produced by a single instruction or statement provided by the programmer.

Irrespective of the method of coding employed, the programmer must 'desk check' his program for coding and clerical errors.

In terms of modern computer usage, machine code programming is very rarely used except in highly specialist applications on very small machines. Assembly language programming is still used but insignificantly compared to high level languages which are now the most popular for commercial and scientific applications. The problem is the proliferation of languages (COBOL, PL/1, BASIC, FORTRAN, ALGOL, RPG, etc.) which presents the modern computer user with a veritable Tower of Babel! Worldwide, however, COBOL is the major language for commercial applications and FORTRAN for scientific work.

Input Preparation and Testing

Usually, a program will be coded on special pre-printed forms. The program must be transcribed on to an input medium; this is usually the punching of the coded program into punched cards or paper tape. The format of the punched program and the punching code will be specified by the language specification.

If a program has been coded in machine code, the punched program will be input and tested. If, however, a programming language has been used the punched source program will be input with a compiler or assembler and the required object program will be produced. Generally, this compilation or assembly process will not only produce the required object program by writing it to magnetic tape or punching it on cards or paper tape, but it will also provide a hard copy or print-out of the source program statements and generated object program instructions. The processor program will 'flag' (i.e. print indicative symbols against) incorrect statements in the source program. Incorrect statements can be, for example, statements which have an invalid format by virtue of incorrect use and positioning of punctuation, the use of numeric or alphabetic characters where such characters are not permitted, the use of invalid or illegal 'operation codes' or operands. Once the source program has been 'debugged' (i.e. once errors have been located and rectified) as far as is possible from the source/object program printouts, the source program is again input for compilation or assembly. This process continues until the object program appears to be correct.

When a machine code program has been produced and is ready for input, the next stage is that of program testing. This is the running of the program on specially prepared test data. The test data is input and processed by the program: the test data is so prepared that the expected effect of the conditions and results induced in the program as a result of processing the data are known beforehand. The actual running conditions and results are compared with the expected conditions and results. Where discrepancies occur, the program is inspected for errors which are then located and rectified. When the program has been proved, i.e. it processes test data in the required manner, it can be used with confidence on live data as required.

Running a Proved Program

Having seen how a program is developed, let us consider some of the problems and solutions in running the developed and proved program.

Firstly, there is the problem of program loading. Since a peripheral device is usually operated under the control of program instructions, there is the problem of 'how can a program be read into internal store if there are no input peripheral instructions in store which can be obeyed?' The solution is the provision of a 'bootstrap'. This is the means of reading a program into internal storage. The bootstrap can be hardware and the program is input and entered by means of external switches and internal electronic circuitry. Alternatively, the bootstrap can be a series of instructions permanently held in the internal storage of the computer. The bootstrap program can itself be input by means of special circuitry activated by, say, the engineers.

When the program is to be input, it is loaded on an input device, the appropriate manual controls are set, and the program is input and stored by means of the bootstrap. When the program has been input it can be entered, again by manually operated controls, and obeyed.

Before considering some general problems of program preparation and running, the operating aspects of a modern digital computer may be briefly described. Manual operating controls, called the *console*, are usually provided as part of the central processor. Also, each peripheral unit has its own operating switch panel. The console is used to facilitate general 'operator to computer' and 'computer to operator' communication. The console can be a panel with switches and indicator lamps as shown in Plate 4. Alternatively, a console typewriter may be fitted in place of the central processor switch panel as shown in Figure 74. The console, be it panel or typewriter, serves

Fig. 74. Console Typewriter

two purposes. Firstly, it enables the operator to be notified of any special hardware condition requiring attention. In terms of the switch panel console, this can be the illumination of a special indicator lamp while, in terms of a console typewriter, a special message will be typed. Note that by the phrase 'special hardware conditions' is meant conditions of the mechanical components and electrical circuits; examples are an internal store parity error, a card wrecked or misread on a card reader, or the end of a reel of magnetic tape being reached.

The second main purpose of the console is to provide a means for the *program* to communicate to the operator and vice versa. In terms of a panel console, messages can be output by the program in the form of a series of numbers displayed by means of indicator lamps. Similarly the operator may input a message to a program by setting a series of multipoint switches, thereby generating a message in numeric code which is input to the program. If a console typewriter is attached to a central processor, reasonably comprehensive messages may be used to facilitate operator/computer communication. A console typewriter is invariably used with a master control program, sometimes called an executive or monitoring program, stored within the internal storage of the central processor. A 'special hardware condition' as defined previously can be detected by the master control program and an appropriate message can be generated and typed out. Similarly, a message such as a request for special parameters may be produced by the user program and presented to the master control program which outputs the message on the console typewriter. All input messages typed in by the operator are accepted by the master control program. An input message will either result in special action being taken by the master control program or the input message will be 'passed' to the user program for inspection and action. Usually, the master control program also serves other functions, such as the 'initiation and supervision' of peripheral transfers; see page 203.

SUBROUTINES AND SOFTWARE

So far in this chapter, we have considered in general terms what is meant by the term 'program' and the various functions encompassed by the term 'programming'. In conclusion, some general aspects connected with the provision of programs for modern digital computers can be discussed.

Firstly, there is the *subroutine*. Consider the following example. In one particular program, it is required to convert input data from character (decimal) form to serial binary form as described on page 84. Now, the set of instructions to perform this conversion process can be included in the program for each item of data to be converted. However, the same set of instructions can be applicable in all instances of conversion; only the addresses of the items of data to be converted will change. A subroutine will enable *one* set of instructions to be used in a number of instances where the same operation is to be performed on different data at different times. The principle of a subroutine can be explained by reference to the 'character to binary conversion' used above. A basic set of instructions is prepared to perform the conversion process. Suppose that ten instructions are required to perform the conversion which is to be performed four times on different items of data at different times in one program. The basic set of instructions could be included, with the appropriate addresses, four times in the program; this can be shown diagrammatically as in Figure 75a. The alternative is to 'separate' those program instructions which perform the conversion and to obey the same instruction set four times; see Figure 75b. There are two problems. Firstly, the address of the items of data which are to be converted may be different at each entry to the 'conversion instructions'. Secondly, once the conversion process has been performed, control must be returned to the main program.

There are two solutions to the first problem. The data to be converted can be placed in the same location prior to the conversion instructions being performed. Alternatively, the address of the data

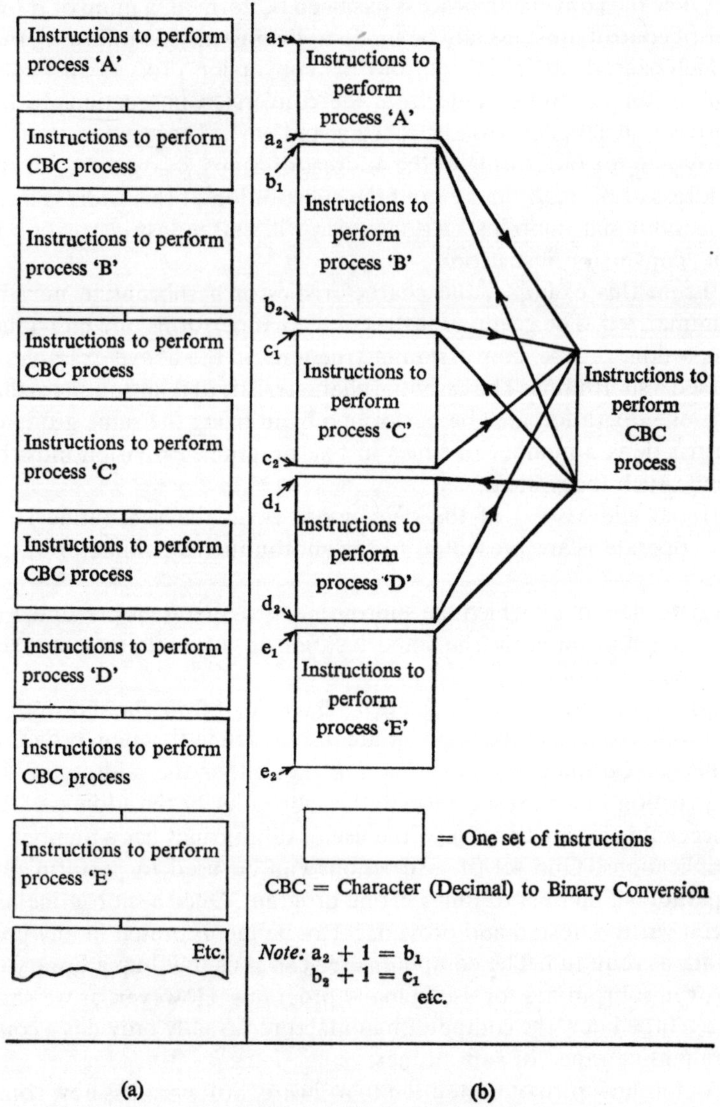

Fig. 75. The Concept of a Subroutine

to be converted can be presented to the conversion instructions as a parameter prior to these instructions being obeyed. The instructions which perform the conversion must therefore be modified by the address(es) presented as a parameter prior to entry.

Once the conversion process has been performed, a jump or transfer of control must usually be made to the instruction following that which caused the initial jump to the conversion process. In Figure 75b a jump is to be made from the conversion instructions to the instruction labelled (b_1), (c_1), (d_1) and (e_1). There must thus be provision for the storing of the address of a_2, b_2, c_2 d_2 and e_2 or the address of b_1, c_1, d_1 and e_1 and the substitution of this address in an unconditional jump instruction which will be the last instruction in the 'conversion instruction'.

From this example, the characteristics of a subroutine may be summarized. The group of instructions that performs one individual operation, i.e. the 'conversion instructions' in the above example, is called a subroutine. The essential characteristic of a subroutine is that the one operation may be performed by utilizing the same group of instructions a number of times in one program. Provision must be made such that either:

(i) the address(es) of the data upon which the subroutine is to operate is/are presented to the subroutine as parameter(s),

or,

(ii) the data upon which the subroutine is to operate is presented to the subroutine in the same location in internal store on each occasion of entry.

Further, provision must be made so that on exit from the subroutine, control is passed to the appropriate instruction in the main program. This can be made by storing a *link*, i.e. either the address of the instruction which caused entry to the subroutine or the address of the succeeding instruction. Now, the use of subroutines has a number of implications. One set of instructions can be used to perform one operation a number of times in one program. Once a subroutine has been written, tested and proved, it can be incorporated in any program as required. The computer user can thus build up a library of proved subroutines for use in many programs. However, as we shall see a little later, the computer manufacturer usually provides a comprehensive range of subroutines.

Let us now turn our attention to *software*. Software has now come to be a generic term which refers to standard programs and subroutines provided by the computer manufacturer. Some examples of manufacturers' software have been seen already; there are the compilers and assemblers which must be provided for the computer's repertoire of programming languages. A range of subroutines will probably be provided and these will include mathematical and arithmetical subroutines, input/output subroutines and commercial subroutines.

In addition to subroutines, the manufacturer also supplies a range of complete and tested programs or *routines*. The standard routines will include utility programs such as:

card to magnetic tape transcription
paper tape to magnetic tape transcription
magnetic tape to magnetic tape transcription
magnetic tape to printer transcription
sorting programs.

Some mathematical programs may also be offered such as statistical analysis and linear programming.

Thus, a comprehensive range of software for a computer or range of computers would be:

assemblers and compilers
subroutines e.g. commercial, input/output and mathematical
routines i.e. complete programs
operating systems (executives).

The provision of software is becoming more and more important in the use of modern digital computers. The potential computer user is just as critical of the range of software as of the computer's hardware facilities, in the selection of a computer.

Operating Systems

One of the most important pieces of software in a modern computer is the *operating system*. An operating system (also known as an *executive*) is a master control program which is held in core storage throughout the time that the computer is in use. Most modern computers have such a control program and, indeed, many computers cannot operate without one. It bridges the gap between hardware and user programs (software); this dependence is often reflected in the general term 'firmware'. The operating system is usually supplied by the computer manufacturer, although there are specialist companies who write and sell them independently of the equipment suppliers. The purpose of an operating system is to make programming and machine operations more efficient and simpler. The functions of the operating system depend on the size and complexity of the machine. Basic functions include the following:

finding and loading the required programs

operator/machine communications via console typewriter messages

performing general housekeeping functions, such as initiating and controlling peripheral transfers, checking parity errors, etc.

opening and closing magnetic tape or disc files.

There are several extensions to these basic functions. Some operating systems produce accounting information about the jobs which have been processed on the computer. If an internal clock is available (i.e. a clock within the central processor which can be inspected by program) the operating system can produce reports such as:

name of program
name of user
time job started (hour/minute/second of the day
time job completed (hour/minute/second of the day)
elapsed time (how long the job took to process)
cost, with which the user should be charged.

More sophisticated applications of the operating system including controlling *interrupts* and *multiprogramming*. An interrupt occurs when an outside signal is received at the central processor indicating that an input message is available. This is the situation which occurs when there are a number of terminals, such as input/output typewriters connected to the central processor. Consider the case where there are ten typewriters linked to a central processor. A user, such as a development engineer, may wish to input a message at any time. When a message is to be sent to the central processor, the user presses a special control key. This causes an interrupt signal to be sent to the central processor; the signal is a notification to the central processor that a message is ready to be sent. The interrupt signal is detected by the operating system and the appropriate action can then be taken by a program to receive the message into core storage. Further, several engineers may wish to send messages at more or less the same time; this will mean that the central processor receives a series of interrupt signals in a relatively short space of time. The operating system is continually monitoring all incoming signals and ensuring that all messages are being serviced in the appropriate sequence.

Multiprogramming is a technique in which a number of programs are held in the central processor at the same time. The operating system will maintain a record of where each program is held in the core storage, the peripherals being used by each program and so on. The operating system ensures that each of the programs are executed according to established priorities. Each program is executed according to the state of processing and the availability of the appropriate machine facilities at any one time.

Operating systems are thus a powerful adjunct to the basic hardware. Without their use, the complex modern computer could not function efficiently and effectively. They bridge the gap between the programmer and the machine. The programmer's task is made easier because many routine operations (all of which will require programs) are dealt with by the operating system and do not need to be catered for in every individual program.

5. Basic Computer Techniques

The aim of this chapter is to indicate some basic techniques of computer usage. For simplicity, two types of program can be considered. Firstly, there are the programs which have the simple structure of 'read input data – process – output results'. Secondly, there are the programs which process files; here, the structure is still fundamentally 'read input data – access file and process – output results'. Most of this chapter will be concerned with file processing.

The basic form of a program can be considered as one in which the structure is:

read input
process
output results

and uses, say, one input device and one output device. In fact, a program need not read input data; a mathematical program, for example, may contain a number of constants and a range of values assumed by variables. Of course, it is the *structure* of the program which is basic; the processing part of the program may perform exceedingly long and complex calculations. On the other hand, the processing may be virtually non-existent as, for example, in a program which merely reads a number of cards and writes the contents of these cards to magnetic tape.

Some tasks performed by the computer require the mass storage of data on-line to the central processor. Selected items of data are accessed, i.e. retrieved from the storage device and 'processed'. The basic units of data are the *file*, the *record* and the *field*.

A file is a collection of associated groups of data called records, each record being identified by a *key*. The record comprises a number of character groups called *fields*. This may be illustrated by a simple example.

A company keeps the details of all items of stock being marketed on a file storage device. The details of one item of stock form a record. Since each item of stock must be identified, all items of stock have a key; the key is a numeric stock item code. Each stock record has a number of entries related to that stock item identified by the key. These entries include: an alphanumeric description, present quantity in stock, re-order level, quantity to be ordered when the re-order level is reached and the name and address of the supplier. The file is shown diagrammatically in Figure 76.

Once a file has been constructed, a desired record can be retrieved, i.e. brought into internal storage, by means of the key. Consider again the stock file described above. As stock is sold (issues), the balance must be reduced accordingly and as the stock is replenished (receipts), the balance must be increased accordingly. Each time the balance is reduced, it must be compared with the re-order level and if it is reduced below this level an order for the appropriate quantity must be sent to the supplier. A stock file record may be updated by a movement record. At the end of each day, a movements (issues/receipts) file is created. Each issue and receipt results in a corresponding movement record. The stock master file is updated as shown in Figure 77.

Two major problems of file processing must be considered. Firstly, there is the method of holding the file on a storage device and secondly, there is the method of accessing or retrieving a record from the file storage device. The former consideration is secondary to the latter. Two methods of file processing will be described in this chapter: serial file processing and non-serial (sequential and random) file processing.

SERIAL FILE PROCESSING

Serial file processing is based on the existence of two files; one file comprises the master records and the other comprises records which contain data to be applied to the master file. The former file will be called here the master file and the latter the movements file.

An outline flowchart for serial processing is shown in Figure 78. Both files are read into internal store in their entirety. As a movement record and a master record are held in core store, there is a comparison of record keys. If there is agreement, the master record is updated by the data held in the movement record.

The prime requirement for serial processing is that the records in

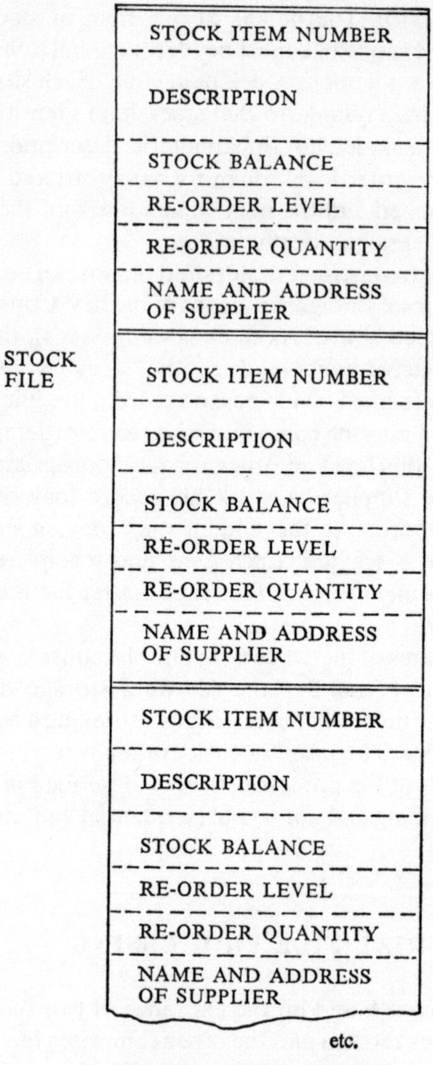

Fig. 76. An Example File

both files are in the same sequence. By sequence is meant that the records are arranged so that the keys are in ascending order.

The files may now be related to a particular file storage device – magnetic tape. For explanatory purposes, the processing procedure is assumed to be that shown in Figure 77. Three programs are required to perform this process of serial file updating.

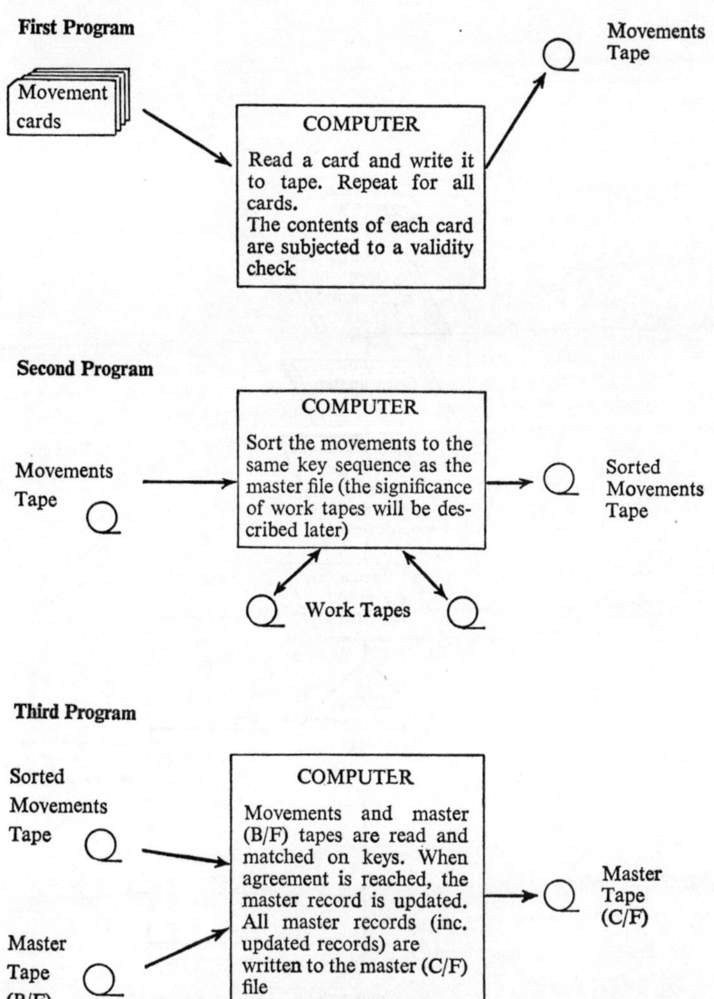

Fig. 77. A Serial File Processing Procedure (Magnetic Tape)

The first program reads all the movements cards and writes the data to magnetic tape. This is a simple transcription process which also includes the vetting of the input data from cards before writing it to magnetic tape. This *validity checking* can include, for example, the checking of the format and content of the movement records.

The second program sorts or arranges the movement records into

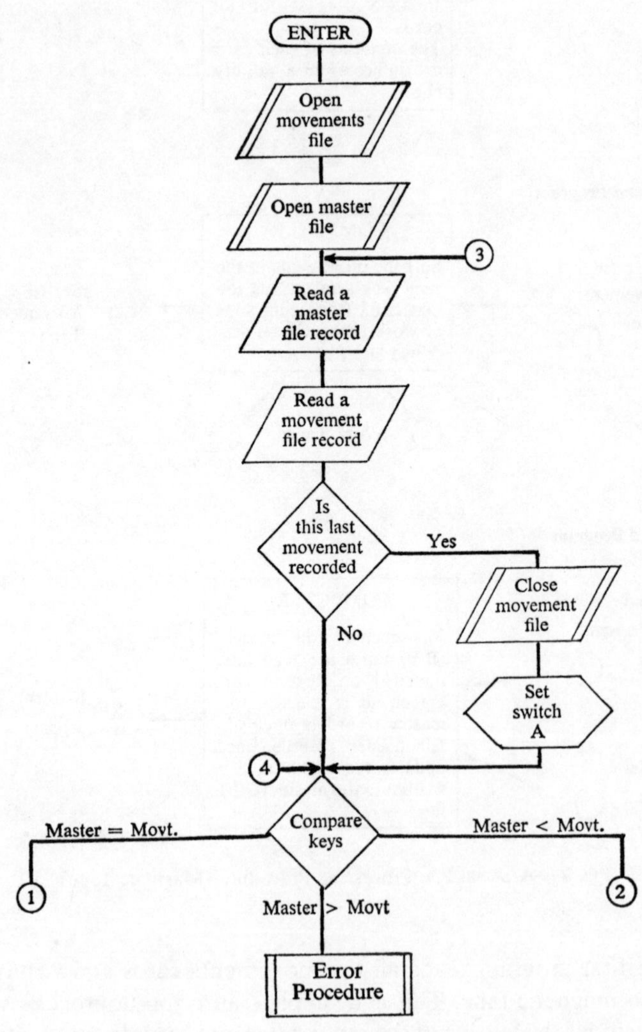

Fig. 78. Outline Flowchart for Serial File Updating

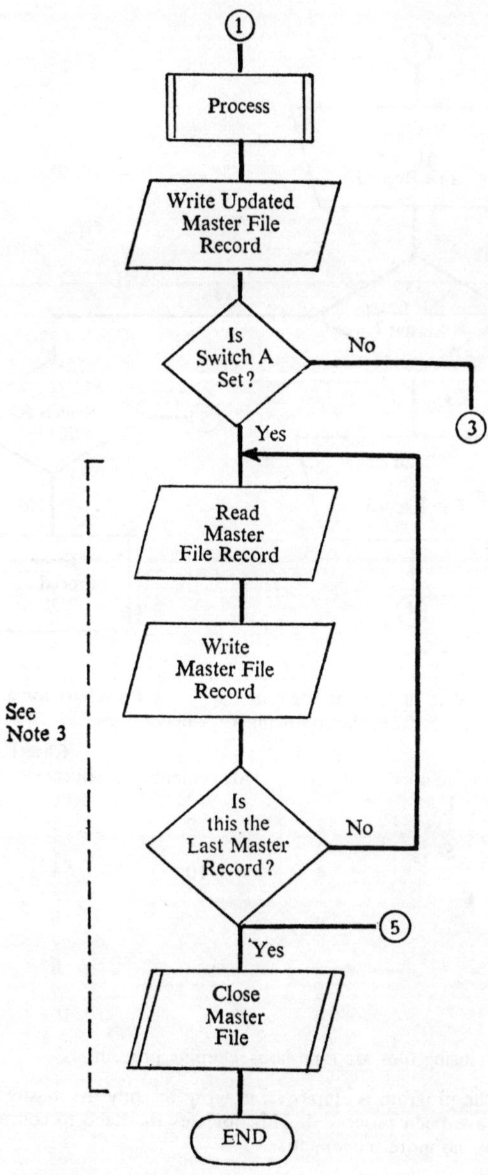

Fig. 78. – *continued*

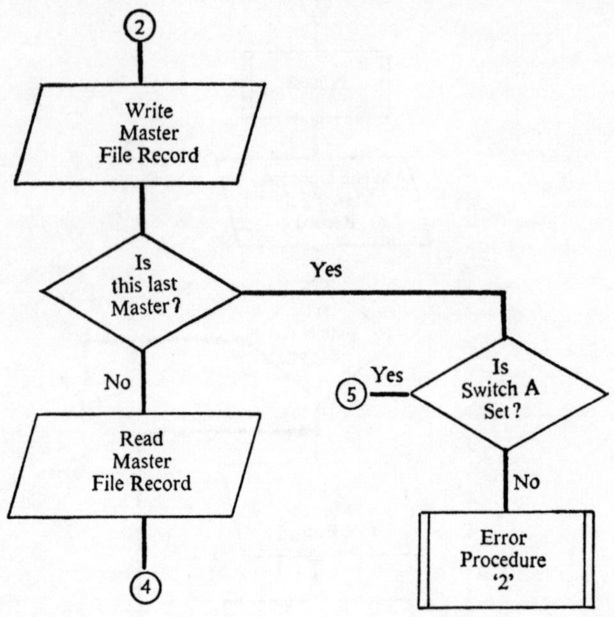

Notes:

1. If the reader wishes to test the logic of the above flowchart for a clear understanding of the procedure, the following keys may be used.

Case I		Case II		Case III (Error)	
Master	Movements	Master	Movements	Master	Movements
1	1	1	2	1	2
2	4	2	7	2	8
3	5	3	8	3	7
4		4	10	4	9
5		5		5	
6		6		6	
7		7		7	
8		8		8	
9		9		9	
10		10		10	

2. Opening and closing files are tape housekeeping procedures.

3. This part of the program is employed to write or copy the master file when all movements have been processed. This obviates the need to compare keys etc. when there are no more movements.

Fig. 78. – *continued*

ascending order by record key. Methods of sorting will be discussed later in this chapter.

The third program performs the serial file updating; the movements and master files are read record by record, the keys are matched and when there is agreement the master record is updated from the movement record. A brief description of how this updating program operates will indicate the principle of serial processing.

Note that in Figure 77 the third program employs *three* magnetic tapes: a movement tape, a carried forward master tape and a brought forward master tape. The reason for having the two master tapes, one for reading and one for writing, will become clear when the reading/writing process is considered. It will be remembered that data is recorded on magnetic tape in blocks, one block being written in response to one write instruction. Similarly, a read instruction will cause one block to be read into internal storage. The block size in writing will be decided by the user programmer but will usually be dependent on the amount of internal store available to hold data. Thus, one block, say 500 words, can hold a number of records, say ten records of fifty words each. In the reading of the master file therefore, a complete block representing one or more records will be read into the internal store. If a block contains more than one record, the program must be capable of locating the relevant fields within all records in the block currently in store. When all the appropriate records have been updated, the revised records must be written to tape. It is usually mechanically impossible to rewind the master tape from which the data has been read and to write the revised block back on to the same tape in the space occupied by the existing record. Thus, the revised block must be written to another reel of tape. This tape will become the input on the next updating run and yet another edition, or generation of the file must be output on another reel of tape and so on.

Software (e.g. programs supplied by the computer manufacturer) can play a very important role in magnetic tape operations as described above. For example, the user program may exploit 'record present', 'record write' and 'tape housekeeping' subroutines. The user need not be concerned with the reading or writing of tape. When a master or movement record is required, the user program may call or enter a record present subroutine. The subroutine will read a block from tape into a reserved area of storage. Provided the user specifies the size of records (or specifies how the size of a record may be determined) to the subroutine as a parameter, the next record in the block (i.e. the first and subsequent records in a block) is transferred to an area in store again specified to the subroutine by the user. Similarly, when a master record is no longer required by the user program because there is no corresponding movement record or the master record has been updated, then another subroutine is entered and the record for output is transferred by the subroutine to a special output area in internal storage. When this area is full, in that it cannot hold the next record presented to the user program, the subroutine writes the contents of that area to tape as one block.

When using magnetic tape, there are a number of basic organizational or *housekeeping* procedures. For example, all magnetic tapes must have two special identification blocks written, one at the beginning of the tape and one at the end of the tape. Housekeeping subroutines will write these labels, containing data provided by the user, on to output tapes. Similarly, an input tape can be identified by housekeeping software by comparing the details of the tape required by the user with identification data contained in the label at the beginning of tape.

The principles of serial processing may be summarized as follows. Serial processing requires that a complete file must be read, record by record, and that the keys of the records in this file must be compared with the key or, more usually, with the *keys* of the movement records. Both the master file and the corresponding movement file must have their records in the same key number order.

There are two very important considerations in serial processing; these are the batching of movements and the hit rate or *file activity rate*. Serial file processing would be extremely uneconomical if only a very small percentage of the total number of records in the master file are to be accessed. For example, a file comprising 40,000 records may be stored on tape; if only 1% (400) records are required, the complete file must usually be read and in the case of magnetic tape, recreated. An alternative method of file processing which solves this problem of low hit rates is non-serial processing on a *direct access* device (sometimes called a *random access* device).

NON-SERIAL PROCESSING

Non-serial processing is the selective retrieval of records from a file without reading the complete file in a serial search. It is also known as *direct access*; it is only possible with direct access devices, such as magnetic discs and magnetic drums. The important characteristic of these devices is that they are constructed so that the total recording surface is sub-divided into small addressable units. In a disc device, for example, data could be accessed by quoting the surface, track and sector. There are several methods of organizing the layout of data on a track. One of these methods is the *bucket and record*.

A bucket has many of the characteristics of a block on tape. There are however some important differences. A bucket is related to the physical characteristics of the device. For example, the area under a read/write head on one disc surface may form a bucket. Alternatively, the area under a read/write head may for example be divided into blocks thus:

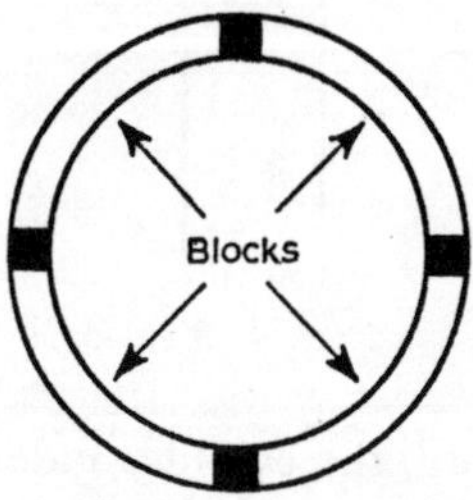

In this case, a bucket may be equal to four blocks, two blocks or one block.

An alternative method is the variable track format. In this system the two divisions are the *track* and the *record*. There is no hardware division into fixed blocks. Records are recorded one after another on a track. Small gaps are left between records. In addition, various special control codes are recorded with the data records for identification purposes. For explanatory purposes, the bucket/record method will be used in the following examples.

A file stored on a direct access device may be accessed serially, sequentially or randomly. Serial processing will be simply the accessing of each bucket in sequence, equivalent to reading successive blocks into internal store from magnetic tape.

Sequential processing requires that the records are stored in sequence by key. A direct access file can be considered as divided into a number of layers or levels. For example, a disc device may be considered as comprising a number of cylinders (e.g. the area of the disc beneath all read/write heads at any one time, assuming that all read/write heads move in unison), each cylinder comprising a number of buckets. The most common method of accessing records sequentially is the *table look-up* technique employing an index. The index gives a broad picture of how the records are stored in the cylinders in the buckets. For example, two levels of indexing may be employed: a cylinder index and a bucket index. Assuming that the cylinders and buckets are numbered, the indexes may take the form of

CYLINDER

Cylinder Number	Highest Record Key in Cylinder

PER CYLINDER

Bucket Number	Highest Record Key in Bucket

When a record is required, the cylinder index is quickly scanned in internal storage and the appropriate cylinder holding the record is located. Reference to the bucket index for that cylinder will give the number of the bucket holding that record. If the keys of the records to be retrieved are in the same sequence as the keys in the file, sequential processing becomes the relatively simple procedure of index inspection, bucket fetching, processing and, if necessary, *bucket return*. It will be remembered that serial processing of magnetic tape files in which the master file was updated, required that a new tape be produced. This was a 'mechanical' problem of magnetic tape positioning. Use of a direct access device however, permits an updated bucket to be written back into the same bucket location of the file. The process of finding, accessing, processing and writing back to a bucket is commonly called the *overlay* technique.

Random processing of a direct access file is characterized by the order in which the records are to be accessed from the file. If the keys of the records to be retrieved from the file are *not* sorted or if the file is to be interrogated randomly (as in the example shown in Figure 64), then an address generation technique will probably be more economical, in terms of access time, than index searching per record. An address generation scheme may be shown diagrammatically thus:

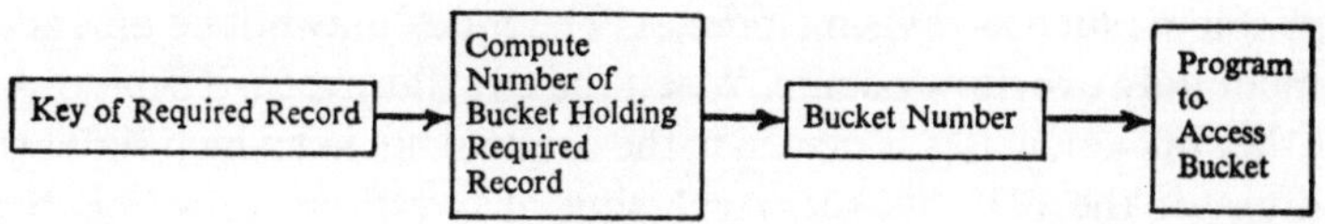

The address generation procedure will be used to allocate records to buckets and retrieve the correct buckets according to a given record key.

There are a number of problems associated with file storage and record retrieval using direct access. These problems are rather complex and cannot be fully explained here; however, some may be briefly introduced. Most of these problems are related to the fixed bucket size and the storage of a number of records per bucket. Depending on how many records are stored in a bucket (the packing density) there may be a problem of *overflow*. For example, as records are updated, fields may increase in size and new fields may be added. If a record overflows its home bucket, then the record may be deleted from that bucket and stored in another bucket. This, of course, results

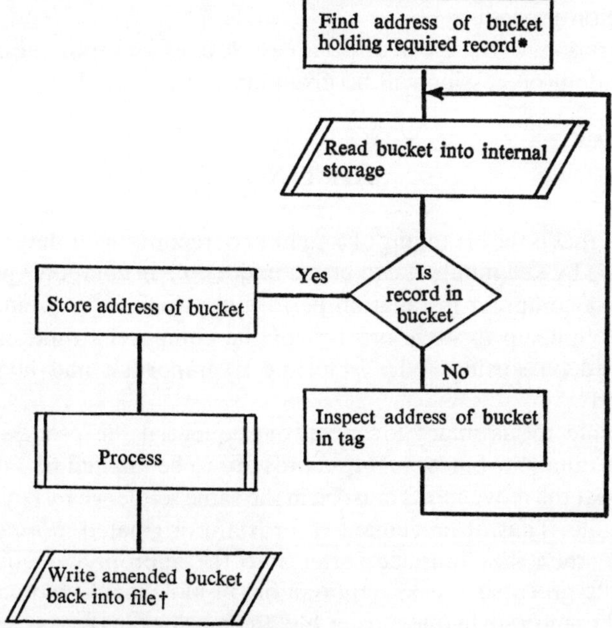

* By index or address generation.

† This procedure must detect overflow caused by the processing and be able to write the record to another bucket and to tag the home bucket.

in problems such as revising indexes. The index may not be amended immediately overflow occurs. When the overflow record is placed in another bucket, a 'tag' is placed in the original bucket which states the address of the new bucket. Accessing of overflow records is then carried out by the procedure shown on page 217.

Note that a 'chaining' effect may be produced where a number of buckets must be accessed (after inspection of overflow tags) before the actual bucket holding the data is located. This can be uneconomical in terms of record access times, and the file may have to be reorganized periodically.

The address generation procedure must be carefully designed. Records must not be under-packed in a bucket thereby wasting storage space and similarly, records must not be so tightly packed that overflow will become a major problem in a high activity or expanding file. The design of the address generation algorithm is a fascinating but complex task. If the optimum packing density is y records per bucket, then y record keys must generate the same bucket address x. If more than y record keys generate bucket address x, then tagging and chaining may become an uneconomical part of the address generation procedure.

Illustrations of the use of direct access devices for serial, sequential and random processing will be given later in this book.

SORTING

Sorting, that is the arranging of a number of records in predetermined sequence by key number, can play a major role in computer processing. In a computer installation performing work for a commercial organization, up to 40% or 50% of the computer's time may be employed on sorting. Why is sorting so important and how is it achieved?

A prime requirement for serial or sequential file processing in which a number of movement records are to be applied to a master file, is that the movements must be in the same sequence by key as the master file. Thus, if movement records are originated in a random manner, then they must be sorted into the appropriate sequence. Some file processing tasks require a file of movement records to be applied to more than one master file, the master files having records identified by different keys. Consider the case where a file of movement records is to be applied to two master files, File A in key (a) sequence and File B in key (b) sequence. Firstly, the movement records must be sorted to key (a) sequence and applied to File A, and secondly they must be resorted to key (b) sequence and applied to File B. An example of this procedure is shown in Figure 79. In this example, movements are sales orders or transactions which must first be applied to a stock file and then to a customer file as shown in outline in Figure 22. Note that, on input, the basic order records read from cards are expanded with the customer number associated with each item ordered. This is very necessary since the orders are first to be sorted to item number, the stock file accessed and updated, and an 'expanded orders' file produced. The expanded orders file is then to be sorted again, this time to *customer order number*; the customer file can then be updated and the invoices produced.

Of course, the use of sorting is not restricted to arranging a movement file to be applied serially or sequentially to a master file. Output from a program may be sorted before being printed. For example, the reorder notices produced as a result of updating the stock file shown in Figure 76 may be sorted to, say, item number sequence within supplier.

How is sorting achieved? The most common methods of sorting use punched cards or magnetic tape. Punched cards may be sorted off-line from the central processor by a sorter, an example of which is shown in Figure 80. Cards are placed in a hopper and are usually read one column per pass. According to the character read in one column, the card is channelled to one of the stackers. By reading each column of the key field over a number of passes, cards may be sorted into the required sequence. Naturally, off-line card sorting is only possible when one card contains one record identified by one key. Magnetic tape sorting is far more flexible. There are many methods by which data may be sorted on tape. Two will briefly be considered here: classical and polyphase sorts.

The simplest classical sort is the 'two-way merge sort'. An example of the two-way sorting procedure is shown diagrammatically in Figure 81. Four magnetic tapes are required to perform the sort and the procedure is as follows.

First Pass: The tape containing the records to be sorted is loaded on a tape deck; three other magnetic tapes are also loaded and these are called 'work tapes'. The program reads the records to be sorted and writes them in sequenced pairs to two work tapes. Each pair of sequenced records is called a *string*. At the conclusion of this pass, work tapes 1 and 2 each contain a number of two record strings.

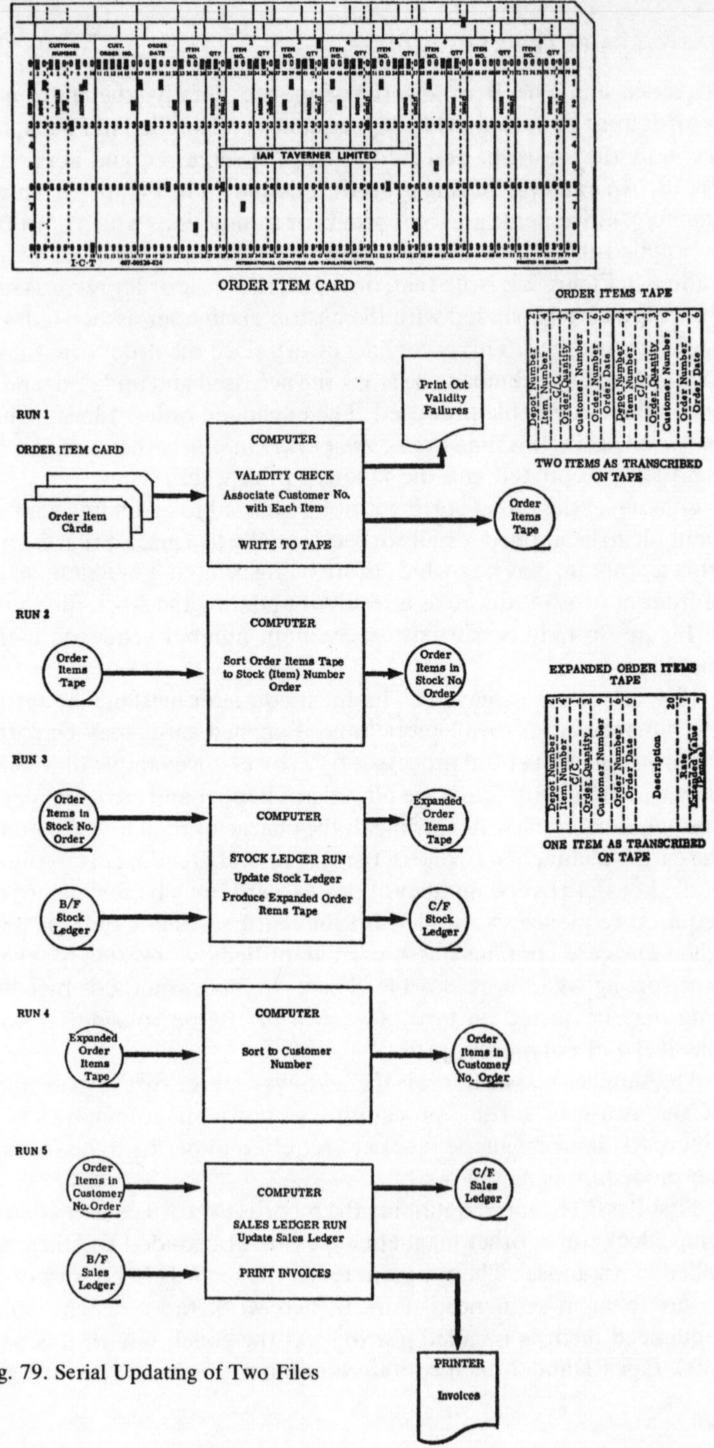

Fig. 79. Serial Updating of Two Files

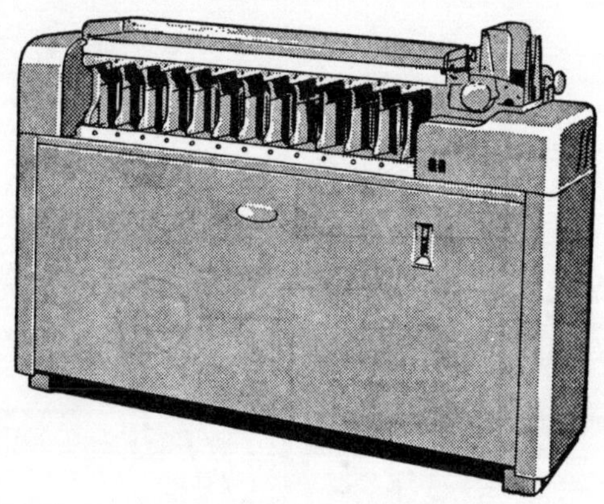

Fig. 80. A Punched Card Sorter

Second Pass: The tape which originally held the records to be sorted is unloaded. This is purely a security measure and makes provision for recovery if one of the work tapes is damaged or inadvertently overwritten during the subsequent passes of the sort. A fourth work tape is loaded. The program reads two strings of two records, one from work tape 1 and one from work tape 2, places the records in sequence and writes the new four record string to either work tape 3 or work tape 4. As the new four sequenced record strings are created, they are written to work tape 3 and work tape 4 alternately. At the completion of the second pass, work tapes 3 and 4 contain a number of four record strings.

Third Pass: A four record string is read from work tape 3 and from work tape 4. The two strings are merged to form one eight sequenced record string. This process is repeated until all four record strings have been read, merged and eight record strings created. The eight record strings are written to work tape 1 and work tape 2 alternately.

Fourth Pass: On the last pass in this example, the two eight record strings are read, merged and written to work tape 3 to give the required sixteen sequenced record string. The sort is now complete.

The number of passes to sort N records is equal to Log_2 N. Thus the above sort of 16 records takes $\text{Log}_2\ 16 = 4$ passes. If further magnetic tapes are available, a 'three-way merge' may be performed. This requires six work tapes and the number of passes to sort N records is equal to Log_3 N. The principle of operation is essentially the same as a two-way merge sort, i.e. *three* strings of sequenced records are created, merged and written until one string of sorted records is produced. Similarly, a four-way merge sort requires

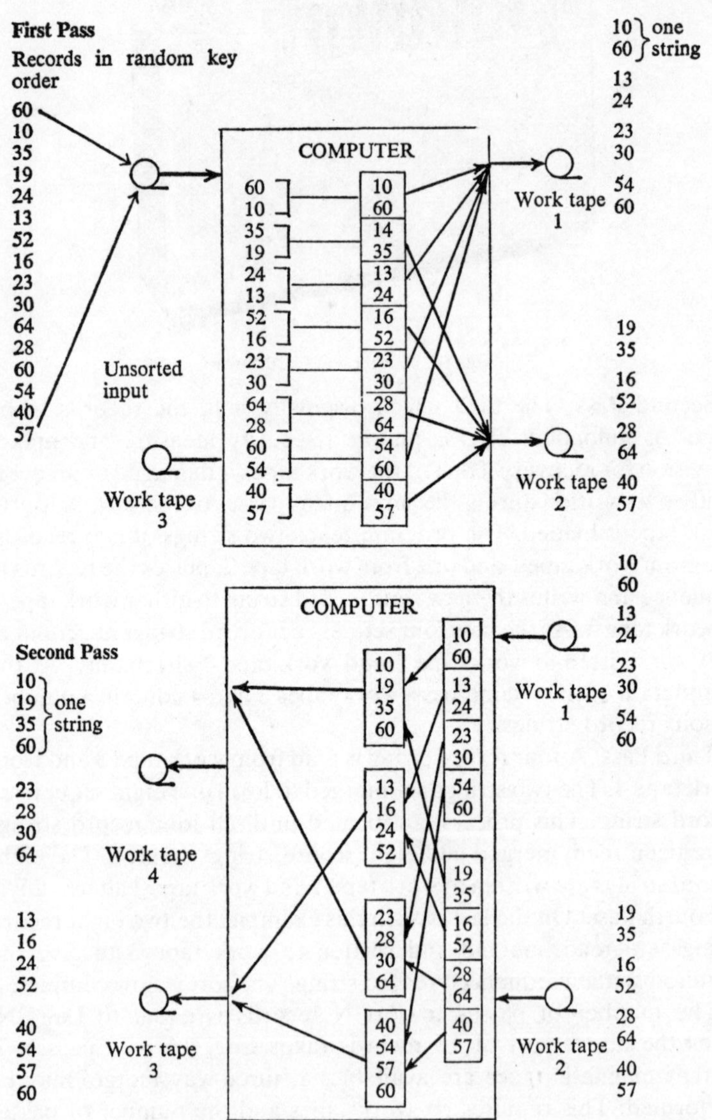

Fig. 81. An Example Two-Way Merge Sort

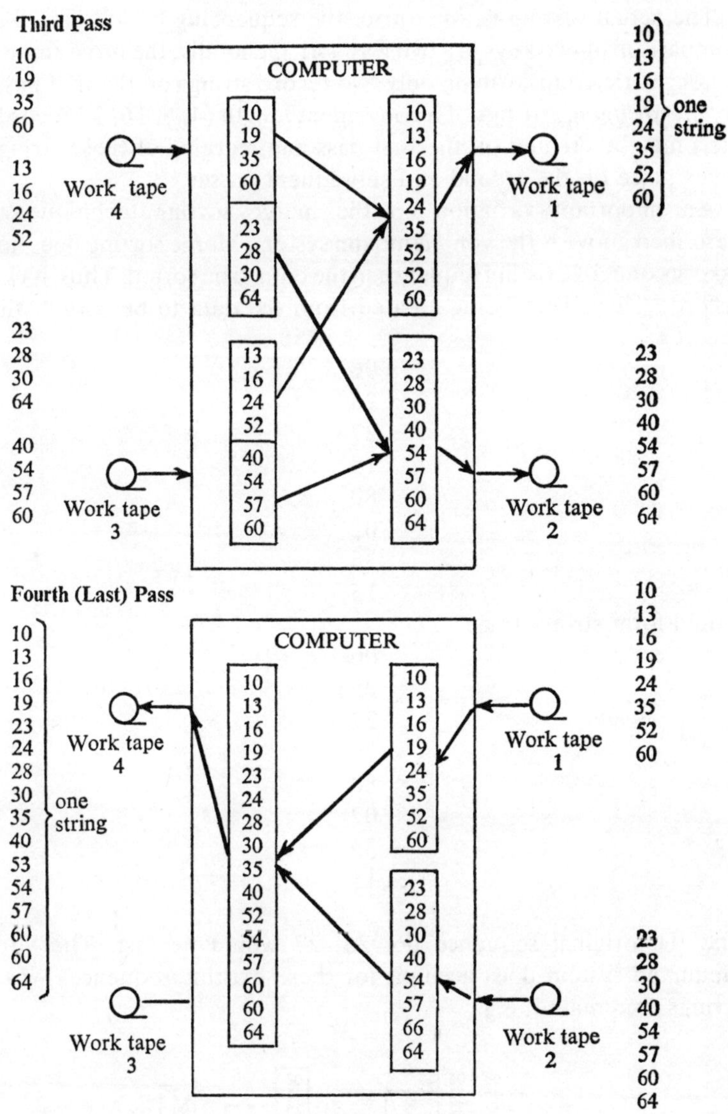

Fig. 81. – *continued*

8 work tapes and the number of passes required to sort N records is equal to Log_4 N and so on.

The actual sorting is, of course, the sequencing by merging, i.e. comparison of two keys in a two way sort. Generally, the programmer is not restricted to forming only two record strings on the first pass. By *pre-stringing*, strings of a convenient length (4, 8, 16, 32 records etc.) may be created on the first pass and merging of these strings takes place on the second and subsequent passes.

An important variation on the merge sorting technique as described above is the von-Neumann system. Merge sorting does not take account of existing sequence in the data to be sorted. Thus, if two record strings were being created from the data to be sorted, the records

06
25
27
15
80
02
35
15

would form strings thus:

06
25
27
15
80
02
35
15

and the original sequence 06, 25, 27 would be lost. The von-Neumann system does account for these existing sequences when strings are created; e.g.

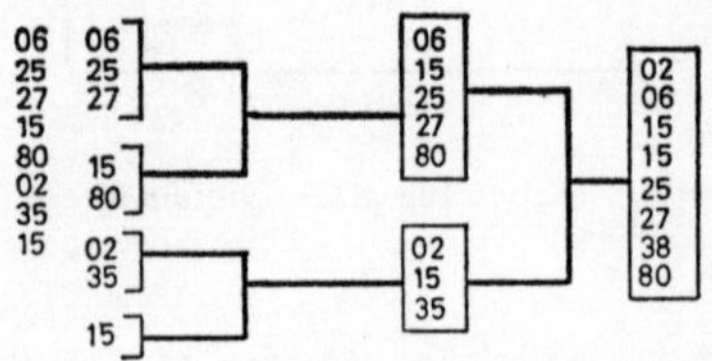

Polyphase sorting is rather more complex than the basic classical merge sorting. The tape holding the records to be sorted is read and strings of a convenient length are prepared and written to a number of work tapes. The number of strings written to each tape is critical. When all the strings have been written to the work tapes, the process of merging the strings commences. A 'blank' work tape must be provided and a certain number of strings are read from the work tapes, merged and written to the 'blank tape'. The principle of polyphase sorting is best illustrated by means of a simple example.

A number of records are to be sorted using four tape decks. The records to be sorted are read, formed into 31 strings and written to three work tapes (see Figure 82). The number of strings written to

Tape 'A'	Tape 'B'	Tape 'C'	Tape 'D'	
0	7	11	13	←—Allocation of Strings
				7 Strings on Tapes B, C and D are merged clearing Tape B and written on Tape A. Tapes A and B are then rewound
7	0	4	6	←—Result
				4 Strings on Tapes A, C and D are merged clearing Tape C and written on Tape B. Tapes B and C are then rewound.
3	4	0	2	←—Result
				2 Strings on Tapes A, B, and D are merged clearing Tape D and written on Tape C. Tapes C and D are then rewound.
1	2	2	0	←—Result
				1 String on Tapes A, B and C are merged, clearing Tape A and written on Tape D. Tapes A and D are then rewound.
0	1	1	1	←—Result
				Tapes B, C and D are merged, clearing Tapes B, C and D and written on Tape A
1	0	0	0	←—Result
1				←—Tape A now contains the Sorted Records

END OF SORT

Notes

1. A string is a collection of records arranged in key number sequence.
2. As the number of strings *decreases*, so the string length *increases* accordingly; the string length is, of course, the number of sequenced records forming that string.

Fig. 82. An Example Four-Tape Polyphase Sort

each of the three work tapes is 13, 11 and 7. The tapes are rewound to the beginning. The 7 strings on tape B are read as are 7 strings from tapes C and D. The strings are merged and written to tape A. (Note that tape A is shown as having 7 strings but, of course, the string length is equivalent to three times the length of the original strings.) Tapes A and B are then rewound; 4 strings are read from tapes A, C and D, merged and written to the rewound tape 6. This process of reading a number of strings, merging and writing continues until one string is produced and all records have been sorted.

The initial sequence or number of strings written to the three work tapes permits at least one tape to be 'cleared' at each pass.

The discussion of sorting has indicated the principles of sorting and outlined some of the methods. Magnetic tape sorting programs are usually supplied by the manufacturers as utility routines or in the form of a tape sort generator. The type of magnetic tape sort employed will depend on many factors such as: the number of tape decks available, the amount of internal store available for program and data, the read and rewind speed of the tape decks, the availability of a read reverse facility and so on.

6. The Role of Computers in Commerce and Industry

The digital computer, as previously described, is a complex arrangement of electronic circuits and electromechanical devices such that vast quantities of data may be stored and selected items of data can be processed at high speed. It has been shown (at the end of Chapter One) that computers are eminently suitable for calculation, especially for the complex and lengthy calculations in advanced scientific applications. However, the relevance of computers in the modern business world was demonstrated by placing less significance on the calculation aspect; data storage and handling procedures becoming the major factor. It is important to realize that the modern digital computer is a versatile and powerful tool; the onus is on man's ingenuity and imagination to harness this power and to use the tool to his best advantage.

What we must now consider is how computers are, and should be, used in commerce and industry. Naturally, the question of how computers *should* be used depends on the interpretation of 'man's best advantage' in the context of modern business. Since the computer is a tool, any discussion on the use of a computer must be preceded by a brief examination of the environment in which the computer is to be used. Let us first examine the characteristics of a commercial and industrial organization and then indicate the areas in which a computer can be employed.

The problems of *electronic business data processing* are extremely varied and often complex. It is possible to introduce only some of the aspects of business data processing and to point out the relevance of computers.

Firstly, consider a manufacturing company with the following functions:

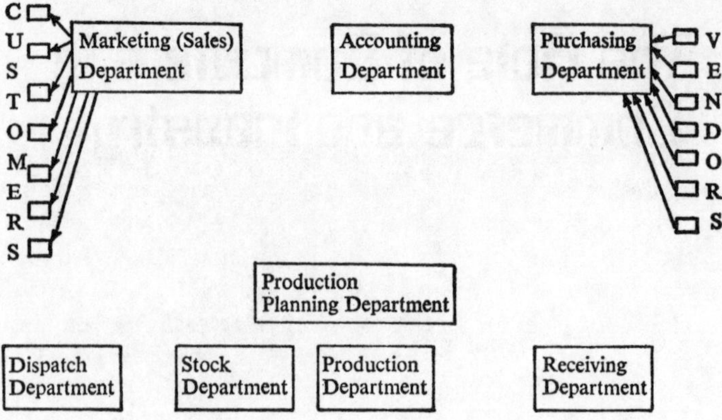

As yet, no link has been shown between the functions. If each functional operation, e.g. selling, purchasing, dispatching, was performed as if by an autonomous unit, then the company would be reduced to a state of anarchy and would be a collection of uncoordinated individuals, each serving his own ends. Such a company cannot of course exist for long in practice. It would be ludicrous, for example, for the purchasing department to operate in complete isolation, excluding the present quantity and type of raw materials being held in the receiving department or consumed by production. The ordering of tons of raw material for a product for which demand has dropped and for which production is to cease would be ridiculous. Within our example company, therefore, there must be information recording and control.

Consider now the information flow in the company:

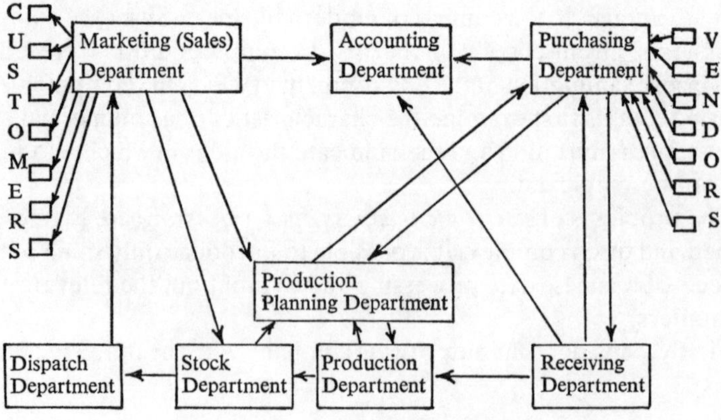

The pattern information flow may be described briefly as follows. Orders originate from customers and are passed, via the sales office by the appropriate documentation, to the stock department. When the order is filled, the goods are sent to the customer via the dispatch department. Copies of filled orders go to the customer, the sales office and the accounting department. The production planning department must initiate the production of required quantities of goods, and the orders and existing stock figures are used to make the decisions: what to produce and when to produce. Production orders must therefore be sent from the production planning department to the production department. Similarly, production planning must specify to the purchasing department the amount of raw materials required and the purchasing department will, in turn, place orders with the vendors. Copies of the 'purchase requirements' must be sent to the receiving departments so that the incoming material can be identified. When the raw materials arrive, the production planning department must be informed by means of 'materials-received' notices. The accounting department must be notified for all transactions for which the company will be charged or for which the company makes a charge. Thus, bills and invoices must be sent to the customers; records maintained of payment; orders placed with the vendors must be paid for; production costs must be assessed; company employees must be paid; and so on.

This *simplified* company structure illustrates the complexity of information flow or communication between the various functions operating within the company. Let us briefly inspect two aspects of these functions: the function of management control and the function of recording.

Some of the functions in the example company above are clerical procedures; pure and simple paper work. Two notable examples are the accounting department's payroll procedure and the invoicing procedure. Both are simply the recording of entities, e.g. personnel to be paid and how much, or events, e.g. a transaction and subsequent payment. Thus, a number of clerks can be performing a purely routine mechanical procedure of record keeping. Such procedures are ideally suited to processing by modern digital computers. This does not mean, however, that the introduction of a computer to perform the manual clerical work will be advantageous in terms of effectiveness, efficiency and economics; but this will be discussed later. We have thus seen one application of computers: the replacement of manual clerical workers performing paperwork record-keeping functions which are vital to the working of the company. Each department contributes information for the upkeep of files and the production of input information. Thus, for example, the production of payslips and the making of payments will be subject to data supplied from, say, production department (overtime and piece work or productivity bonus data), sales or marketing department (sales commissions) and personnel and accounts department (employee identifying data, pay and tax rates). When the payroll procedure is to be performed on the computer, all relevant input data must be collected and prepared, possibly coded and punched, so that it can be read by the computer. Standard files brought forward from the last

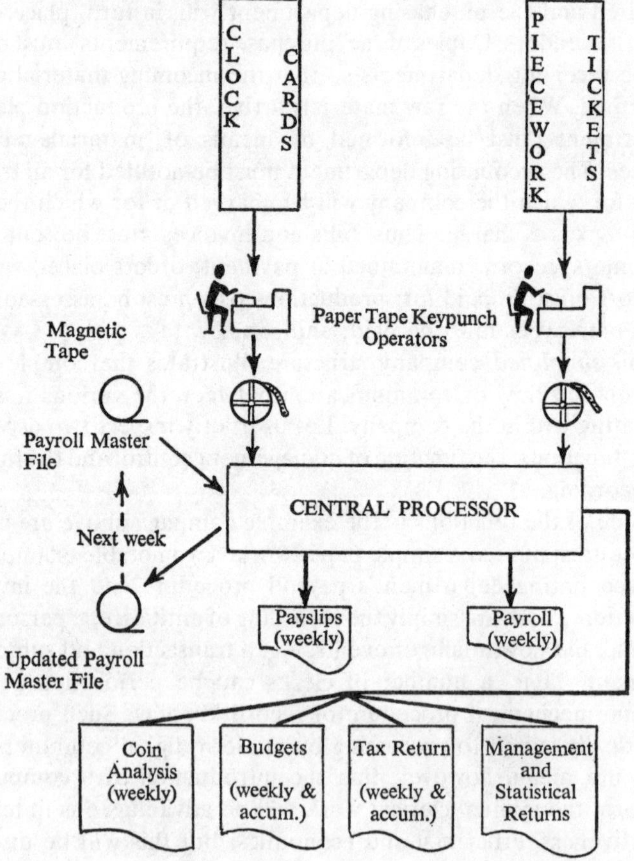

Fig. 83. An Example Payroll Procedure

time the payroll procedure was performed must be available in a form for computer acceptance, and a dispatch procedure must be established to hold carried forward files and disseminate printed output. An example payroll procedure illustrating the above characteristics is shown in Figure 83.

Such jobs as invoicing, payroll, sales ledger and sales analysis may be classed as the 'bread and butter' work undertaken in the company by a computer; the computer can simply replace existing clerical workers.

Let us now consider another function in an organization, the function of management control. In terms of the company structure as shown on page 228, the information flow provides a basic link between departments. Some of the information from a number of departments is received by one department and transformed or processed according to a given procedure. Most of the information can be considered as the recording of observed events, e.g. the present stock in hand, the quantity of product ordered by a customer, the quantity of product ordered by a customer, the quantity of raw materials received from a vendor and so on. Naturally, some sort of control must be exercised and this exercise of control must be based on facts, i.e. the recorded events. For simplicity, we may consider that control is based upon the comparison or correlation between results achieved (the recorded events) and the goals or objectives sought. Consider the servomechanism concept of control:

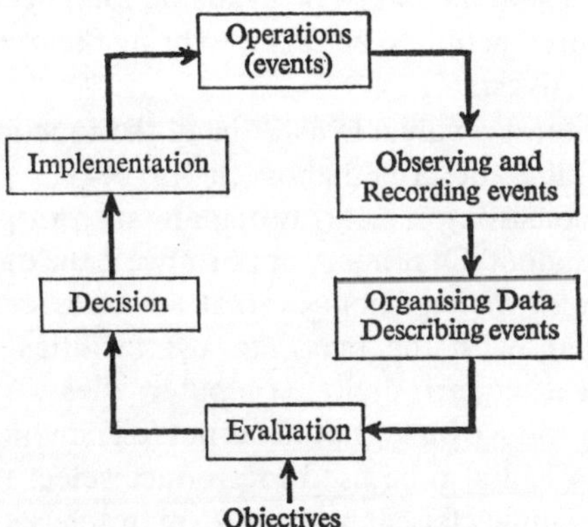

The operation of the control loop may be likened to the operation of a thermostat. Let us say that the objective of a certain operation is to maintain an oven at a temperature of 500°F. The thermostat is set to 500°F and let us say that a tolerance of ±5°F is acceptable. When the device is switched on the heating system is activated and when the temperature reaches 500°F, the heating device is switched off. The procedure for maintaining the required temperature may be viewed as:

operation	–	heating oven
observing operation	–	taking temperature
evaluation	–	comparing current temperature with required temperature
decision	–	activate heating device if temperature less than 495°
implementation	–	activate heating device.

Note that, in this analogy, there is no corresponding operation for 'organizing data describing events' since the raw information (the temperature as recorded by the thermometer) is in a form which can be directly compared with the objective, the temperature set on the thermostat. However, in business it is more likely that considerable organization of data may be required before it is in a form which can readily be compared with the proposed objectives. For example, the objective for a company may be a certain profit level on a specified product. The determination of current profit level will require a considerable amount of organizing and processing of data (e.g. income and expense data) from a number of sources before the data can be expressed in a convenient form for comparison with the goals. Similarly, sufficient data must be available for a decision to be made as to the required action to be taken to bring the operations into line with the objectives.

The computer is a valuable asset in all the functions in the simple single control loop described above; in practice, a company may be visualized as consisting of an array of many such loops, all interwoven and interdependent. Of primary importance is the data collection and manipulation for management evaluation and decision making. We have seen that, with the mass storage facilities and high speed processing of a modern digital computer, files may be stored and processed to produce bulk printed output (e.g. invoices and payslips). The computer can also be used to produce select reports and summaries. In a manual clerical procedure, many clerks may be engaged in producing summarized data or selective reports as requested by management. In fact, the amount of labour and time involved in producing such reports may be prohibitive and management may have to act in ignorance of some of the facts. The processing of files on the computer can be achieved rapidly and efficiently; the repetitive actions of inspection and accumulation of data from many records is an application suited to the modern digital computer. There are still the problems of collecting the data for computer analysis according to management's requirements, the preparation of that data for computer processing and the preparation of the programs to process the data. At a basic level, files which exist and are updated for one purpose may also be analysed for the other purpose of providing management with required summaries. For example, orders and sales ledgers may be kept for the preparation of invoices but these same files may be processed by another program to show volume of sales by product within area at specified times in the year. Naturally, the files must contain the required information in a form which can be inspected and accessed by program. An example of summarized reports for management inspection for the determination of policy is in the field of sales forecasting. The trends of present sales will, of course, assist in determining the type and volume of products to be manufactured. But consider the wider implications – what should be the distribution of the product on a national or international scale – what sort of advertising campaign should be mounted? – and so on. A case may be quoted in which a large chain store, for example, discovered that:

Large salesmen tend to be more successful in selling large sized garments;
Black underwear sells better in ports than in inland towns;
Larger numbers of white gloves are sold in Liverpool but only a meagre amount is sold in Birmingham;

and many other interesting facts. All the factors are of immense interest in determining sales policy. Note that considerable effort would be required to produce data to give the above conclusions by manual methods. If sufficient data is available in file form on the computer, however, a program may be produced to analyse selling trends. From the mass of individual events, summaries are produced and trends ascertained.

The two cases described above, namely the replacement of standard manual clerical activities by a computer and the use of a computer to provide information for management decisions, have been related to 'office' procedures. What influence has the computer had, and what can it have, on the production side? Firstly, there are applications, such as production control, which organize the production function. Secondly, there are applications in which the digital computer actually performs or enhances part of a production process.

Production control is perhaps the most important application of digital computers in the organization of the production functions.

The general concept of a production control system is shown in Figure 84. There are seven basic steps in the system:

1. Finished Product Order Analysis and Programme Analysis
2. Order and Programme Breakdown
3. Assemblies and Component Parts Stock Control
4. Plant Loading and Progress Control
5. Shop Documentation
6. Raw Material Stock Control
7. Purchase Control.

Production control by computer is too complex a system to be described in detail in this book, but the relevance of computers to performing this function may be described briefly. The production control system is concerned with the co-ordination of three interrelated factors: men, machines and materials. There are many variables involved in establishing, implementing and progressing a production programme. The calculations required to monitor and organize a complex production control system can require much time, and time is a vital factor. However, all industrial activities are dynamic. Changes in demand, material shortages, labour problems and many other factors require rapid responses from a production control system. In view of the complexity of the calculations which are necessary to determine the action required and the inevitable problems of communication in implementing decisions, the computer solves the problem of maintaining adequate control of the production processes in respect of the time function. A well designed and programmed production control system must provide a breakdown of the production programme such that positive precise working instructions are available.

Procedures must be available to permit a feedback of data, so that the production processes can be monitored by the computer. Thus, the details of the action taken by the personnel may be compared with the original plans. The flow of data in an example production control system is shown in Figure 85. Note that one criteria for judging a production control system is the degree of responsiveness of the various operations within the control cycles according to varying conditions.

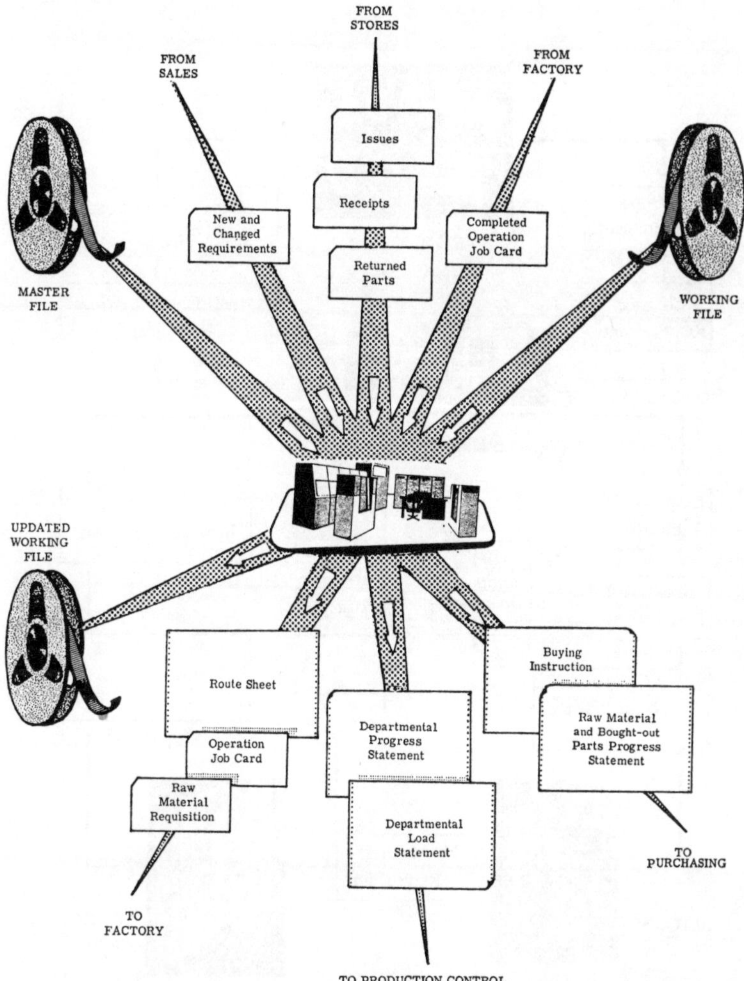

Fig. 84. General Concept of a Production Control System

The modern digital computer can also aid the production process directly. Two examples of the employment of computers in this capacity are the fields of numerical control of machine tools and automatic typesetting. Some machine tools can be controlled by instructions punched in paper tape; this control tape can be produced by a computer. The machine tool control program specifies: operations to be performed (milling, drilling, tapping, etc.); the size of tools to be employed; movements of the part to be machined and the

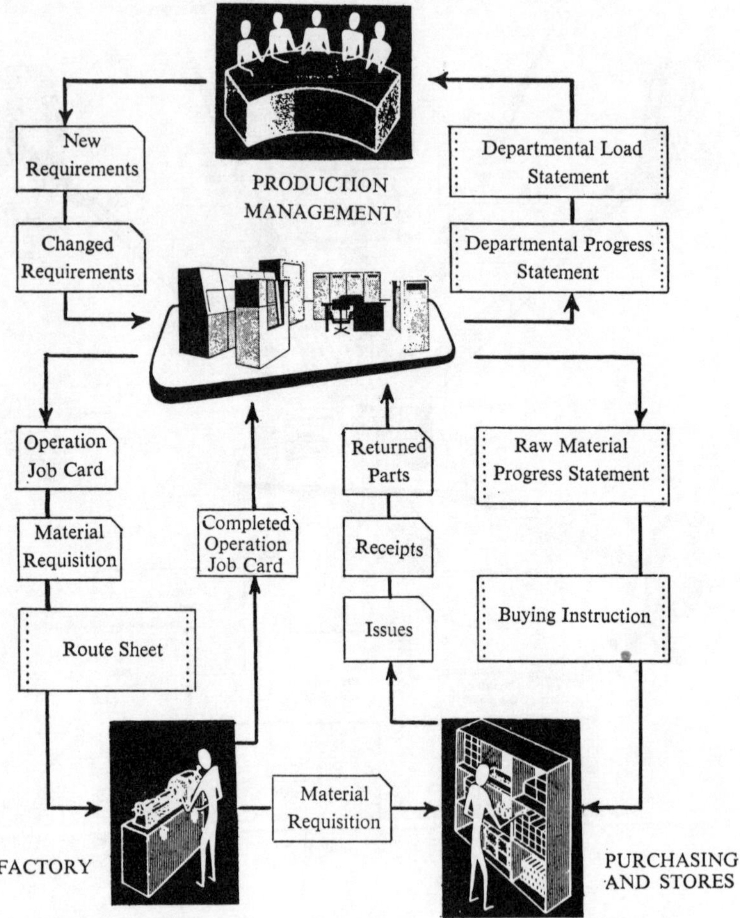

Fig. 85. Flow of Data and Documentation in a Production Control System

location on the part at which machining is to take place; the rate of part movement during machining and the speed of rotation of a tool according to the material being machined and so on. The preparation of a control tape can involve very lengthy, and often complex, calculations. An *example* system for the numerical control of machine tools is shown opposite:

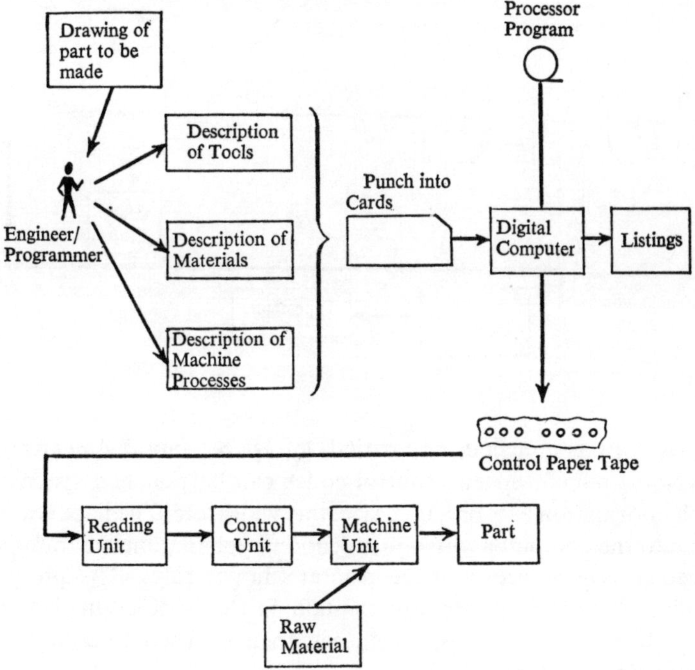

The documentation prepared by the engineer and the production of the control tape can be compared, in this example, to the production of a machine code object program from a user oriented source program with a processor program performing the conversion process.

The second example of digital computer participation in a production process is in the field of automatic typesetting and justification. Many publishing and printing companies are now realizing the potential of computers in this field.

Automatic typesetting using a computer again depends on the production of a control tape by the computer for the control of an off-line machine. It is a convention that most printed matter should be justified, that is, pages should comprise printed lines of equal length thus giving a straight margin to the right as well as the left. This is achieved by varying the space between the words and, if necessary, by 'hyphenation'. The basic process of using a computer for justification is shown overleaf:

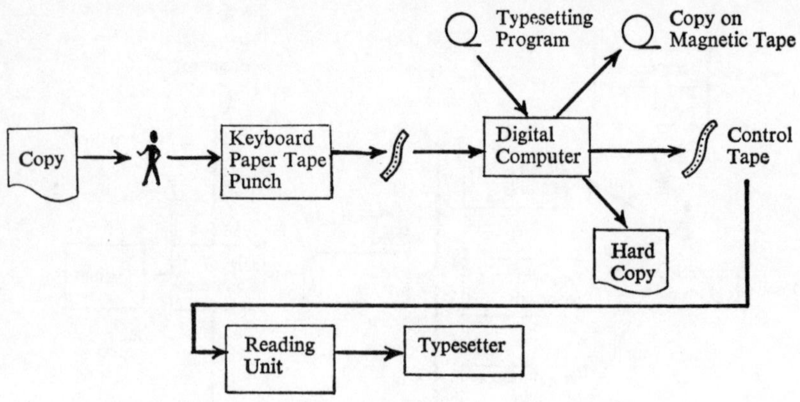

The copy is punched, unjustified, into paper tape by means of a keyboard punch. Special control codes can be punched specifying such information as fount, type size, line width, etc. The paper tape is fed into the computer with a justification/hyphenation program prepared in accordance with the printer's house rules. The program produces punched paper tape containing the justified/hyphenated copy, with control codes, which can then be used to control the typesetting machine.

The two applications described above do not require special purpose computers. The same general purpose digital computer used for the preparation of payroll, control of stock, production control, etc., can be used to produce output to control the productive processes in the plant. However, some special purpose digital computers have been developed for direct digital control (DDC). The computer receives data direct from a processing operation, and makes an assesment of the operation and outputs instructions to control the operation. The structure of a control system is usually:

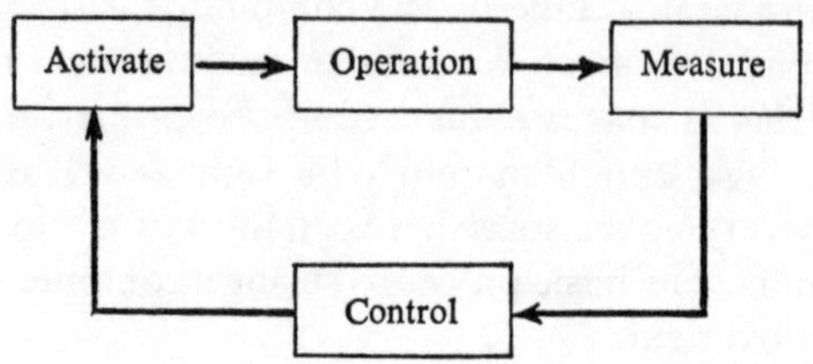

Usually, plant control systems monitor the quality and quantity of output. Various conditions such as temperature, pressure, acidity, viscosity, hardness, texture, etc., can be measured, inspected and compared with the required conditions and the plant activated automatically to achieve these conditions. In direct digital control systems, there is analogue measurement and an analogue actuator; control is exercised by a digital computer with analogue/digital converters forming a link thus:

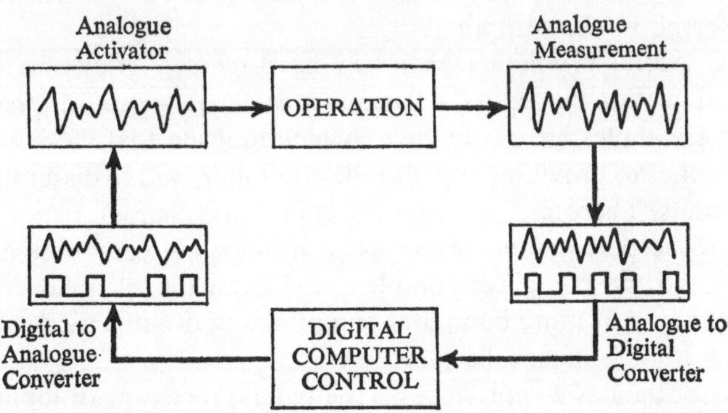

The direct digital control system provides a compromise or bridge between the purely analogue system and the purely digital system. In a purely analogue system a number of analogue computers may be required to control a process, each computer controlling one aspect of the process. With a digital computer however, all input is in a digital form and a separate program may be used for controlling each aspect of the process; thus only one computer need be employed to control all aspects. However, the range of digital measurement instruments and activators is limited and few, if any, plants can be controlled by a purely digital measurement and activation system. The DDC system, with intermediate analogue/digital converters, appears to offer the best all round solution. Providing input and output signals are matched between the converters (virtually peripheral units) and the central processor, there is, theoretically, no reason why a general purpose digital computer cannot be used for DDC systems. However, so much time may be consumed by process control, that the computer may not be available for other work as described above.

Finally, we may consider two general problems of computer usage in commerce and industry. The generalized example company structure as shown on page 228, suggests that there is considerable overlap and interaction between all functions. In production control, for example, sales forecasts, customer orders and stock despatches are vital in the preparation production programme. There is thus the case where the output from one procedure becomes the input to one, or more, other procedures. As will be seen later, the integration of systems and procedures throughout the company can be a viable proposition since considerable analysis of existing company procedures may be necessary when work undertaken by clerical effort is transferred to the computer.

The second problem which may be discussed briefly is that of communication between the various user departments and the computer. Examples have been given which indicate that there are two approaches to providing input to the computer, and to disseminating the results. There are two considerations: the characteristics of the work to be performed, the physical distance between user departments and the computer complex, and even the physical distance between two or more computer complexes between which an interchange of data must take place.

One of the basic approaches is the batch processing of input from user departments i.e. information sources. For example, the various sales offices must submit customer orders. If the processing of orders is on a daily basis, and orders are to be processed by a centralized computer unit, the orders must be sent to the computer unit, prepared for computer input, encoded on a computer input medium and processed. Similarly output, say despatch notices, invoices etc., must be dispatched to the appropriate recipients. If the time delay between the origination of the order by the customer and the processing of the order on the computer is critical, a telecommunications network may be provided. Thus, data may be transmitted from source to computer and, similarly, urgent output (e.g. dispatch notes to a number of localized depots) may be transmitted from computer to destination. At its simplest, the data transmission link may be by teleprinter. The source terminal operator types the orders on a keyboard machine, the orders are carried over telephone land lines to the destination where a receiving unit punches the orders into paper tape. This paper tape is then input to the computer for processing.

Some commercial applications call for file interrogation or '*real-time*' processing. In these applications, the time delay between the source originating data or initiating a query and the provision of a response by the computer is critical. Individual transactions and queries are considered rather than large batches of such transactions and queries. Since immediate access to the computer is required by the source and a response must be given quickly by the computer, real-time processing generally requires: a keyboard enquiry terminal at source on-line to the computer via a communications system; direct access devices, such as magnetic discs or magnetic cards, to hold the relevant files; a printer or display unit at the enquiry terminal, again on-line to the computer via a communications link to the central processor. Let us consider two simplified examples of real-time processing. The first is that of management enquiries, or real-time information retrieval. An enquiry is accepted by the computer from a remote terminal; the message is inspected and the appropriate program is activated. Files are searched and accessed according to the given key in the message. The information required is printed or displayed at the appropriate enquiry terminal for immediate inspection and action.

Alternatively, the input message, rather than merely accessing data from a file, may update the information in the file. A simple combination of the retrieval of information from a file and updating information within a file was shown in the example in Figure 64. The potential applications of real-time processing are many and varied.

There are airline reservation procedures, for example, in which the records of bookings are stored on-line to the computer. The reservations file, stored on a direct access device, can be interrogated directly from a number of remote terminals (at booking desks), vacancies on selected flights determined and reservation placed.

Finally, we must consider the use of computers for solving general commercial or industrial problems. Two problem solving methods are described here: operational research techniques and critical path analysis. It must be stressed that the techniques for solving problems described below are not peculiar to computers. Manual methods can be applied to the calculation processes in these techniques. But, as will be seen, the calculation processes are often very complex and repetitive and manual calculation is often impractical for solving large and complex problems. The results of a problem-solving attempt may become purely 'historic' because of the time delays in the calculation processes. Another disadvantage is that the probability of errors in many manual calculations is considerable.

A simple definition of operations research (O.R.) is the use of mathematical and scientific methods in managerial decision making. In commerce and industry, the primary aim of O.R. is greater efficiency in all company operations resulting in increased profitability. Just as the computer is a tool which can be used by the modern business man, so O.R. is the tool to be used by the modern manager. Operational research aids management; it suggests a course or courses of action, but the decision to take any course of action is still in the hands of management. Thus, the use of O.R. techniques does not replace management's decision-making function. Before considering some of the O.R. techniques, let us briefly consider the stages in problem solving.

It is difficult to give a formal outline of the stages of an operational research investigation but a basic approach may be considered in five stages:

1. Formulation of Problem Definition
2. Investigation and Analysis
3. Construction of a mathematical model
4. Derivation of a Solution
5. Implementation

One of the aims of O.R. is to extract the maximum of information from the minimum of data. Thus, the problem must be carefully defined so that the investigation results in only the required information being collected. Time must not be wasted on collecting irrelevant or superfluous information, yet if insufficient information is collected, the solution will be erroneous, assuming that any solution will be reached from insufficient data. When sufficient information is available it is analysed to establish the relationship between the various factors involved, and a mathematical model is created.

The model will contain a number of *variables* and it may be manipulated by applying selected values to the variables; the consequences of various courses of action, dictated by the substitution of values for variables, may be established by inspecting the 'reactions' in the model. The reactions will of course be nothing more than sets of figures. Management may thus be presented with sets of figures which indicate reactions to decisions. Naturally, the relevance or accuracy of the figures will be determined by the validity of the model.

We come now to the questions: what is the nature of the mathematical model, how is it manipulated and what is the significance of the results?

These questions may be answered by considering briefly a number of O.R. problems and techniques.

One set of problems can be given the name 'allocation'; problems of allocation have the characteristic that there are a number of operations to be performed but there are restrictions on resources or on the distribution of resources such that each operation cannot be performed in the most efficient manner.

One type of allocation problem is that of assignment. A number of discrete resources can be assigned to a number of operations or activities. A cost is associated with each resource-to-activity assignment. Resources must be assigned to activities so that overall cost is minimized.

For example, a specified number of operations are to be performed in a machine shop comprising a specific number of machines all capable of performing the operations but with varying degrees of efficiency, where efficiency may be equated with cost. Consider an instance in which there are five machines: M1, M2, M3, M4 and M5 and five operations or jobs to be performed, J1, J2, J3, J4 and J5. The cost of performing each job on each machine may be measured and given a figure, e.g. machine 1 performing job 1 = 6, machine 1 performing job 2 = 3 and so on. The costs for performing all five jobs on all five machines may be shown in a table thus:

		Jobs				
		1	2	3	4	5
Machine	1	6	3	8	4	5
	2	2	3	6	7	7
	3	3	5	4	6	6
	4	5	3	6	8	4
	5	6	7	7	6	8

Note that in this example there are 5! (meaning factorial 5 or 5 × 4 × 3 × 2 × 1) or 120 ways of assigning jobs to machines. Similarly for 15 jobs to be assigned to 15 machines there are 15! or 1,307,674,368,000 possible ways of job machine assignment. It is possible to simplify the procedure of establishing the assignment of jobs to machines on an optimum cost basis without resorting to testing each combination. The creation of the array to solve an assignment problem (resources to operations) and the inspection of the possible assignments can be accomplished on the computer.

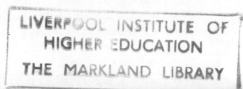

The transportation problem is an extension of the assignment problem. Given a number of origins or sources holding a number of items and a number of destinations having a requirement for items, what is the most efficient manner, in terms of transportation costs, by which destinations may be supplied from origins? There can be restrictions on the resources available at any one source and a destination may not be supplied by the same source for all resources. Thus, a destination may not be supplied from the specific source which will give the *minimum* transportation cost. The problem is to find a pattern of supply such that the requirements of all destinations may be met at the minimum *overall* transportation costs.

The data collected during the investigation stage must reflect the transportation cost of supplying each destination from each source. A model of the supply system is created and manipulated to produce the required solution.

Yet another type of allocation problem-solving technique is 'linear' programming. In fact, both the assignment and the transportation problem are simple applications using linear programming techniques. However, these two problems were identified by particular characteristics, i.e. the assignment of discrete resources to a number of operations and the supply of resources from origin and destination. Linear programming can be applied to more generalized problems in which the resources are assumed to be freely divisible and any combination of resources may be required for any activity. For example, consider a factory producing three products and using three machines. The characteristic of the plant and product are shown below.

Product	Profit per Unit	Time to Produce Item			Machine Availability (hours per day)		
		Machine 1	Machine 2	Machine 3	Machine 1	Machine 2	Machine 3
A	£2	2		1			
B	£3	1	3		8	10	10
C	£5		2	3			

A production program is to be determined which gives the maximum profit.

This problem has the following characteristics which apply to problems to be solved by linear programming techniques.

Firstly, there is a number of unknown quantities or variables, in this case the number of products A, B and C which are to be produced. Secondly, there are constraints such as the number of hours that machines 1, 2 and 3 are available for production. Thirdly, there must be an optimizing function; in the above example this is the maximizing of profits within the limits of the constraints.

The complexity of the calculations to solve the problem will depend on the number of constraints and the number of variables. The calculation is an iterative process, i.e. a repetitive process in which a final result is reached after repeating a calculation procedure a number of times, each time obtaining a result which is nearer the optimum than the previous one. It is impractical to solve complex problems by hand but linear programming solutions are easily obtained by using a computer.

There are many other O.R. techniques but one, that of simulation, will serve to round off this brief discussion on the relevance of computers to O.R. and the relevance of O.R. to modern business. Simulation is basically imitation; it is the creation of a model which represents on a smaller scale a situation in the real world. We are all familiar with experimentation by model; for example, the aircraft designer studies the action of a model in a wind tunnel, the ship designer studies the action of a model in a water tank simulating conditions at sea and so on. In both these cases, of course, the model is created by building a physical replica. However, systems or operational procedures may be simulated by means of sets of rules and mathematical relations.

Consider the problem in which we require to know the probability of scoring a selected number (say eight) with a perfect pair of dice. There are three ways of finding the answer. We may acquire two perfect dice and throw them many thousands of times, noting the number of times that eight results. We may calculate the probability mathematically (i.e. by mathematical analysis) or we may simulate the conditions of throwing the dice by using random number tables. In the latter case, two numbers in the range of one to six are picked at random thousands of times and the number of instances in which the sum is eight is noted. With this simple example, the use of simulation by a mathematical model is easily illustrated. Obviously, it would be extremely cumbersome to throw the dice many thousands of times just as it would be extremely inconvenient and costly to build a complete ship for *initial* experimentation in hull design! In some cases, mathematical analysis is impractical; insufficient data may be available or existing theory may be too incomplete or impractical to apply to the problem. Simulation therefore is a convenient method of experimentation and problem solving when mathematical analysis has been attempted and abandoned. Naturally, simulation will not automatically produce an optimal solution; the user who creates the model must apply his selected policies and select the policy which appears to produce the most acceptable results.

Although simple calculations can be made by means of desk calculators using random number tables and pencil and paper, obviously computers are a great asset in performing the repetitive work once a simulation has been programmed for a digital computer. The development of a simulation program requires considerable effort but the development of general software by, for example, manufacturers, is tending to relieve the programmer of much of the coding work, etc.

Simulation on a computer provides management with a laboratory for testing new ideas such as the organization of plant and labour in a manufacturing process or the behaviour of a proposed stock control system and so on.

Another application in which the modern digital computer acts as an aid to management is in critical path analysis; one technique will be considered here – PERT (Programme Evaluation Review Technique).

Many projects consist of a number of interdependent activities. PERT is a technique for planning, co-ordinating and progressing these interdependent activities to achieve the desired objective. For example, it can be applied to the building of a house, a battleship or a spacecraft; it can be applied to the installation of a complex defence communications network or to installing a computer or even producing a film.

The basic elements in using PERT are the *activity* and the *event*. An activity is a time or resource consuming element in the execution of a project. An event is a meaningful accomplishment in the execution of a project. Although it can be recognized at a particular point in time, an event does not consume time or resources. A project is analysed in terms of the activities to be undertaken to enable it to be completed. A network, showing the relationship between the various activities and events is drawn up. The network will resemble a road map with the roads or lines representing activities and the towns or nodes representing events. A single activity, commenced and terminated by events, is shown below.

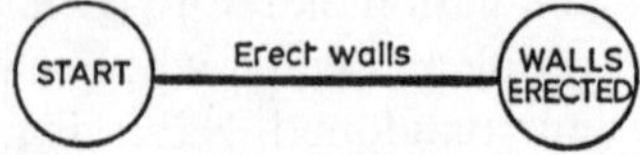

The activity, i.e. the erection of walls, will take time and resources while the event, 'walls erected', merely identifies the accomplishment of the activity. Now let us consider a very simple network for making a cup of tea; see Figure 86. For the moment, resources may be ignored and only time may be taken as being significant. The commencement of one activity is restrained or restricted by the completion of another activity. For example, the activity 'pouring milk into cups' cannot take place until after the event 'cups available'. The broken lines represent dummy activities which do not consume time but place a restraint on the commencement of an activity until another activity has been completed.

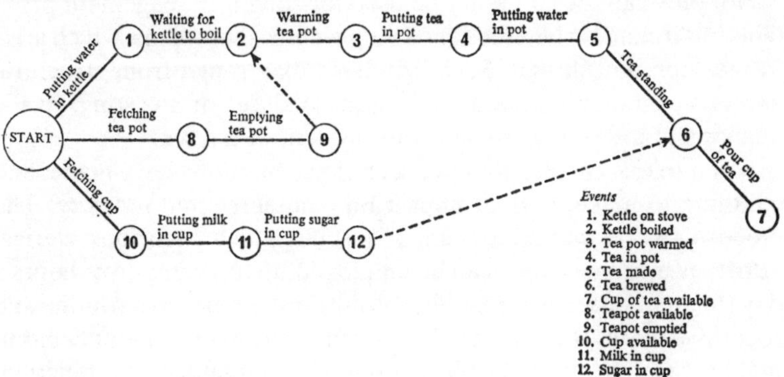

Fig. 86. An Example PERT Network

Once the network has been drawn, and the activities have been qualified by the time or resources consumed by the activity, the network can be processed and much important information gathered. If the information on the network is, say, punched into cards or paper tape and processed by a PERT Program, the critical path may be established. The duration of each activity is noted in terms of weeks and days by adding up the times allocated to the activities along all the paths in the network. (Note there are three paths in Figure 86.) The PERT program can calculate : (a) the shortest time in which the project can be completed, (b) the critical activities and (c) the 'ancillary' activities. The critical path is the route through the network which takes the longest time to complete and is therefore equivalent to the shortest time to complete the project. If a date is given to the start event, the date for each of the events given on the network can be calculated by the PERT program from the duration of the activities. In fact, PERT accepts three time estimates for activities;

optimistic-time, most-likely-time and pessimistic-time. The critical path is calculated on the weighted average of these estimates. Once the critical path has been established, the PERT program can print out a list of those activities which lie on the critical path (b) above and those which do not (c) above.

The PERT program can also calculate the *slack* time which is an estimate of the time that the activities can be delayed before another critical path is established. In addition to a time analysis, analyses may be made which will help to ensure an economic use of a company's resources under management control and to minimize possible bottlenecks.

Not only can the computer be used for solving management problems but it can also be used for solving technical problems which arise in research and design. Such problems may range from structural analysis of a dam or the metallurgical analyses of a casting, to the analyses of a drainage or sewerage system in a town.

So far in this chapter we have seen that computers have made, and continue to make, a great impact on commerce and industry. The modern digital computer can undertake much laborious clerical effort; as machines, they can be employed up to twenty-four hours a day (maintenance and reliability permitting) on the most routine and repetitive work. It can be a valuable aid to the management decision making function, for while the computer cannot replace this function, more manageable and precise information can be provided as a result of file processing, e.g. statistical and general summaries. The use of real-time processing and telecommunications especially by employing remote enquiry terminals, brings the computer closer and closer to the user at source or operation it is controlling. It has been seen too that the computer can be valuable as a management decision aid by making use of operational research techniques. Software packages for performing standard operations are becoming more important in spreading the use of computers in commerce and industry since potential computer users may well be deterred by the amount of programming effort that must be expended; more will be said about this later.

COMPANIES WITH COMPUTERS

Having seen the role of computers in commerce and industry, we may now investigate such topics as 'why do some organizations employ computers while others do not?', 'what sort of companies use computers?', 'what sort of people are engaged in computer work?' and so on.

The hardest question to answer factually is why and how does a business organization make the decision to install a computer. Note that the term 'install' is used in the previous sentence; there are many ways in which a business organization may use a computer. For example, computer time may be bought from a special computer bureau or from an existing user with spare computer time. Alternatively a number of organizations may jointly purchase a computer, which is placed in one, or a specially created, organization. Finally of course, a company may buy (direct or hire purchase), or lease, a computer from a manufacturer.

Once a company decides to consider using a computer, a feasibility study is made. This may be made with the aid of consultants or selected computer manufacturers. Obviously, it must be established whether or not a computer is a viable technical proposition, i.e. can the required work be performed by a computer. The answer is invariably yes, but at a price. The computer must, of course, be able to perform the work undertaken by manual methods; not only must it do this but it must undertake the work more efficiently and effectively. Justifying the installation of a computer on economic grounds is, of course, an important factor. Firstly, there can be a comparison of the cost of the manual data processing system with the cost of a proposed computer or electronic data processing system. However, this is an extremely narrow outlook. For example, to compare the cost of employing x clerks at a rate of y pounds per hour to perform job A for z hours consuming materials costing w pounds, with the cost of employing a computer to perform the same job in terms of the cost of the computer and associated staff and equipment at y pounds per hour for z hours, consuming materials valued at w pounds. This may give a misleading impression, especially if job A is only one of many to be performed on the computer. One would also have to consider the financial benefits (or otherwise) obtained as a *result* of employing electronic data processing. (There may be a question of survival against competitors who already have computers!) With more timely reports of greater accuracy, the extraction of relevant information from large volumes of data and improved management control, a number of benefits may be obtained. For example, increased management control can result in reduced costs, increased sales, more effective control over existing products and more reliable assessment of potential of proposed products. A better service to customers as a result of less time to process orders and to service products will enhance the company's image and so on.

If a business organization decides that a computer will be beneficial what range of computers are available and how can a choice of machine be made? Ideally, the business organization should be able to define the requirements in reasonable detail and then select the machine which is best suited to these requirements. With the introduction of the 'series' concept of computers, the prospective user has a wide choice. Manufacturers are tending to design and market a comprehensive range of central processors and peripherals. If the user selects his equipment from the range of one manufacturer, and should wish to expand his computer configuration at a later date, he may select further compatible units from the manufacturer's range. Thus we may say, quite simply, that modern digital computers come in all shapes and all sizes! Three example configurations are shown in Plate 5. Given a number of computer configurations from one or more manufacturers all capable technically of performing the user's work, not only will a user compare capital cost or monthly rental of the computer equipment, but also the range and suitability of software, the quality of maintenance service and general customer support offered by manufacturer, the cost of housing the equipment and, if necessary, the cost of installing special power supplies, air conditioning, etc.

Assuming that a company has decided to install a computer on a rental or outright purchase basis, what sort of organization must be established to service the computer and where in the company will the organization exist? It is extremely difficult to generalize on either point. Consider, for example, a manufacturing company with the traditional functions of production marketing, accounting and research and development. We have seen that a constant interchange of information takes place between the various functions, and data will be processed in each area of responsibility. One course of action may well be to place the computer in the area of responsibility, production or accounting, etc., which makes most demands on the computer. Alternatively, a 'central computing department' may be established outside the existing areas of responsibility; the production, marketing, accounting and research and development functions may then use the computer on a company service basis.

A more pertinent point for consideration here is the type of personnel functions that must be established to install and run the computer.

To answer this question we must first take a closer look at the tasks associated with the development and implementation of a computer-based system.

The development of a system is a time consuming, expensive and complex job. To produce a successful computer system requires the close co-operation of all user personnel and the data processing technicians. The term 'user' in this context means all people associated with running the business: its management, clerical staff and manual workers. A successful computer system can be defined as one which meets the following three criteria:

(i) *economic feasibility:* that it is worthwhile from a business point of view to put the application on a computer in a particular way;
(ii) *technical viability:* that it is possible to run the application on a computer that way, given the current state of hardware/software technology and the expertise in the company;
(iii) *operational suitability:* that the system is geared to the aptitude, attitude, knowledge and experience of all user staff who will work with it.

An example systems development cycle is shown in Figure 87. This shows eleven basic tasks that must be done from the first inception of the system, through its development, to its implementation, and thereafter to its operational running and support. These eleven tasks can be grouped for administrative convenience and management control, into four project phases as shown in Figure 87.

The first task, as its name implies, is a clear definition of the business problems from the user's point of view, and an implied request for assistance in solving these problems. This means that the relevant user managers must look first to their *business*, not to the technical capability of the digital computer. The Problem Definition/User Request forms the basic terms of reference for the remainder of the project work and is thus, perhaps, the most critical task in the whole project. It requires the user management to do the following:

(i) Define clearly the objectives of any new system.
(ii) Study the current corporate environment to determine the problems which must be solved if the objectives are to be met, now and in the future.

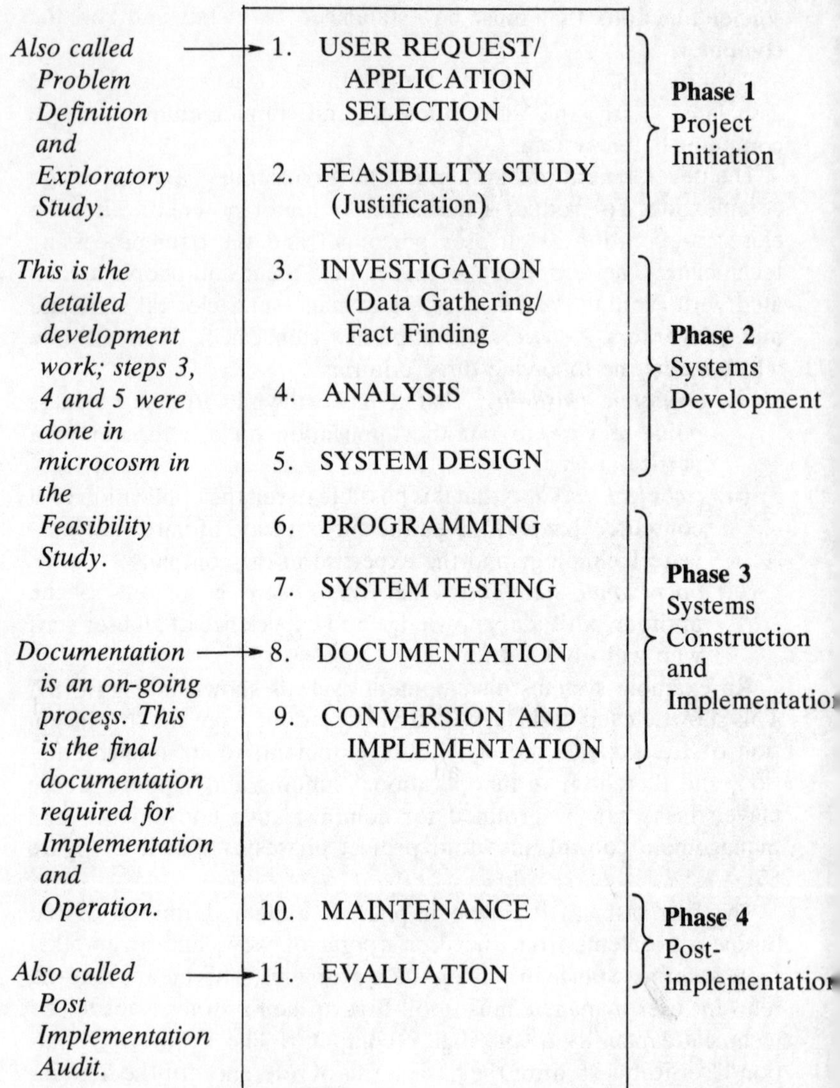

Note that there can be considerable overlap between steps in the development process.

Also, authorization and approval checkpoints are not shown.

Fig. 87. Systems Development Cycle

(iii) Identify the potential benefits of solving the problems, as in (ii), and thereby meeting the objectives, as in (i).

(iv) Establish the ground rules for the development of a solution, such as cost, timescale, potential solutions to be evaluated.

If task 1 defines the *problems*, task 2 determines the *solution*. The Feasibility Study will include an investigation of the user area, an analysis of the results and the design, in outline, of possible solutions. Note that because the project is still speculative at this stage, all work carried out in this task is in outline: a company cannot be expected to commit extensive effort and resources (and therefore money) until a prima facie case is established that a computer can indeed help. Each solution is described in the report together with an appropriate development plan. From this a cost/benefit analysis is derived. If the user opts for a computer-based solution, then the detailed project work can be planned and performed.

It is essential that the computer system works within the user environment, that it is geared to business needs, business methods, business people and business organization. Thus, the next two tasks, 3 and 4, are a detailed investigation and analysis of the user environment: people, procedures and data. The information from these tasks feeds systems design.

Systems design is usually done in two stages: first business/outline, then technical/detail. It is the definition of *all* manual procedures and computer programs. The latter includes the description of the content, format and media of all inputs, files and outputs. This is documented in a System Specification, the definitive description of the new system. User acceptance at this stage is essential; agreement of the System Specification is the final go/no go decision point before really big amounts of money are spent on the actual construction and implementation of the new system.

For each program in the system, a Program Specification must be prepared. This is a clear and unambiguous description of *what* the program must do and the data (contents, format, organization, media, etc.) available to be processed. The programmer's job is to decide *how* the program will do the required processing. This is achieved through logic design, coding, testing, etc., as described in Chapter 4. Having proved each program individually the whole system must now be tested.

Systems Testing, task 7, establishes that all the programs will work together. Suite or linkage testing attempts to prove that the output from one program is acceptable to another, that a file created by one program is accessible by another program. Not only are the computer programs tested, but *all* the manual procedures as well.

Documentation is shown in Figure 87 as one task (8). It is, however, an on-going process which must be done during and at the end of each task in the systems development cycle. Task 8 is *final* documentation before the system is ready for live running.

Task 9, Conversion and Implementation, can be very expensive indeed. It includes all the work necessary prior to the changeover to the computer system and the actual cut-over itself. Conversion can include:

(i) preparation and issue of user procedure manuals;
(ii) user trainer in new methods;
(iii) printing and distribution of new forms;
(iv) installation of new equipment;
(v) file conversion, e.g., translation of paper-based files to magnetic files.

The actual cut-over to the new system must be very carefully planned. If possible the impact of the introduction of the new system will be cushioned by *parallel* running. This means that the existing and new system will be run side by side until the new files are established and the staff are familiar with the new methods. The old system is then discontinued and the new system runs alone. Alternatively, the new system may be introduced by *pilot* implementation. The whole of the new system is introduced into part of the organization. This enables the system to be nursed into the company without major disruptions to the whole of its business activities. On some occasions, however, neither parallel nor pilot running may be possible in which case *immediate* conversion must be used: literally, the existing system is abandoned at one minute and the new system is adopted the next.

Tasks 1 to 9 are thus concerned with the development and implementation of the computer system; 10 and 11 are concerned with the post-implementation tasks.

Maintenance, task 10, can be a very expensive, time-consuming process. It is the modification and enhancement of the operational system to keep it in step with changes in the business and technical environments. There are many causes of maintenance, such as;

(i) bugs (errors) in the system which were not detected during testing;
(ii) changes in the hardware/software available;
(iii) new business methods;

(iv) 'tuning' the system to make it more efficient;

(v) user realization of how the system can be further exploited.

The final task is the Post-Implementation Audit. This is a review of the system after it has been running for a significant period of time. It assesses the system on the three grounds of economic feasibility, technical viability and operational suitability. The review may lead to an enhancement or major redevelopment of the system, which means that the whole cycle is repeated.

It can thus be seen that a considerable amount of work must be done to design and implement a computer-based system. What type of staff will work on these tasks?

Most companies establish a Data Processing Department under a Data Processing Manager. In this department are all the technical personnel who will undertake the research and development activities in the system development cycle. It will also include the operations facilities: the people and hardware to run the new systems.

The role of the user in systems development must not be overlooked: experience has shown that without user participation, a successful computer system just cannot be developed. There is a strong case for the creation of a 'steering committee', comprising the senior and line managers of departments who will utilize, directly or indirectly, computer time. Without the direction of senior management, computer systems development will become an isolated 'technical-problem solving' activity, remote from the realities of business.

The organization of the Data Processing Department will depend on the size and structure of the company and the types of systems being developed. Most organizations make a distinction between the work of a systems analyst and that of a programmer. The role of the programmer can be defined reasonably precisely: it starts with the receipt of a Program Specification and finishes with the handover of a coded, tested and documented program. Programmers will also provide technical assistance in changing the programs during subsequent maintenance.

The role of the systems analyst is, however, much harder to define. The term systems analyst is probably the most misleading title in data processing. Examination of the systems development cycle in Figure 87 shows, for example, that he is variously an investigator (task 3), an analyst (task 4), a designer (task 5), a trouble-shooter (task 7), a resource manipulator (task 9). He is the vital link between the non-technical user and highly technical specialist, such as the programmer. His role is to interpret user business requirements into computer technical terms.

The very large organizations (who can afford it!) recognize that it is unrealistic to assume that one person can be thoroughly proficient in *all* these tasks. A proliferation of job titles then results; an example is shown in Figure 88. The medium-sized organization will probably strike a balance between the simple analyst/programmer approach and the multiplicity of functions as in Figure 88.

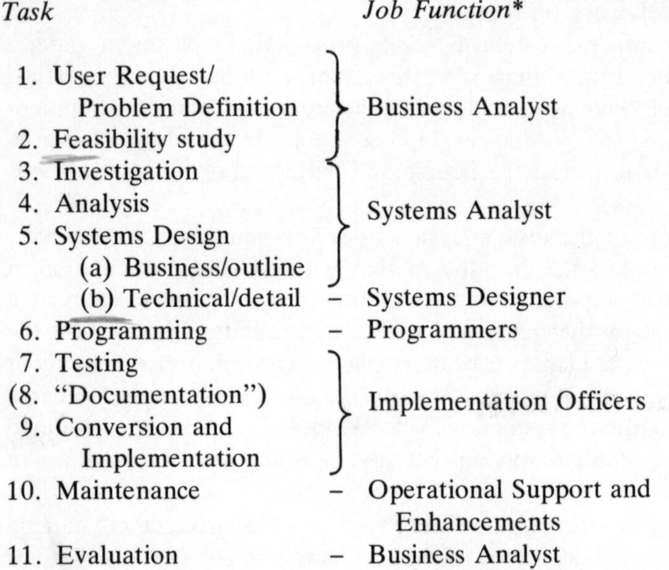

Task	*Job Function**
1. User Request/ Problem Definition 2. Feasibility study	Business Analyst
3. Investigation 4. Analysis 5. Systems Design (a) Business/outline	Systems Analyst
(b) Technical/detail	– Systems Designer
6. Programming	– Programmers
7. Testing (8. "Documentation") 9. Conversion and Implementation	Implementation Officers
10. Maintenance	– Operational Support and Enhancements
11. Evaluation	– Business Analyst

* Note that "Job Function" shows primary responsibility; *assistance* may be given by many other functions during each task.

Fig. 88. Data Processing Department Job Functions – Large Organization

7. The Use of Computers for Scientific Work

Computers are today accepted as an everyday tool for the scientist and engineer. Historically, the search for good aids to calculation has always been motivated by the scientist rather than the business man. The first computers were developed for scientific work – their application in commerce was a later step. As early as 1671, Leibniz, the German philosopher and mathematician, was writing:

> . . . the astronomers surely will not have to continue to exercise the patience which is required for computation. It is this which deters them from computing or correcting tables, . . . working on hypotheses, and from discussions of observations with each other. For it is unworthy of excellent men to lose hours like slaves in the labour of calculation, which could be safely relegated to someone else if the machine were used.

In 1876, Kelvin was writing in the same vein of 'substituting brass for brain in the great mechanical labour of calculation'. Let us first look at the general characteristics of computing in scientific work.

Characteristics of Scientific Computing

In Chapter One, a basic distinction was made between commercial and scientific computer applications. This was on the grounds that calculation, or complex calculation, was the major characteristic of scientific work and input/output and file storage were the major characteristic of commercial work. In Chapter Six, however, the relevance of mathematics and complex calculation in commercial work was demonstrated by the introduction of 'management science'. This chapter is concerned with the computer as a general purpose problem solving machine in scientific research.

Early computers were developed almost exclusively for performing complex calculations to solve mathematical problems. For example, Eniac (*E*lectronic *N*umerical *I*ntegrator and *C*alculator) built at the University of Pennsylvania during the Second World War was used exclusively for calculations. Relatively slow unsophisticated peripheral units could be used and the major area of concern was the development of the central processor with large internal storage and rapid speed of operation.

There are further grounds for distinguishing the 'scientific' from the 'commercial' applications of computers. Relatively few mathematical or scientific tasks require, by their nature, to be repeated in their entirety. Considerable preparatory work may be necessary before a mathematical data processing task can be performed on a computer. Once the job is run on the computer successfully it is not usually repeated. In commercial applications, however, there are many repetitive processes. Thus, for example, once a payroll program has been written, master files created in computer form and a procedure for collecting and encoding raw input data established, the payroll program is run as often as is required.

Perhaps of greatest importance is the difference in the relationship between the computer and the commercial or scientific users. We have seen that in the commercial field, the computer cuts across many areas of responsibility in a company. Many people are involved with a computer project; the systems analyst interprets management's requirements for a proposed system and, in turn, the programmers interpret the systems analyst's specification for the programs and so on. In many scientific applications, however, the problem can be planned, operated and results deduced, under the control of only the scientists or engineers. In some cases, the originator of the problem may define it in detail and prepare the program himself using a programming language. This requires, of course, that the user, besides being fully conversant with his own field, must be conversant with computer techniques and programming.

Before considering some scientific applications of computers, let us examine the characteristcs of a modern digital computer which make it an indispensible tool for the scientist and engineer. The relevance of high speed of processing and large storage capacities has been demonstrated earlier. In addition, the modern computer can deal with very large and very small numbers at high speed.

A basic process may be repeated at high speed and, with the aid of program or instruction modification, one set of instructions may be used to operate on many items of data. Two examples may be given to illustrate the relevance of these two factors.

Firstly, let us consider the computation of square roots; suppose it is required to find $\sqrt{75}$. One method by which this problem may be solved is as follows. We make an intelligent guess as to the approximate result. In this case we guess 8 and the division

$$75 \div 8 = 9$$

shows the 8 is too small and 9 is too large. However, it is reasonable for the next trial to take the arithmetic average of 8 and 9,

$\frac{8 + 9}{2} = 8{\cdot}5$. On the next attempt

$$75 \div 8{\cdot}5 = 8{\cdot}82$$

the result is still to large and we thus repeat the process

$$\frac{8{\cdot}82 + 8{\cdot}5}{2} = 8{\cdot}66$$

$$75 \div 8{\cdot}66 = 8{\cdot}6605$$

The process is repeated until the desired degree of accuracy is reached.

Figure 89 shows a general flowchart of a computer program for evaluating the square root of a given number, x. This is based on the iterative method described above (commonly known as 'Newton's process'). Note that it consists of a number of calculation steps such as 'COMPUTE $b = a - y_0$'. The first test (branch) is inspecting the difference between two successive approximations. If the difference is smaller than the acceptable error e (where e has been given by the user as a parameter), the process is stopped (Figure on page 260).

Our second example is the solving of quadratic equations. Suppose we are seeking a root of the equation

$$x^2 = 5{\cdot}6 - 14 = 0$$

This equation may be written as

$$x(x + 5{\cdot}6) = 14$$

and thus

$$x = \frac{14}{x + 5{\cdot}6}$$

This may be rewritten as

$$x_{n+1} = \frac{14}{x_n = 5{\cdot}6}$$

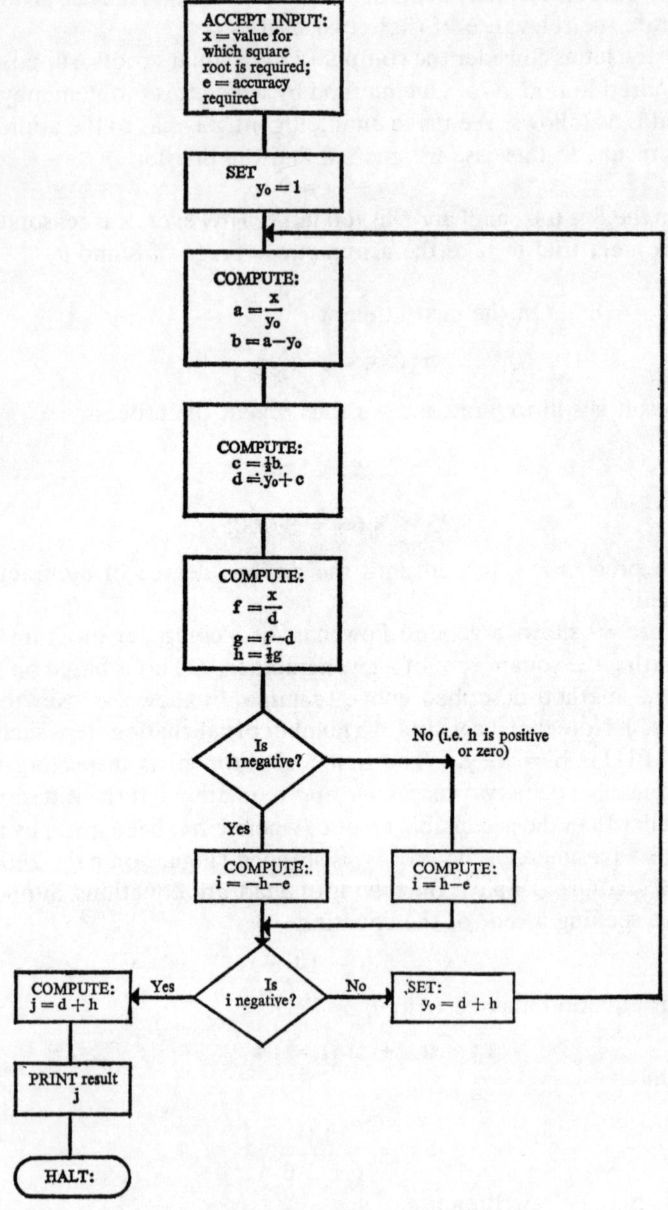

Fig. 89. Evaluation of Square Root

Now, we may attempt to guess the solution and our guess is, say, 2. Setting n = 0, the guess is substituted for x_0 on the right:

$$x_1 = \frac{14}{2 + 5{\cdot}6} = 1{\cdot}84$$

If the initial guess is exact, then x_1 will equal x_0; in the example this is not the case since x_0, 2, does not equal x_1, 1·84. Substituting x_1, we have

$$x_2 = \frac{14}{1{\cdot}84 + 5{\cdot}6} = 1{\cdot}87$$

This process is repeated until a result of sufficient accuracy is obtained. For example:

$$x_0 = 2$$

$$x_1 = \frac{14}{2 + 5{\cdot}6} = 1{\cdot}84$$

$$x_2 = \frac{14}{1{\cdot}84 + 5{\cdot}6} = 1{\cdot}88$$

$$x_3 = \frac{14}{1{\cdot}87 + 5{\cdot}6} = 1{\cdot}875$$

$$x_4 = \frac{14}{1{\cdot}875 + 5{\cdot}6} = 1{\cdot}874$$

$$x_5 = \frac{14}{1{\cdot}874 + 5{\cdot}6} = 1{\cdot}873$$

$$x_6 = \frac{14}{1{\cdot}873 + 5{\cdot}6} = 1{\cdot}8734$$

$$x_7 = \frac{14}{1{\cdot}8734 + 5{\cdot}6} = 1{\cdot}8733$$

or 1·873 carried to four significant figures.

This process is known as *iteration*, i.e. repetition using different numbers, each repetition producing a more accurate result. The relevance of a computer in performing iterative processes is clear. A basic number of instructions are created to perform one simple calculation. This set of instructions is then repeated as many times as required.

In the realm of science, computers have not only replaced the tedious work of calculation; new techniques have been developed which enhance the methods of calculation. Computers have ceased to be a luxury and have become a necessity. Computers have made, for example, a great impact on the field of numerical analysis. This field is concerned with the control of errors, operations on matrices, methods of successive approximation to solutions and so on.

Methods of Applying Computers in Scientific Work

Some years ago I was preparing a paper on the impact of the computer in scientific development. During the research period I traced a large number of papers describing various applications of computers. However, over the years there were less and less references to the special application of computers. This did not mean that computers had ceased to be used. Rather, the computer had been accepted as an everyday tool, so much so that it now no longer merited special reference in scientific and technical journals.

Beyond saying that the computer is a problem solving device for the scientist and engineer, and indicating the reason for the significance of computers, it is difficult to describe applications without going deeply into their scientific background.

In the field of physics, there are many areas in which the computer can be employed. As a tool in the hand of the physicist, the computer can be used to solve quantum mechanical calculations. Calculations of electron (and other charged-particle) paths inside synchrotrons and wave guides have been performed by computer.

The research work of chemists has been advanced rapidly with the aid of computers. For example, in the advanced analysis of the structure of proteins by X-ray crystallography computers have become invaluable.

In the social sciences, statistical analysis by computer is becoming standard practice. In economics, national economic models for simulation purposes have been created and manipulated on computers.

One application of computers in scientific work has been in the use of input/output terminals for basic calculations. For many years the tools of the scientist for calculation consisted of reference tables, slide rules, or desk-top calculators or very small computers. With the advent of terminals, such as input/output typewriters and visual display units, the computing power of the modern computer has been brought into the scientist's office. An example of the organization of computing facilities in a scientific environment is shown in Figure 90. In this case typewriter terminals are provided at strategic points in the building; these are linked to a very large and powerful central processor with massive file/backing storage. All scientists thus have access to a powerful computer, in much the same way as they had access to a desk-top calculator. The scientists can input numeric data, together with a processing program, and receive the results back in their own office. Subject to inspection of the results, further data may be input and processed. The central processor will be controlled by an operating system (as described on page 203) which will monitor the interrupts and ensure that the appropriate results are output on the right terminal. In many instances, programs will be repeated as new data becomes available. In this case it will not be necessary to input the processing program for each set of data to be processed. The program is entered once; the user gives the program a name, let us say 'PROCX/', and the operating system is requested by an appropriate message to hold the program in the program library. The program library is the collection of all programs in the system which may be required more than once. The library is held on the file/backing store, such as magnetic drums and discs. As the operating system inserts a program in the library, it builds up a catalogue of program name/file storage location. Let us suppose that more data is to be processed using 'PROCX/'. The procedure followed by the user scientist will be as follows. The scientist goes to a terminal with his input data noted on a piece of paper. Let us suppose that the input data consists of three values, a, b, and c; these three values are to be subjected to considerable calculation processes. The scientist is interested in one result, d, which is calculated by the program 'PROCX/'. The scientist presses the 'INTERRUPT' key on the terminal typewriter. The operating system detects the interrupt in the central processor, and sends a message back to the terminal; 'IDENTIFICATION?'. The scientist types in his name and reference number. This is accepted by the operating system and checked for authenticity. This is a basic security procedure; the message will also be used for accounting purposes to record the use of machine time to a project. When the operating system has processed this message and it has been found to be in order a message is typed back to the user notifying him that he may proceed with his job. The user types in his request for a program, together with a suitable instruction to the operating system to find and load that program. For example, the message could be: 'LOAD PROGRAM PROCX/.' The operating system locates the program in

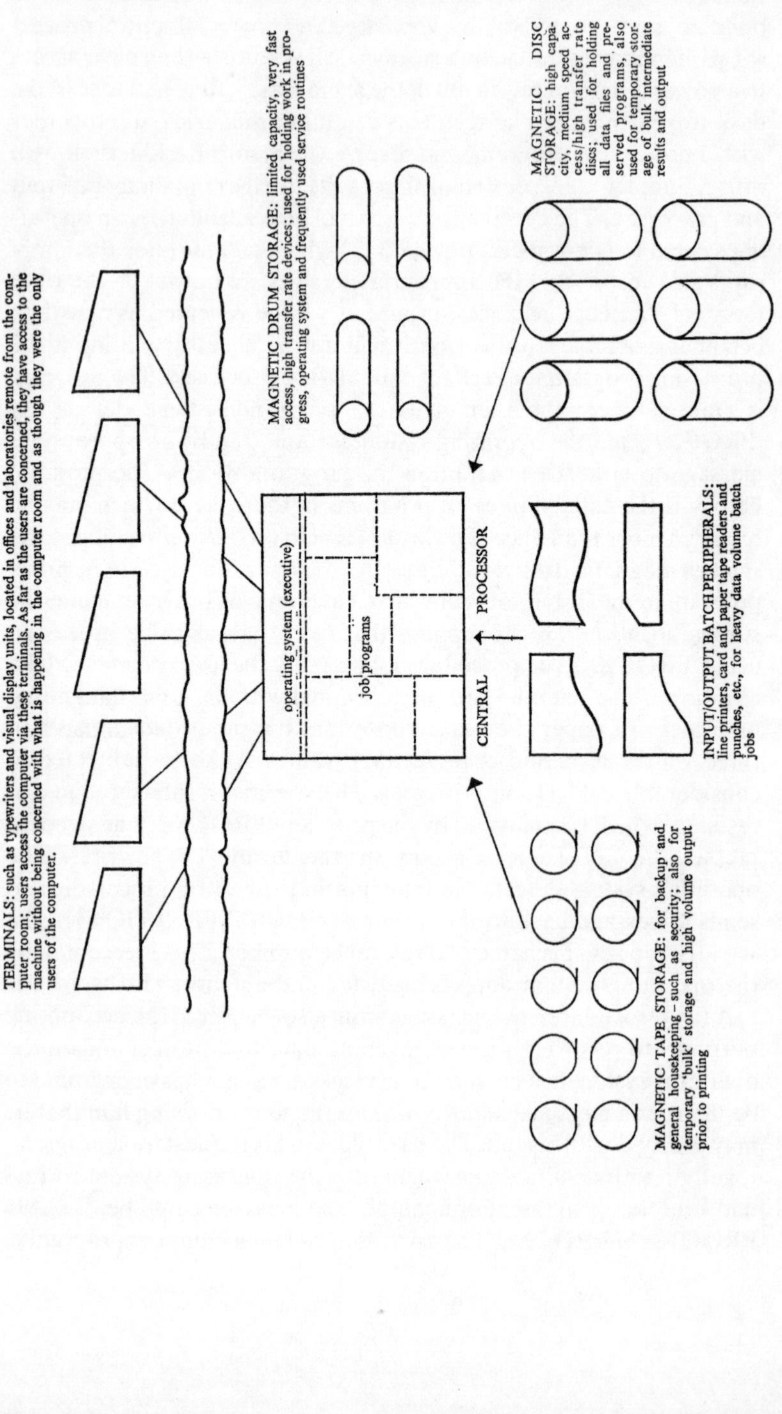

TERMINALS: such as typewriters and visual display units, located in offices and laboratories remote from the computer room; users access the computer via these terminals. As far as the users are concerned, they have access to the machine without being concerned with what is happening in the computer room and as though they were the only users of the computer.
operating system (executive)
job programs
CENTRAL PROCESSOR
MAGNETIC DRUM STORAGE: limited capacity, very fast access, high transfer rate devices; used for holding work in progress, operating system and frequently used service routines
MAGNETIC TAPE STORAGE: for backup and general housekeeping – such as security; also for temporary 'bulk' storage and high volume output prior to printing
INPUT/OUTPUT BATCH PERIPHERALS: line printers, card and paper tape readers and punches, etc., for heavy data volume batch jobs
MAGNETIC DISC STORAGE: high capacity, medium speed access/high transfer rate discs; used for holding all data files and preserved programs, also used for temporary storage of bulk intermediate results and output

Fig. 90. On-line Working in a Scientific Environment

the library via the appropriate catalogues, and reads that program into core. When the program is loaded the operating system notifies the user accordingly; e.g. a message is typed out at the terminal: 'PROGRAM PROXC/ LOADED.' The user then gives the operating system a message so that the program can begin: 'GO PROGRAM PROCX/.' Control is now passed to the processing program. The first action taken by the program will be to request the appropriate input data from the user. An example of the messages which will pass between user and program on the terminal will be as follows:

```
*PROCX/DATA REQUIRED AS FOLLOWS
*VALUE A?
        0·0089765
*VALUE B?
        3456·0098756
*VALUE C?
        0·000567
*WAIT
*VALUE D = 5674·000789
        DELETE PROCX/
*PROCX/ DELETED
        CLOSE
*TERMINAL 45 LOGGING OUT
```

In the above list of messages, those which were typed under the control of the user program (PROCX/) and the operating system are prefixed by an asterisk. Those values and messages which are typed in by the user are indented. After each generated message has been typed, the user checks the typing and presses an 'INPUT' key. This causes the messages to be actioned by the program. The program thus requests the input data from the user, the user types it in, checks it and presses the input key. The program calculates the required result and sends it to the terminal. The user examines it and decides that he does not wish to do any further processing at this time. He therefore types in a message deleting the program. He does not wish to use any other program so he types in an instruction to close down his terminal. The operating system acknowledges this message and terminates the link.

This method of processing is called *on-line* working. It can be seen that through the use of simple messages the user scientist has access to a very powerful computing aid. The central computer services all the calculation requirements of the establishment. As described in Chapter Three, however, input/output terminals are relatively slow peripherals. The quality of the results produced must depend to a certain extent on the typing capabilities of the user. If there are many values to be input (such as the results of many experimental observations) then terminals become slow and rather unwieldy. Where there is a large volume of input, therefore, the user scientist will use the more conventional means of *batch processing*. That is, the results of the experiment will be recorded on forms, and the contents of these documents punched into cards or paper tape and processed in the normal manner in the computer room.

The modern scientist is not only concerned with complex calculations. More and more, the volume of data which must be collected and processed is creating administrative and data handling problems. In this respect, the scientific uses of the computer are similar to those described in the previous chapter. Consider the following example. A group of scientists are working on an analysis of the effects of using certain chemical sprays in agriculture. During the development of the chemical products, considerable research and tests will take place. Before release, however, field trials must take place in which the sprays are used in a real life environment. During the field trials considerable data will be generated, all of which must be coded and processed. The actual processing may be quite simple, in terms of the mathematical techniques used. The problem will be one of data handling rather than complexity of calculation. For example, the sprays must be used in a hundred selected sites. Field research workers will record the effect of the sprays at the same time as carefully documenting information about the environment in which they are being used. These conditions can include:

soil
climate
irrigation
flora/fauna
etc.

The results of the application of the sprays must be correlated with the characteristics of the site in which it is used. The computer will be useful here in the actual handling of the data; the problem is one of volume and correlation of many items of data rather than the actual process of correlation itself. File storage and handling techniques will be as important in this application as in commercial data processing.

So far we have looked at the computer as a valuable aid to calculation as in the processing of experiment results. There is another vital role that the computer can play. This is the use of the computer as a model builder. In effect, a theory can be simulated on the computer by means of various mathematical model building techniques. This application of computers has had a direct impact on the economics of scientific research. For example, without a powerful computing aid, many experiments can only be performed by empirical techniques – setting up the experiment and using direct observation of the results. Given a machine capable of performing complex calculations and data handling procedures, an experiment can be simulated rather than actually performed. In this role, therefore, the computer is used as an *actor* rather than a calculation instrument. If a mathematical model of a theory can be created then the theory becomes dynamic. Various conditions can be applied to it and the results inspected. Several experiments may then be set up based on the manipulation of the model. This is especially important when direct measurement is difficult (almost impossible) and certainly very expensive. The simulation of physical phenomena has proved invaluable in many areas of scientific research, such as in the study of protein structures, in chemistry, in fluid dynamics and so on.

The computer of itself is merely a tool. There is a common trend throughout its use in scientific research – this is that the computer takes the 'drudgery' out of research, leaving the scientist free to concentrate on those areas in which there can be no substitution for human endeavour – intuition and creative development.

Glossary

ACCESS: pertaining to the ability to obtain information from or place information into storage.

direct access: a store in which data are accessed *non-serially* and in which the time taken to approach a storage area does not depend on the location of data in store; i.e. there is no search and data is accessed merely at the provision of an address;

immediate access: a form of direct access storage in which the access time is especially short, and usually the data transfer rate is relatively fast. Storage of this type is referred to as core storage or internal storage or I.A.S.

random access: (U.S.A.) synonym and alternative for **direct access**.

ACCESS TIME: the time that elapses between the moment the command to access a location or area is given, and the moment when the transfer of data to or from that area can commence.

ACCUMULATOR: a register or specific location in store in which arithmetic or logic results can be formed. In some computers, one of the operands in an arithmetical or logical operation is required to be an accumulator.

ACTIVITY: 1 a measure of the time and resources needed to complete part of a project – **network**, i.e. the passage of time and employment of resources that are necessary for progress from one **event** to the next;

2 a measure of the proportion of the **records** in a **file** that are processed during one **run** (i.e. file activity).

ADDRESS: the characters or bits that identify a register or a specific location, word or area of storage.

absolute address: a precise address, corresponding to the machine code for the area of storage indicated, identifying that address uniquely and unambiguously;

address generation: the process of deducing, from its key or other item of data, the position of a record in a direct access file;

address replacement: a technique of addressing in which the address in an instruction is not that of the location holding the operand, but that of a location which in turn holds the address of the location in which the operand is stored. This technique is supplementary to that of **modification**, and is sometimes known as *indirect addressing*;

double address: descriptive of computers in which the instructions contain two addresses (also known as *two-address*); see **instruction format**;

relative address: an interim address to which another address will be added at the appropriate time, thus forming an **absolute address**;

single address: descriptive of computers in which the instructions contain only one address. Such machines usually have a single **accumulator** that is automatically used without being specifically addressed; see **instruction format**;

three address: descriptive of computers in which the instructions contain three addresses; see **instruction format**.

ALGORITHM: a sequence of statements defining a computational procedure.

ALPHANUMERIC: appertaining to the full character set of a machine that processes alphabetic and numeric data.

ANALOGUE: the representation of numerical quantities by means of physical variables such as rotation, voltage or resistance; or, the representation of physical quantities by others more conveniently generated or measured.

ASSEMBLER: a computer program that operates upon another program, written in symbolic form, to produce a complete program in machine language. Basically, assembly will consist of:

1 translation of symbolic operation codes and addresses to machine language form;

2 assembly of the resultant machine language program from its constituent parts, i.e. inclusion of library software, consolidation of program segments, etc.

ASSEMBLY LANGUAGE: the symbolic language used in conjunction with a particular assembler.

BAD PATCH: an area of a magnetic recording medium in which it is impossible to record data to the required degree of accuracy owing to a fault in that area.

BASE: synonym for **radix**.

BINARY: of two.

binary coded decimal (B.C.D.): a binary representation of the individual digits in a decimal number rather than the whole value being expressed to the base of two;

binary digit (bit): a digit (0 or 1) of a scale-of-two number;

binary notation: representation of numbers in the scale of two.

BLOCK: 1 a unit of information of convenient size for processing;

2 the area of storage in which a block of information is recorded;

3 a unit of computer construction (building block).

interblock gap: blank storage locations or time interval required between blocks to suit the logical design of the system.

BOOTSTRAP: a programming technique for initiating a program, where a few instructions are used to pull a longer routine into storage.

BRANCH: see **jump**.

BUCKET: a term peculiar to direct access storage; a quantity of storage with a fixed position and size dictated by the physical characteristics of the storage device.

BUFFER: a hardware device for matching the speed and/or code of information handling between a peripheral and a central processor.

CARD PUNCH: 1 an output device **on-line** to the computer, which punches patterns of holes into cards to store information for subsequent input to the same or other data processing system; the punching may be performed *serially* (column-by-column) or in *parallel* (row-by-row), or the cards may be *block punched*. Block punching is effected while the card is stationary, all the required holes being punched simultaneously, i.e. there is one punch knife per punching position.

2 a keyboard machine operated manually, used to prepare punched cards from **raw data** (e.g. *source documents*).

CARD READER: a machine that senses the information recorded as punched holes in cards. The direction of reading may be *serial* (column-by-column) or *parallel* (row-by-row), or the cards may be *block sensed*. Block sensing is effected while the card is stationary, all punching positions being sensed simultaneously, i.e. there is one sensing mechanism per punching position.

CARRY: propagation from one digit position into the next more significant position when the value in the first position has become equal to or greater than the **radix**.

CHARACTER: one of the set of symbols that can be used by a particular data processing system, such as the numerals 0 to 11, letters A to Z and additional symbols; see **code, character**.

CHARACTER RECOGNITION: the machine-reading of characters that are designed to be easily read by human beings; the characters may be in magnetizable ink and read by *magnetic ink character recognition* (M.I.C.R.) equipment, or in normal printing ink and read by *optical character recognition* (O.C.R.) equipment.

CIRCULATE: to shift information along a register that operates as a ring; that is, as a digit is moved beyond one end of the register an identical digit is inserted at the other end.

CLEAR: to erase the contents of a storage area; in the case of equipment capable of distinguishing between zero and blank.

CLOCK PULSE: one of a train of pulses occurring at fixed time intervals, used to check or control the speed of operation of a peripheral device and/or a central processor.

CLOCK TRACK: a track on a magnetic storage medium (e.g. drum, tape or disc), used to check or control the speed of operation of the medium or the computer.

CODE, CARD: the scheme of punching columns in a punched card used to represent individual characters.

CODE, CHARACTER: the relationship between the representation of characters in different media.

CODE, INTERNAL: the combinations of bits in the store of a computer used to represent individual characters.

CODE, PAPER TAPE: the pattern of holes in a punched paper tape, used to represent individual characters.

COMPILER: a computer program that operates on symbolic data in a **source program** to produce an object program with machine language function codes and absolute addresses.

COMPLEMENT: the result of subtracting one number from another, fixed, number. In binary computers, for example, negative numbers are often stored as their complement with respect to two. For example, the complement of a binary number where the word length is 24 bits is the difference between the number and 2^{24}. The integer +44 is represented in binary as follows:
0 0 0 0 0 0 0 0 0 0 0 0 0 0 0 0 0 0 1 0 1 1 0 0
whereas the integer −44 is represented by
1 1 1 1 1 1 1 1 1 1 1 1 1 1 1 1 1 1 0 1 0 1 0 0

CONSOLE TYPEWRITER: an electrical typewriter that is one of the computer's on-line peripheral devices and is used by the operator to control the computer. Messages typed in are accepted and interpreted, and action is initiated by an **executive program**. The executive program in turn types out directions and messages to the operator via the console typewriter. It is *not* an input/output (interrogating) typewriter.

CONTROL, TRANSFER OF: see **jump**.

CORE STORE: The now preferred term for I.A.S.

CRITICAL PATH: the sequence of inter-connected **events** and **activities** between the start of a project and its completion that will require the longest time to accomplish. This gives the shortest time in which the project can be completed; see also **PERT**.

CYCLE TIME: 1 the duration of a complete logical process in respect of a single storage location;
2 the duration of any complete repetitive sequence of operations;
3 of core store, the minimum time which must elapse between two successive references to a store to insert or extract a word or character.

DATA: the general term meaning information relative to a given heading. Literally 'those things which are given'.

DATA PREPARATION: the process of recording raw data in or on an input medium preparatory for input to a computer, etc.

DEBUG: to locate and correct any errors in a computer program.

DEMODIFY: see **modification**.

DIGITAL: pertaining to the representation of data in numerical form.

DIGITIZE: to convert an analogue measurement to digital form.

DIRECT ACCESS: see **access**.

DIRECTIVE: a statement from a prescribed list, which is entered in a **source program** and used to control the working of a compiler or assembler.

DISC FILE (Disc Store): a direct access storage device in which data are recorded on a number of concentric circular tracks on magnetic discs; the required disc and track are selected by electromechanical and electronic controls. Once accessed, the information is read sequentially.

DROP OUT: 1 a condition in which a bit, supposedly held in store, is not recorded there, thus resulting in an error;
2 a bit so lost.

DRUM: a magnetic storage unit in the form of a cylinder which revolves at high speed past multiple read/write heads.

EDIT: to arrange data into some desired format. For example, to rearrange and select pertinent data, insert symbols and constants, suppress unwanted zeros and apply predetermined format rules.

ENCODE: to apply code, usually before machine processing or data transmission.

ERASE: to replace the contents of a storage area by binary zero; see also **zeroise**.

EVENT: a specified project accomplishment at a particular instant of time (i.e. no resources are involved) in a project-**network**.

EXECUTIVE PROGRAM: a program that takes care of housekeeping and allocates priorities, particularly in conjunction with multiprogramming, providing essential facilities that cannot economically be provided by hardware; also called an *operating system*.

FEEDBACK: the use of a closed loop for controlling a process; the technique of controlling a process or system by extracting information at one point and using it as a supplementary input, possibly after some processing, at an earlier stage in the cycle of operations.

FERRITE: a special ferrous compound which has the property of retaining its magnetism after the magnetizing force has been removed. **ferrite core:** a small ring of ferrite; one of the cores in a **core store**; **ferrite core matrix:** a three-dimensional array of ferrite cores threaded on wires, forming all or part of a **core store**.

FIELD: a portion of a peripheral medium, storage location or source document used to hold one item of data.

FILE: an organized collection of information, e.g. a series of records stored in key number order.

FLAG: a special symbol used on an **object program** printout or listing to indicate invalid statements and violations of format rules in the preparation of the **source program**.

FLOATING-POINT: a form of representation of numbers in which the number is represented in two parts, the *argument* or fixed-point part, and the *exponent*. The exponent is that power of the radix by which the argument must be multiplied to give the true value of the number. The use of floating-point representation and arithmetic in a computer facilitates storage and manipulation of numbers in a wider range of magnitudes than is normally practicable and with a consistent relative degree of precision.

FLOWCHART: the diagram showing the main steps in a program or system and their sequence.

FORMAT: 1 the layout of a printed document, e.g. with regard to the predetermined printing area, spacing and punctuation;

2 any other predetermined arrangement of data, e.g. instruction format, file format.

FORMAT CHECK: part of a **validity check**; the check, usually applied by a program, determines whether input data conform to a specified format, permitting rejection of some incorrectly prepared data.

FRAME: a transverse section of magnetic tape or paper tape that consists of one bit position for each tape **track**. The term *row* may be used in place of frame when reference is made to paper tape.

FUNCTION CODE: the field in an instruction which specified the operation to be performed.

HARDWARE: the physical units from which a computer is built (see also **software**).

HOUSEKEEPING: the organizational activities necessary to maintain control of a process.

I.A.S. (Immediate Access Storage): that form of storage within a computer which has the shortest access time and where no delay occurs before or during the execution of instructions; at the present time I.A.S. is usually core storage or monolithic circuits.

INDEXING: see **modification; key**.

INDEX TABLE: a collection of data arranged for ease of reference to the item corresponding to a given key.

INDICATOR: 1 a visual signal to the operator, e.g. a panel light;

2 a two state device which may be set or unset by program, or automatically, or by manual switch setting or other operator action, and can be tested by program.

INFORMATION: a collection of facts or ideas; the meaning conveyed by data.

INPUT/OUTPUT TYPEWRITER: an on-line peripheral device whereby data can be entered directly into a computer store by means of a keyboard, the data not being recorded on an intermediate peripheral medium. In many applications, a reply generated by the program is automatically output (typed-out) on the same device, though other forms of output display are sometimes used. Also known as an interrogating typewriter.

INSTRUCTION: the group of characters or bits that defines an operation to be performed by the computer, usually including one or more addresses where data can be found and/or placed.

instruction code: the set of instructions relative to a particular computer;

instruction format: the arrangement of operation codes and addresses within an instruction, which may be *single address, double address*, etc. depending on the machine logic;

illegal (invalid) instruction: an instruction that specifies an address outside the range the program is permitted to use, or an instruction that for some other reason contravenes the logical rules of the machine;

macro-instruction: an instruction that, although written as a single instruction in the source language, is compiled into a sequence of machine instructions and is obeyed as such;

pseudo-instruction:

1 a symbolic representation of an instruction in the form associated with an assembler or compiler;

2 a group of characters complying with the format rules of an instruction, but not intended to be executed as such by a computer.

ITERATION: a method of solution of certain types of problem in which, given an approximation of the true solution, a closer approximation is calculated therefrom, the process being repeated until a prescribed degree of accuracy is achieved.

JUMP: to transfer control of the computer to an instruction that is not necessarily the next in sequence; the jump may be *unconditional* (e.g. to enter a subroutine) or *conditional* upon the result of a test, and conditional jumps appear as branching on a flowchart. The word *branch* is sometimes used as an alternative.

JUSTIFY: 1 to bring the significant digits or characters of a quantity into some prescribed position in relation to the boundaries of the field in which it lies, e.g. if a quantity is left justified, then its left most significant digit or character is at the left-hand boundary of the field;

2 to propagate **carry** from one word of a multiple-length number into the next more significant word.

KEY: 1 a field, such as an item code, that is used to identify a record;

2 a parameter required by a subroutine.

LABEL: 1 legible information attached to, for example, the spool of a reel of magnetic tape to identify it;

2 one or more blocks recorded on a peripheral medium identifying the data on the medium;

3 a symbolic address, usually written on the same line as some statement in a source-language program, used to identify that statement, so that, for example, it can be referred to in an instruction.

LEAST SIGNIFICANT DIGIT: the right-hand end digit of a number or computer word, often referred to by the abbreviation L.S.D.

LINEAR PROGRAMMING: a technique of operations research (not necessarily computer programming) where an optimum value or ratio of values is to be found in a situation involving many variables and for which there is no unique solution.

LINE PRINTER: an output peripheral which prints data one line at a time.

LINK: a form of **pointer**; a word or series of characters that contains the address of an instruction and is used by the appropriate instruction to cause a jump to the addressed instruction or one close to it. For example, a link is employed for returning from a subroutine to an appropriate position in the main program. Frequently a link contains other data, such as the condition of the program at the time the link was created.

LIST: a series of records each containing a reference, such as an address, to its predecessor and/or its successor.

list processing: processing records that are in the form of a list.

LOOP: a series of instructions that is repeated until a terminal condition is reached, often coupled with the techniques of **modification** and counting or **iteration**.

loop stop: a condition in which the same instruction in a program is unproductively obeyed repeatedly. On older computers, this was often an accepted way of stopping a program when it had completed its task or when some insuperable fault had been discovered in the program. On more recent computers, a loop stop is almost always the result of a programming error.

MACRO-INSTRUCTION: see **instruction**.

MAGNETIC INK CHARACTER RECOGNITION (M.I.C.R.): see **character recognition**.

MAGNETIC TAPE: the tape of any material coated or impregnated with a magnetizable substance upon which information can be recorded by magnetic flux.

magnetic tape deck: the mechanism used for feeding magnetic tape, with the reading and writing heads and circuitry relative to

one such assembly (also known by engineers as the *tape drive* or *tape transport*);
magnetic tape group: a number of magnetic tape decks mounted in one physical unit, and/or connected to a common control unit;
magnetic tape system:
1 an unspecified number of magnetic tape decks, of a particular speed range or size, e.g. 1900 half-inch (96 kch/s) magnetic tape system;
2 the assemblage of magnetic tape decks attached to a particular computer.

MASK: 1 a computer word of known value that is used during logical operations to achieve editing, packing or unpacking;
2 to protect parts of words from the effects of an instruction.

MEMORY: synonym for core storage or internal storage (I.A.S.), or sometimes for storage in general.

MICROSECOND: one one-millionth part of a second (10^{-6} second), abbreviated μs. or microsec.

MILLISECOND: one one-thousandth part of a second (10^{-3} second), abbreviated ms. or millisec.

MODIFICATION: the technique of augmenting one or more of the addresses in an instruction by the addition of a *modifier*. Modification may be effected by changing the value of the address *in* the stored instruction. Alternatively, the modification may be performed automatically at the time the instruction can be obeyed, without altering the stored form of the instruction. In the former instance, *demodification* is the application of a *demodifier* to the address with the result that the address is now in its original unmodified form.

MODULE: 1 an interchangeable unit of computer construction, sometimes called a *brick*;
2 an additional unit offered for sale with the computer, such as extra storage, usually corresponding to a construction unit.

MONITOR: to supervise.

MONITOR ROUTINE: see **executive program.**

MOST SIGNIFICANT DIGIT: the left-hand end digit of a number or computer word, often referred to by the abbreviation M.S.D.

NANOSECOND: one one-thousand-millionth part of a second (10^{-9} second), abbreviated ns. or nanosec.

NETWORK: 1 a schematic representation of **events** and **activities** that shows their inter-relationship;

2 a number of terminals with interconnecting paths.

NUMERICAL CONTROL: descriptive of systems in which digital computers provide discrete instructions for the control of automatic machines or operations (see also **process control**).

OBJECT PROGRAM: see **program**.

OFF-LINE: pertaining to those data processing machines or operations that are part of a system but are not directly controlled by the central processor.

ON-LINE: pertaining to peripheral equipment of the computer, attached to and controlled by the central processor.

OPERAND: a quantity used in an arithmetical or logical operation.

OPERATION CODE: see **function code**.

OPERATIONS RESEARCH (O.R.): the analytical and mathematical study of human enterprises as an aid to management strategy (see also **linear programming**).

OPTICAL CHARACTER RECOGNITION (O.C.R.): see **character recognition**.

ORDER CODE: synonymous with **instruction code**.

OVERFLOW: the condition arising when the result of an arithmetic operation is greater than the capacity of the register or storage area in which it is to be stored.

overflow indicator: an indicator that is set when a result larger than the capacity of a store location is produced by one of certain instructions; its being set shows that an incorrect arithmetic result has been stored.

OVERLAY: a section of program, held in a backing store, that is transferred to the core only when it is actually required for immediate execution.

PACK: to store several small items in the area normally provided for one word or record.

PACKAGE: 1 a board carrying electronic components connected together, forming one of the basic units from which an electronic computer is built;

2 a set of subroutines that may be incorporated as a whole into a program to perform certain processes, usually with the object of easing the task of writing the program. Examples include packages concerned with handling files on magnetic tape, and input and output of data.

PACKING DENSITY: the amount of information that can be recorded in a given space; for example, the density in digits to the inch on magnetic tape.

PARALLEL RUNNING: the method of conversion testing in which the system is run concurrently with the pre-existing method of performing the procedure, using the same raw data and comparing the results.

PARAMETER: 1 a value that must be supplied to a subroutine by the main program to ensure that a process is performed in the required manner;

2 a value that is constant for a given process and time, i.e. a parameter may take any value within prescribed limits but for any given operation remains constant for the duration of that operation.

PARITY BIT: a check-bit that is appended to a character, word, frame or block when necessary to ensure that the total number of bits in the series to be checked is odd or even, according to the logic of the system.

PASS: part of a computer **run** in which one logical unit of program is obeyed, e.g. a sorting *run* may consist of a number of *passes*.

PERT (Programme Evaluation Review Technique): a system of network analysis designed to trace the critical path and to predict the effects of any redeployment of resources (see also **activity; critical path; event**).

PROCESS CONTROL: descriptive of systems in which computers are used for the automatic regulation on a continuous basis of processes or operations (see also **numerical control**).

PROGRAM: 1 the complete sequence of instructions for a job to be performed on a computer;

2 to devise a procedure and list the steps necessary for a job to be performed on a computer.

automatic programming; a technique that provides for the translation by computer of programs written in symbolic form into machine language (see also **assembler; compiler**);

object program: the program produced by automatic translation of a **source program**;

source program: a program written in a symbolic language designed for the easy expression of problem-solving procedures; the source program is input to an **assembler** or **compiler** and the output is an **object program** in machine language.

PROGRAM LIBRARY: the collection of utility programs, subroutines, compilers, etc., appropriate to one computer.

RADIX: the quantity of characters for use in each of the digital positions of a numbering system, e.g. decimal notation uses radix 10.

mixed radix: a form of number representation in which different radices are used for various digits; time, for example, uses a mixed-radix system (e.g. hours (24), minutes (60) and seconds (60)).

RANDOM: a sequence in which it is impossible to predict, from a knowledge only of the preceding members of the sequence, what the next member shall be.

RAW DATA: data in its original form as collected for processing, i.e. before any data preparation has taken place.

READ-AFTER-WRITE CHECK: a form of checking applied to data written on to a magnetic recording medium, in which the data are read back after they have been written and the two sets of data (that written and that read) are compared.

REAL TIME PROCESSING: the processing of data for immediate use in controlling the data source, i.e. involving feedback, and such that the time taken for the processing is commensurate with the rate at which the input is changing.

RECORD: 1 a group or block of related data treated as a unit;
2 to place data in storage.

REGISTER: a hardware device comprising storage elements with special significance in the logical design of the computer, for example one word of parallel storage in a serial machine (see **accumulator**). Also, any of the locations in an immediate access store.

ROUTINE: any part of the program that deals with the particular aspects of the overall procedure (see also **subroutine**).

RUN: 1 the performance of a complete computer program through to its end condition;
2 any complete automatic sequence.

SEARCH: to examine a series of items for any that have a desired property or properties.

SEEK: to look for data relative to a given key.

SELF-INDEXING: a form of file arrangement in which the position (addresses) of a record can be deduced directly from part of the record itself, such as its key.

SENTINEL: an information bit whose function is that of an indicator.

SEQUENCE CONTROL NUMBER: the address of the instruction currently being obeyed. Abbreviated as SCN; also known as *control number, order number* and *instruction number*.

SEQUENCE CONTROL NUMBER REGISTER: a hardware unit in which the sequence control number (SCN) is held; facilities associated with the SCNR are that of automatically increasing the SCN by 1, and that of replacing the current SCN by a different value if a successful jump instruction is obeyed, and of transferring to the store the SCN or sometimes the SCN + 1 as part of the link.

SHIFT: to move the characters or bits in a storage area to the left or right; in the case of a number having all its digits in the same radix a left shift is equivalent to multiplying, and a right shift to dividing, by a power of that radix (see also **circulate**).

SIGN: an arithmetic symbol that distinguishes positive and negative quantities.

sign bit: A **sentinel** whose function is to indicate the algebraic sign of a quantity.

SIMULATE: to imitate by a model or computer routine the performance of a physical or biological system.

SIMULATOR: 1 a working model; an analogue computer or digital computer routine that can be used to predict the performance of the original process or system;

2 a program based on a mathematical model;

3 a routine designed to make one computer behave like another.

SOFTWARE: the library service available to users of a particular computer, e.g. subroutines, assemblers, compilers, and other programming aids (see also **hardware**).

SORT: to arrange records according to a logical system.

SOURCE PROGRAM: see **program**.

STORAGE: a mechanical, electrical or electronic unit in which data can be recorded, held and later recovered in its original form.

SUBROUTINE: a routine that is arranged so that control can be passed between it and a master routine, to avoid having to store duplicate copies of similar sequences of instructions and to permit the inclusion in one program of a routine proved in another (see also **link**).

SUPERVISORY PROGRAM: (U.S.A.) synonymous with **executive program**.

SYMBOLIC IDENTIFIER: a character or series of characters used to indicate or identify some quantity (usually in a source program), other than a direct representation of that quantity.

TABLE: an ordered set of data; see **index table**.

TRACK: the path along which information is recorded on a continuous or rotational medium, such as paper tape, magnetic tape or a magnetic drum.

TRANSLATE: to change information from one form of representation to another without significantly affecting the meaning.

UNPACK: to extract several small items from one computer word or record and store them in separate locations.

UPDATE: to revise a master file in respect of current information or transactions.

UTILITY ROUTINE: a routine available for repetitive data-handling procedures such as sorting or dumping data from storage. (Alternatively *utility program*.)

VALIDITY CHECKING: an examination of data for correctness against certain criteria, such as upper and lower cash limits, or the maximum number of items per account (see also **format check**).

VOLATILE: of a store; such that the information in the store is, or must be assumed to be, destroyed when the computer is switched off.

WORD: an ordered set of bits or characters that is treated by the computer as a single logical unit; word lengths may be fixed or variable depending on the particular computer and usually expressed as a number of characters or bits.

WORD TIME: the time required to move a word past a particular point (especially when transfers are performed serially).

WRITE: to record data electronically, e.g. on magnetic tape.

write ring: a device attached by the operator to a spool of magnetic tape when writing is to take place; its absence prevents writing.

ZEROISE: 1 to replace the contents of the storage area by pulses representing zero (see also **erase**);
2 to reset a mechanical register to its zero position.

ZERO SUPPRESSION: the replacement of non-significant zeros by 'spaces' to the left of a number before output takes place.

ZONE DIGIT: the numerical key to a section of code; e.g. 10, 11, and 0 are zone digits relating to the sections of a punched card comprising the letters A to I, J to R and S to Z respectively.

Index